FROM THE SYSTEM OF NATIONAL ACCOUNTS (SNA) TO A SOCIAL ACCOUNTING MATRIX (SAM) – BASED MODEL

An Application to Portugal

COLECÇÃO ECONÓMICAS – 2ª Série
Coordenação da Fundação Económicas

António Romão (org.), *A Economia Portuguesa – 20 Anos Após a Adesão*, Outubro 2006

Manuel Duarte Laranja, *Uma Nova Política de Inovação em Portugal? A Justificação, o modelo os instrumentos*, Janeiro 2007

Daniel Müller, *Processos Estocásticos e Aplicações*, Março 2007

Rogério Fernandes Ferreira, *A Tributação dos Rendimentos*, Abril 2007

Carlos Alberto Farinha Rodrigues, *Distribuição do Rendimento, Desigualdade e Pobreza: Portugal nos anos 90*, Novembro 2007

João Ferreira do Amaral, António de Almeida Serra e João Estêvão, *Economia do Crescimento*, Julho 2008

Amélia Bastos, Graça Leão Fernandes, José Passos e Maria João Malho, *Um Olhar Sobre a Pobreza Infantil*, Maio 2008

Helena Serra, *Médicos e Poder. Transplantação Hepática e Tecnocracias*, Julho 2008

Susana Santos, *From de System of National Accounts (SNA) to a Social Accounting Matrix (SAM) – Based Model. An Application to Portugal*, Maio 2009

COLECÇÃO ECONÓMICAS – 1ª Série
Coordenação da Fundação Económicas

Vítor Magriço, *Alianças Internacionais das Empresas Portuguesas na Era da Globalização. Uma Análise para o Período 1989-1998*, Agosto 2003

Maria de Lourdes Centeno, *Teoria do Risco na Actividade Seguradora*, Agosto 2003

António Romão, Manuel Brandão Alves e Nuno Valério (orgs.), *Em Directo do ISEG*, Fevereiro 2004

Joaquim Martins Barata, *Elaboração e Avaliação de Projectos*, Abril 2004

Maria Paula Fontoura e Nuno Crespo (orgs.), *O Alargamento da União Europeia. Consequências para a Economia Portuguesa*, Maio 2004

António Romão (org.), *Economia Europeia*, Dezembro 2004

Maria Teresa Medeiros Garcia, *Poupança e Reforma*, Novembro 2005

1ª Série publicada pela CELTA Editora

SUSANA SANTOS

FROM THE SYSTEM OF NATIONAL ACCOUNTS (SNA) TO A SOCIAL ACCOUNTING MATRIX (SAM) – BASED MODEL

An Application to Portugal

Foreword by Jeffery Round

ALMEDINA

FROM THE SYSTEM OF NATIONAL ACCOUNTS (SNA) TO A SOCIAL ACCOUNTING MATRIX (SAM) – BASED MODEL

An Application to Portugal

AUTOR
SUSANA SANTOS

EDITOR
EDIÇÕES ALMEDINA, SA
Av. Fernão Magalhães, n.º 584, 5.º Andar
3000-174 Coimbra
Tel.: 239 851 904
Fax: 239 851 901
www.almedina.net
editora@almedina.net

PRÉ-IMPRESSÃO | IMPRESSÃO | ACABAMENTO
G.C. GRÁFICA DE COIMBRA, LDA.
Palheira – Assafarge
3001-453 Coimbra
producao@graficadecoimbra.pt

Maio, 2009

DEPÓSITO LEGAL
291765/09

Biblioteca Nacional de Portugal – Catalogação na Publicação

SANTOS, Susana

From the System of National Accounts (SNA)
to a Social Accounting Matrix (SAM) – based
model : an application to Portugal. – (Económicas. 2ª série)
ISBN 978-972-40-3774-5

CDU 330
338

Contents

Appendixes

List of Tables

Foreword

The use of a social accounting matrix (SAM), as a way of representing the social and national accounts and as a basis for modelling, was pioneered by Sir Richard Stone more than 50 years' ago. Even then there were several important antecedents to Stone in developing systems of matrix accounts and associated models, in particular, through the work of Quesnay and Leontief. Since Stone's pioneering work, there have been other significant proponents of SAM-based analysis, such as Pyatt and Thorbecke (fixed price multiplier models) and Robinson (computable general equilibrium models). Based on their work many other scholars have seen many virtues in combining the means of estimating and representing the accounts of society in a social accounting matrix format and in building associated models of the economy. Many scholars refer to these as SAM-based models.

SAM-based models usually exploit the transparent way in which a SAM exhibits the structural features and interdependencies in an economy, although, beyond that, there is no particular restriction on the kinds of models that might be referred to in this way. SAM-based models are generally simulation models rather than forecasting models and are often used to explore a variety of counterfactual questions, usually about the possible economy-wide consequences of exogenous shocks. More specifically, such models are ideally suited to examining distributional issues, providing the SAM on which it is based contains sufficient detail about social and/or institutional groups. For this reason especially, most of the work on SAMs and SAM-based modelling has been based on developing countries, but there are now many good examples of the use of SAMs in industrialised countries.

The key to constructing a useful SAM and developing an effective SAM-based model is the SAM design. A SAM need not be dimensionally large as long as it represents the most significant features of economy-wide interdependence. More precisely, this means designing the SAM so that the key sectors, markets and institutions are as fully represented as is practicable. Estimation of the transactions between accounts is obviously also important but this needs to go in tandem with the SAM design.

This monograph shows, first, how a SAM can be extracted from the national accounts for Portugal that are in SNA/ESA format and, secondly, how this SAM can be used in developing a SAM-based model. The model is used to examine the distributional impact of two budgetary policies. Although it is a linear model and is inherently based on the structure of the SAM, it is considerably more complex than the standard 'fixed price multiplier' models of this genre. Of course, the lack of an endogenous price response mechanism and, more generally, the necessarily limited endogeneity of such models means that simulation results must always be viewed with a degree of caution. But policy modellers usually know this, and interpret their results accordingly.

It is to be hoped that this interesting monograph, representing painstaking and diligent research, will represent another useful stepping stone in the development of practical policy models based on the SAM approach.

Jeffery I Round

Emeritus Reader in Economics
University of Warwick, U.K.

Preface

This work served as the basis for the lecture given by the author as part of the examination necessary for obtaining the level of *agregação* (a Portuguese post-doctoral degree) in Economics. Part of this same work was also presented at the International Conference on Policy Modelling, held in Berlin, Germany, on 3 July 2008, and has been published in the Working Paper Series of the SSRN (Social Science Research Network), with the abstract number of 1159389, besides being included in the conference proceedings.

This work also embodies the achievement of yet another stage in the author's research into the Social Accounting Matrix (SAM). Beginning in 1993 with her PhD thesis[1], her research into the numerical and algebraic versions of the SAM, almost always with specific applications to Portugal, has followed a path whose results have been presented at several conferences and published in working papers and articles. The fruits of this research are now being published in a book that represents the synthesis of a methodology with a corresponding specific application, the main purpose of which is to study the impacts of government policies.

As stated in Chapter 3 (Section 3.1.), the author would like to emphasise that both the numerical and algebraic versions of the SAM presented here are understood as representing a stage coming after the traditional multiplier analysis, which still needs to be tested, improved upon and afforded its own theoretical justification in the future.

SUSANA SANTOS

---

[1] "The Social Accounting Matrix as a working instrument for defining economic policy. An application to Portugal during the 1986-90 period, with emphasis on the agroindustrial sector" (only available in Portuguese). PhD dissertation, ISEG-TULisboa, Lisbon, April 1999, 309pp.

Abstract

A Social Accounting Matrix (SAM), in both its numerical and algebraic versions, will be proposed as a working instrument for studying the (macro-)impacts of government policies on the distribution of income, paying close attention to the corresponding response of the different macroeconomic aggregates, balances and indicators.

For the geographical limits of Portugal and a time limit of one year (1 January to 31 December), a SAM is constructed from the SNA 93 (1993 version of the United Nations System of National Accounts) within an ESA 95 (European System of National and Regional Accounts in the European Community of 1995) framework. It will be shown that underlying the SAM are interrelated subsystems that, in its numerical version, provide an analytical picture of the circular flow or the general equilibrium interactions of a market economy (Portugal, in this case) when studied in a particular accounting period, while, in its algebraic version, these same subsystems make it possible to measure and quantify the economy-wide effects of changes in the particular nominal flows represented by the numerical version (injections into and leakages from the system), which might be the result of policy measures.

Key words: Social Accounting Matrix; National Accounts; Economic Planning; Economic Policy; SAM-based Modelling; Macroeconomic Modelling; Income distribution.

JEL classification: C82; D58; E01; E61

Acknowledgements

The author would like to thank Professor Jeffery Round (Warwick University, UK) for the suggestions and comments that he made about the database and the model, which resulted in a significant improvement of the whole work.

Special thanks are also due to Professors João Ferreira do Amaral (ISEG/TU Lisboa – Technical University of Lisbon, Portugal), Fernando Brito Soares (Universidade Nova de Lisboa, Portugal) and Sherman Robinson (Sussex University, UK): the first, for the encouragement that he gave and the comments that he made during the course of this work; the second (who aroused the interest of the author in this subject) for the comments that he made about the model; and the last, for the comments that he made about the model and for the interest that he showed in using the Portuguese SAM in order to carry out some experiments with a balancing method into which he was researching.

As a member of UECE (Research Unit on Complexity and Economics), the author is also grateful for the financial support received from FCT (Fundação para a Ciência e a Tecnologia) – Portugal. This work is itself part of the Multi-annual Funding Project (POCTI/0436/2003).

A special word of thanks is also due to *Fundação Económicas* and its vice-president, Professor António Romão, without whom this publication would not have been possible.

The author would also like to express her appreciation and gratitude for John Elliott's work in revising the English language version.

Abbreviations[1]

CE	– Cross Entropy (method)
CGE	– Computable General Equilibrium
c.i.f.	– cost-insurance-freight
ESA 95	– European System of National and Regional Accounts in the European Community of 1995 (Eurostat, 1996)
f.o.b.	– free on board
GAMS	– General Algebraic Modelling System
GDP	– Gross Domestic Product
INE	– Instituto Nacional de Estatística (Portuguese Statistical Institute)
ISCED	– International Standard Classification of Education
ISEG	– Instituto Superior de Economia e Gestão (School of Economics and Management)
ISWG	– Inter-Secretariat Working Group
LEG	– Leadership Group on SAM
NACE Rev.1	– New Statistical Nomenclature of the Economic Activities in the European Community
NAM	– National Accounting Matrix
NPISHs	– Non-Profit Institutions Serving Households

[1] Besides those used as parameters and variables, which are listed in Appendix F.

RAS	– Richard A. Stone (method)
SAM	– Social Accounting Matrix
SNA	– System of National Accounts
SNA 93	– System of National Accounts of 1993 (ISWG, 1993)
TU Lisboa	– Technical University of Lisbon
UECE	– Unidade de Estudos sobre a Complexidade e Economia (Research Unit on Complexity and Economics)
UK	– United Kingdom
USA	– United States of America

1.

Introduction

The main purpose of this work is to study and test, through its concrete application to Portugal, a working instrument for studying the impacts of government policies, in this case on the distribution of income. Close attention will also be paid to the corresponding response of the different macroeconomic aggregates and indicators. Because of this aim, the author was obliged to work with data that were more than a decade out of date, since 1995 was the only year for which there existed workable data. However, the task to be carried out in this study is seen as an experiment that has never previously been undertaken for Portugal, while, furthermore, it seeks to demonstrate the importance and potentialities of the working instrument used.

The working instrument referred to above is the Social Accounting Matrix (SAM), underlying which are interrelated subsystems that, in its numerical version, provide an analytical picture of the circular flow or the general equilibrium interactions of the market economy when studied in a particular accounting period. On the other hand, in the algebraic version of the SAM, it is possible to measure and quantify the economy-wide effects of changes in the particular nominal flows represented by the numerical version (injections into and leakages from the system), which might be the result of policy measures.

Thus, Chapter 2 presents a numerical version of the SAM, constructed in perfect consonance with the System of National

Accounts (SNA) through a top-down approach, and highlights how the data collected from other sources of information have been adjusted to the data collected from that system.

In turn, Chapter 3 presents an algebraic version of the above--mentioned SAM, within a static short-term framework, adopting a computable (numerically solvable) general (economy-wide) equilibrium (macroeconomic balance) approach.

Like the numerical version, this algebraic version of the SAM, which will also be referred to as a SAM-based model, is constructed in perfect consonance with the SNA, with each cell being defined through a linear equation or system of equations, whose components are all the known and quantified transactions of that system. This model will be calibrated using parameters and exogenous variables calculated from the database, i.e. the numerical version of the SAM, presented in Chapter 2.

Chapters 4 and 5 show how macroeconomic aggregates and balances, as well as the structural indicators of the distribution and use of income (which can be constructed from the available information), can be calculated from both versions of the SAM.

Chapter 6 defines and analyses scenarios arising from experiments that have been carried out into the distributional impact of government policies. For this purpose, some parameters and the exogenous variables used to calibrate the model will be subjected to shocks, the SAMbased model will then be processed and the impacts will be studied by considering the relative differences between the aggregates, balances and indicators presented in Chapters 4 and 5, after and before the experiments.

Chapter 7 ends the paper with a summary and some concluding remarks designed to emphasise the importance of the SAM as a working instrument.

2.

The database[2]

2.1. The SAM as a complete account of the circular flow in the economy

A Social Accounting Matrix (SAM) is a square matrix in which each transaction is recorded only once in a cell of its own. As is conventionally agreed, the entries made in rows represent resources, incomes, receipts or changes in liabilities and net worth, whilst, the entries made in columns represent uses, outlays, expenditures or changes in assets. So, for each row there is a corresponding column, with the totals of each of these being equal. These figures will include both production and institutional accounts, which are subdivided into yet other accounts.

The taxonomy used in a SAM depends on the available data and the purposes of the study underlying its construction. It is, however, fundamental for the success of any analysis that there

---

[2] A preliminary version of this chapter was presented to the International Conference on Policy Modelling, promoted by EcoMod (Global Economic Modelling Network), held in Hong Kong, China, on 29 June 2006, under the title: "Constructing a database for economic modelling from the System of National Accounts: a Social Accounting Matrix for Portugal". The paper presented at that conference is also published in the Working Paper Series of the Social Science Research Network (Santos S., 2006).

should be a definition of an appropriate classification and a characterisation of the production and institutional subsectors.

While being constantly concerned with providing a mutually exclusive and, in a certain way, exhaustive classification, the adopted disaggregation should, on the one hand, respect the functional criterion, describing the production processes and pointing out the existing technical-economic relationships between the various productive units, and, on the other hand, it should also respect the institutional criterion, describing distribution, accumulation and financing activities, and showing the relationships to be found in economic behaviour. We therefore have "Production" divided into factors of production, activities and products, and "Institutions" divided into current, capital and financial accounts, as well as the "rest of the world" account.

In a general way, the order of the accounts does not obey any specific rule; it simply obeys the criterion of the person who works with them. The criterion of the author for ordering the accounts was the one that lies behind the basic SAM represented in Table 1.

Table 1 – Portuguese basic SAM (Social Accounting Matrix) for 1995 (in millions of euros)

	Incomes (receipts) \ Outlays (expenditures)	Production and Trade: Factors (1)	Production and Trade: Activities (2)	Production and Trade: Products (3)	Institutions: Current A. (4)	Institutions: Capital A. (5)	Institutions: Financial A. (6)	Rest of the World (RW) (7)	TOTAL
Production and Trade	Factors (1)	0	Gross Added Value, at factor cost (70 725)	0	0	0	0	Compensation of Factors from the RW (3 243)	Aggregate Factors Income (73 968)
	Activities (2)	0	0	Production (154 394)	0	0	0	0	Production Value (154 394)
	Products (3)	0	Intermediate Consumption (84 102)	Trade and Transport Margins (0)	Final Consumption (64 898)	Gross Capital Formation (19 623)	0	Exports (24 433)	Aggregate Demand (193 056)
Institutions	Current A. (4)	Gross National Income, at factor cost (70 542)	Net taxes on production (-346)	Net taxes on products (10 283)	Current Transfers (42 145)	0	0	Current Transfers from the RW (3 960)	Aggregate Income (126 583)
	Capital A. (5)	0	0	0	Gross Saving (17 291)	Capital Transfers (4930)	Net borrowing (40)	Capital Transfers from the RW (2 320)	Investment Funds (24 582)
	Financial A. (6)	0	0	0	0	0	Financial Transactions (35 030)	Financial Transactions from the RW (9 257)	Total financial transactions (44 287)
Rest of the World (RW) (7)		Compensation of Factors to the RW (3 426)	Net taxes on production (-87)	Imports + net taxes on products (28 127 + 252)	Current Transfers to the RW (2 249)	Capital Transfers to the RW (29)	Financial Transactions to the RW (9 217)		Transactions Value to the RW (43 213)
TOTAL		Aggregate Factors Income (73 968)	Total Costs (154 394)	Aggregate Supply (193 056)	Aggregate Income (126 583)	Aggregate Investment (24 582)	Total financial transactions (44 287)	Transactions Value from the RW (43 213)	

Source: Portuguese National Accounts (Appendix A)

As far as the flows of money are concerned, the following outline shows us the connections that can be established between the various accounts of the basic SAM.

Outline 1 – Flows of money between the accounts of the basic Portuguese SAM

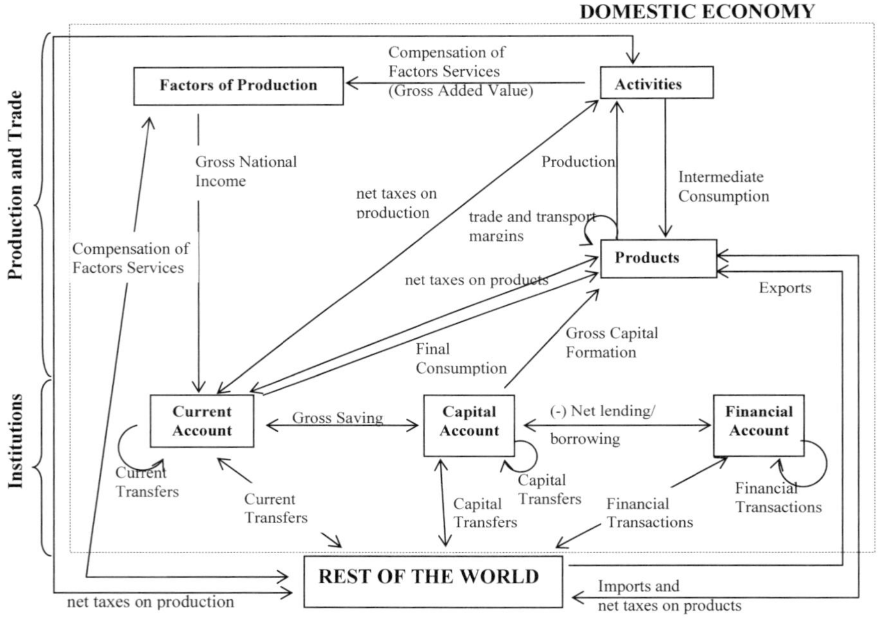

This outline "provides a schematic portrayal of the circular flow of income in the economy" (Devarajan et al., 1991), representing all the transactions recorded by the SAM within the (domestic) economy, as well as those taking place between it and the rest of the world. The latter transactions are represented by the "rest of the world" account (7th column/row), whilst the former are represented by the production and institutions accounts, as described below.

On the one hand, production activities buy "inputs" (intermediate consumption) and the factors of production sell services in order to produce, thereby generating added value. Apart from the subsidies for production (from the government's current account and the rest of the world, i.e. from European Union institutions), which are deducted from taxes (net taxes on production), the only receipts from activities come from the sales of their production, which are then spent on intermediate consumption, the compensation of factors and the payment of taxes (to the government's current account). Therefore, the value of production balances the total costs of the economy (see the "activities" account, 2nd column/row).

On the other hand, the factors of production sell services to (domestic and foreign) production activities, receiving compensation in return. Since the services of the factors are supplied by (domestic and foreign) institutions, outlays can be made to the domestic institutions (current account) through gross national income, as well as to the rest of the world (1st column/row).

Besides gross national income, i.e. the compensation of the factors of production, the other income sources of the institutions are (net indirect) taxes (on products and production) and current transfers, as can be seen from its "current account", which also shows how the income is either spent on final consumption and current transfers or is saved (4th column/row).

Through the "products" accounts, we also have the possibility to study both supply and demand. As sources of demand, we have intermediate consumption, final consumption, gross capital formation and exports. On the supply side, we have production and imports, to which are added the (net) taxes on products and the trade and transport margins (3rd column/row).

The products accounts can be seen as the accounts of those who perform intermediation activities and place products on the market, in other words, those who acquire or import products, organise processing (transport and storage), add the corresponding margins to the price, pay indirect taxes to the government and sell the products to producers, households, government and the rest of the world.

In the "capital account", we can see, on the one hand, investment through gross capital formation and capital transfers, and, on the other hand, the funds available for such investments, resulting from gross saving and capital transfers, as well as from a balance corresponding either to financing requirements or capacity, depending on the respective sign (5th column/row).

The "financial account" reveals the financial transactions taking place in the other accounts (6th column/row).

We can therefore conclude that the SAM is a snapshot of the economy, amounting to a numerical representation of the cycle: production – income – expenditure. It "shows hown sectoral value added accrues to production factors and their institutional owners; how these incomes, corrected for net current transfers, are spent; and how expenditures on commodities lead to sectoral production and value added" (Keuning, Ruijter, 1988) – or, to use the words of Thorbecke (2001 and 2003), "it can readily be seen that it incorporates all major transactions within a socio-economic system".

Thus, the SAM accounts for every transaction taking place between the actors in the economic system while providing a statistical representation of its circular flow. Since "a Computable General Equilibrium (CGE) model describes the whole circular flow of a market economy, while maintaining accounting consistency both at the macro level and at the level of individual actors... CGE models are specially appropriate for operating within a SAM framework" (Abbink et al., 1995). The model that will be developed in Chapter 3, and which is designed to operate within the SAM framework described in this chapter, adopts a CGE approach despite its differences in relation to the traditional CGE models. This approach has to do with the fact that it is numerically solvable (Computable), economy-wide (General) and macroeconomically balanced (Equilibrium), to use the words adopted by Robinson in its presentation, entitled: "A standard general equilibrium approach to national and global poverty analysis", in August 2006[3].

[3] Presentation included in the course "A SAM-Based Single Country CGE Model in GAMS", held at the University of Sussex, Brighton (UK), attended by the author.

2.2. The top-down approach

The SNA that has been used in Portugal since 1995 has been the European System of National and Regional Accounts in the European Community of 1995 – ESA 95 (Eurostat, 1996), which is based on the 1993 version of the International United Nations System of National Accounts – SNA 93, prepared by the Inter-Secretariat Working Group and published by the United Nations Statistical Office (ISWG, 1993). For the latter body, "a SAM is defined as the presentation of SNA accounts in a matrix which elaborates the linkages between a supply and use table and institutional sector accounts" (SNA 93, paragraph 20.4).

By either top-down or bottom-up methods, it is possible to break down or aggregate each account into categories, using on occasions sources of information other than the SNA, without losing the consistency of the whole system. In other words, "a crucial feature is the wide range of possibilities for expanding or condensing such a matrix in accordance with specific circumstances and needs" (SNA 93, paragraph 20.6) – the approach used here will be the top-down one.

Appendix B identifies the items and balances of the various internal accounts of the SNA in the (completely) aggregated SAM, represented in Table 1, in order to show the abovementioned consistency and, at the same time, the perfect consonance between the SAM that will be worked with here and the SNA.

Nowadays, the SNA in general and the Portuguese National Accounts in particular provide several (mutually exclusive) possibilities for the disaggregation of products and activities, a few possibilities for the institutional accounts, and even fewer possibilities for the factors of production.

Therefore, production and trade accounts, which are drawn from supply and use tables (see Tables A.4 and A.5), can be broken down into 60 activities and products, which in the case of some transactions can have yet more levels of disaggregation. Here the products and activities will be worked upon in six groups, described in Tables A.7 and A.8.

Furthermore, in the case of production and trade accounts, the factors of production may only be broken down into labour (employees) and others, which have been given the title of "own assets". The latter category includes the compensation of employers and own-account employees (self-employed), as well as the compensation of capital, such as interests, profits and rents.

In turn, the institutions' accounts can be disaggregated into five institutional sectors, each with a similar economic behaviour: households, non-financial corporations, financial corporations, general government, and non-profit institutions serving households (NPISHs).

General government can be further disaggregated into central government, local government and social security funds, whilst financial corporations can be disaggregated into the central bank, other monetary financial institutions, other financial intermediaries except insurance corporations and pension funds, financial auxiliaries, and insurance corporations and pension funds (see Table A.2). The rest of the world can also be broken down into the European Union (member states and institutions) and non-member countries and international organisations (see Table A.3).

Table 2 shows the part of the Portuguese SAM that it was possible to construct from the SNA, with the particular purpose described in the introduction, and which will be broken down even further, albeit using other sources of information.

This macro-SAM was constructed from blocks of sub-matrices or sets of sub-matrices, whose transactions have common characteristics. These blocks can be specified through the identification of the transactions involved in the National Accounts, which is performed here in Chapter 3 (Section 3.2) on the occasion of their formalisation. Appendix E describes the sources of information and the method of calculation used, but only for those sub-matrices that are not calculated either directly from the sources or whenever there are details that justify a reference to them. An identical, but more systematised, description is provided by Santos in "SAMs and SNA: An Application" (2005) and "Constructing a Database for Economic Modelling from the SNA: a SAM for Portugal" (2006). The first of these also includes a description of the SAM cell contents, although this relates to a SAM calculated for 1999.

As can be seen from its totals, Table 2, which represents the so-called macro-SAM, is a possible disaggregation of Table 1, which represents the so-called basic SAM (the completely aggregated macro-SAM).

It is therefore easy to conclude that "a SAM applies the properties of a matrix format to incorporate specific details on various economic flows" (SNA 93, paragraph 20.26).

Table 2 – Portuguese macro-SAM (Social Accounting Matrix) for 1995 (in millions of euros)

Incomes (receipts) \ Outlays (expenditures)				PRODUCTION and TRADE																
				FACTORS			ACTIVITIES							PRODUCTS						
				Labour - employees	Own assets	Total	Agriculture, hunting and foresty ...	Industry, including energy	Construction	Wholesale and retail trade ...	Financial, real-estate, renting ...	Other service activities	Total	Products of agriculture, hunting, forestry ...	Products from mining and quarrying...	Construction work	Wholesale and retail trade services...	Financial intermediation services, real estate...	Other services	Total
				1	2		3	4	5	6	7	8		9	10	11	12	13	14	
PRODUCTION and TRADE	FACTORS	Labour - employees	1	0	0	0	652	9 258	2 589	8 222	4 212	13 630	38 563	0	0	0	0	0	0	0
		Own assets	2	0	0	0	3 327	8 054	2 303	9 478	5 583	3 417	32 161	0	0	0	0	0	0	0
		Total		0	0	0	3 979	17 313	4 892	17 700	9 794	17 047	70 725	0	0	0	0	0	0	0
	ACTIVITIES	Agriculture, hunting and foresty...	3	0	0	0	0	0	0	0	0	0	0	6 060	379	2	0	19	0	6 460
		Industry, including energy	4	0	0	0	0	0	0	0	0	0	0	0	55 321	69	2	413	48	55 852
		Construction	5	0	0	0	0	0	0	0	0	0	0	0	12	14 191	0	0	0	14 204
		Wholesale and retail trade...	6	0	0	0	0	0	0	0	0	0	0	0	25	13	31 749	683	0	32 469
		Financial, real-estate, renting...	7	0	0	0	0	0	0	0	0	0	0	0	5	14	0	20 967	0	20 987
		Other service activities	8	0	0	0	0	0	0	0	0	0	0	3	81	28	78	852	23 379	24 421
		Total		0	0	0	0	0	0	0	0	0	0	6 064	55 823	14 317	31 829	22 934	23 427	154 394
	PRODUCTS	Products of agriculture ...	9	0	0	0	606	4 640	0	369	0	78	5 693	0	0	0	0	0	0	0
		Products from mining and ...	10	0	0	0	1 756	29 158	5 096	6 608	1 559	3 346	47 524	0	0	0	0	0	0	0
		Construction work	11	0	0	0	30	250	3 394	280	525	128	4 606	0	0	0	0	0	0	0
		Wholesale and retail trade...	12	0	0	0	121	1 198	247	4 193	897	896	7 552	1 236	13 886	0	- 15 122	0	0	0
		Financial intermediation...	13	0	0	0	112	3 019	563	3 092	7 514	2 365	16 666	0	0	0	0	0	0	0
		Other services	14	0	0	0	26	315	38	347	713	623	2 062	0	0	0	0	0	0	0
		Total		0	0	0	2 651	38 579	9 337	14 889	11 209	7 437	84 102	1 236	13 886	0	- 15 122	0	0	0
INSTITUTIONS	CURRENT ACCOUNT	Households	15	38 620	20 994	59 614	0	0	0	0	0	0	0	0	0	0	0	0	0	0
		Enterprises (nonfinancial corporations)	16	0	11 561	11 561	0	0	0	0	0	0	0	0	0	0	0	0	0	0
		Financial corporations	17	0	1 787	1 787	0	0	0	0	0	0	0	0	0	0	0	0	0	0
		Government	18	0	- 2 558	- 2 558	- 135	- 31	- 20	- 96	- 13	- 50	- 346	- 1	7 108	405	1 046	1 347	378	10 283
		Non Profit Institutions Serving Households (NPISH)	19	0	137	137	0	0	0	0	0	0	0	0	0	0	0	0	0	0
		Total		38 620	31 922	70 542	- 135	- 31	- 20	- 96	- 13	- 50	- 346	- 1	7 108	405	1 046	1 347	378	10 283
	CAPITAL ACCOUNT	Households	20	0	0	0	0	0	0	0	0	0	0	0	0	0	0	0	0	0
		Enterprises (nonfinancial corporations)	21	0	0	0	0	0	0	0	0	0	0	0	0	0	0	0	0	0
		Financial corporations	22	0	0	0	0	0	0	0	0	0	0	0	0	0	0	0	0	0
		Government	23	0	0	0	0	0	0	0	0	0	0	0	0	0	0	0	0	0
		Non Profit Institutions Serving Households (NPISH)	24	0	0	0	0	0	0	0	0	0	0	0	0	0	0	0	0	0
		Total		0	0	0	0	0	0	0	0	0	0	0	0	0	0	0	0	0
	FINANCIAL ACCOUNT		25	0	0	0	0	0	0	0	0	0	0	0	0	0	0	0	0	0
REST OF THE WORLD			26	64	3 363	3 426	- 34	- 8	- 5	- 24	- 3	- 13	- 87	1 481	24 689	32	840	1 181	156	28 379
TOTAL				38 683	35 285	73 968	6 460	55 852	14 204	32 469	20 987	24 421	154 394	8 781	101 506	14 754	18 592	25 462	23 961	193 056

Source: Portuguese National Accounts (Appendix A)

Table 2 – Portuguese macro-SAM (Social Accounting Matrix) for 1995 (in millions of euros) (continued)

Incomes (receipts) \ Outlays (expenditures)				INSTITUTIONS – CURRENT ACCOUNT – Households	Enterprises (nonfinancial corporations)	Financial corporations	Government	Non Profit Institutions Serving Households (NPISH)	Total	INSTITUTIONS – CAPITAL ACCOUNT – Households	Enterprises (nonfinancial corporations)	Financial corporations	Government	Non Profit Institutions Serving Households (NPISH)	Total	FINANCIAL ACCOUNT	REST OF THE WORLD	TOTAL
				15	16	17	18	19		20	21	22	23	24		25	26	
PRODUCTION and TRADE	FACTORS	Labour - employees	1	0	0	0	0	0	0	0	0	0	0	0	0	0	120	38 683
		Own assets	2	0	0	0	0	0	0	0	0	0	0	0	0	0	3 123	35 285
		Total		0	0	0	0	0	0	0	0	0	0	0	0	0	3 243	73 968
	ACTIVITIES	Agriculture, hunting and forestry…	3	0	0	0	0	0	0	0	0	0	0	0	0	0	0	6 460
		Industry, including energy	4	0	0	0	0	0	0	0	0	0	0	0	0	0	0	55 852
		Construction	5	0	0	0	0	0	0	0	0	0	0	0	0	0	0	14 204
		Wholesale and retail trade…	6	0	0	0	0	0	0	0	0	0	0	0	0	0	0	32 469
		Financial, real-estate, renting…	7	0	0	0	0	0	0	0	0	0	0	0	0	0	0	20 987
		Other service activities	8	0	0	0	0	0	0	0	0	0	0	0	0	0	0	24 421
		Total		0	0	0	0	0	0	0	0	0	0	0	0	0	0	154 394
	PRODUCTS	Products of agriculture …	9	2 546	0	0	18	0	2 564	185	130	0	3	0	318	0	205	8 781
		Products from mining and …	10	27 967	0	0	628	0	28 595	768	5 282	347	452	246	7 095	0	18 292	101 506
		Construction work	11	74	0	0	0	0	74	4 148	2 816	437	2 552	120	10 072	0	1	14 754
		Wholesale and retail trade…	12	5 467	0	0	37	0	5 504	91	194	19	1	0	305	0	5 231	18 592
		Financial intermediation…	13	6 388	0	0	77	43	6 508	505	1 049	110	8	0	1 671	0	617	25 462
		Other services	14	6 136	0	0	14 272	1 245	21 653	58	91	10	1	1	160	0	87	23 961
		Total		48 578	0	0	15 032	1 288	64 898	5 755	9 562	922	3 018	366	19 623	0	24 433	193 056
INSTITUTIONS	CURRENT ACCOUNT	Households	15	470	1 349	2 051	9 623	13	13 506	0	0	0	0	0	0	0	3 293	76 413
		Enterprises (nonfinancial corporations)	16	1 339	58	363	0	0	1 759	0	0	0	0	0	0	0	23	13 344
		Financial corporations	17	2 125	329	29	4	14	2 501	0	0	0	0	0	0	0	35	4 323
		Government	18	13 883	2 108	229	6 866	7	23 092	0	0	0	0	0	0	0	609	31 081
		Non Profit Institutions Serving Households (NPISH)	19	323	50	34	878	0	1 286	0	0	0	0	0	0	0	0	1 423
		Total		18 141	3 894	2 705	17 371	35	42 145	0	0	0	0	0	0	0	3 960	126 583
	CAPITAL ACCOUNT	Households	20	7 952	0	0	0	0	7 952	0	0	812	206	0	1 018	- 4 023	147	5 095
		Enterprises (nonfinancial corporations)	21	0	9 342	0	0	0	9 342	0	0	0	707	0	707	- 49	896	10 896
		Financial corporations	22	0	0	1 558	0	0	1 558	0	484	328	2	0	814	- 287	0	2 085
		Government	23	0	0	0	- 1 661	0	- 1 661	63	161	3	1 870	4	2 100	4 423	1 275	6 136
		Non Profit Institutions Serving Households (NPISH)	24	0	0	0	0	100	100	0	0	0	291	0	291	- 23	1	370
		Total		7 952	9 342	1 558	- 1 661	100	17 291	63	645	1 143	3 075	4	4 930	40	2 320	24 582
	FINANCIAL ACCOUNT		25	0	0	0	0	0	0	0	0	0	0	0	0	35 030	9 257	44 287
REST OF THE WORLD			26	1 743	108	60	339	0	2 249	- 723	689	20	43	0	29	9 217	X	43 213
TOTAL				76 413	13 344	4 323	31 081	1 423	126 583	5 095	10 896	2 085	6 136	370	24 581	44 287	43 213	X

Source: Portuguese National Accounts (Appendix A)

If we look at the world around us, it is easy to agree with the statement that "the determinants of the distribution of income and the mechanisms by which it changes represent one of the most difficult theoretical and empirical problems facing the science of economics" (Dervis et al., 1982). If it were an easy task, then certainly the world today would be a fairer place. Working on the empirical side, the author doesn't have any doubts that "SAMs provide an invaluable statistical framework for the analysis of the mapping between the different kinds of distributions one may want to consider" (Dervis et al., 1982).

Perhaps in a rather simplistic way, but at least to begin with, the author accepts that the study of the income distribution in a society involves the study of how the national pie is divided up and how it can be sliced. The first aspect can be analysed from one or more snapshots of the economy, provided by a suitably disaggregated SAM, and the second from the modelling of that same SAM. Therefore, of crucial importance here is the way in which the primary and secondary distribution of income, as well as the use that is made of it, are dealt with. As can be confirmed from Appendix B, the factors of production account and the current account of the institutions are the accounts that cover such issues.

"In the SAM, the institution entitled 'households' really represents all the people in society" (Dervis et al., 1982). Its disaggregation therefore needs to be performed. On the other hand, the distribution of the (primary) incomes that accrue as a result of the involvement in processes of production or, as seen above, the ownership of assets among institutions (and activities) is covered by the factors of production account, so that its disaggregation must also be performed.

The question thus arises "how should these disaggregations be performed?" This will not, however, be discussed here, because the dependence of the author on the available data is total[4],

[4] Dervis et al. (1982), for instance, discuss this aspect (see Chapter 12, Modelling Distributional Mechanisms).

although, as can be seen above, despite the fact that the information is not up-to-date, it is nonetheless sufficient for her to be able to at least study some aspects of the distribution of income.

The workable data made available to the author for studying and modelling income distribution in Portugal consisted of an incomplete disaggregated National Accounting Matrix (NAM) (see Tables C.1 and C.2) and a previous (provisional) version for 1995, constructed as a result of the collaboration of the Portuguese Statistical Institute (*Instituto Nacional de Estatística*) in the work undertaken by the Leadership Group on Social Accounting Matrices, under the coordination of Statistics Netherlands (LEG, 2003).

In that NAM, labour was broken down into six types, according to the gender and education level of workers (see Table C.3), and households were broken down into four types, according to their main source of income (see Table C.4). Such disaggregation was performed using specific data sources, such as household budget surveys, the labour force survey and administrative data (employment records, income tax and social security files, etc.)[5].

In this work, gender will not be considered and the factors of production will be disaggregated into two main groups: labour (or employees) and own assets; the latter being further disaggregated into labour (employers and own-account workers) and capital. This disaggregation was based on the data available in the National Accounts, since the primary distribution of income account does not distinguish own-account labour (employers and own-account workers) from capital.

In turn, households were disaggregated into the same four types.

Once again, one of the many advantages of the SAM approach could be referred to here, to use the words of Pyatt

[5] The document resulting from that work (LEG, 2003) highlights the limitations and the methodological details of such a valuable exercise.

(1991): by "reducing the social accounts to the essential", the SAM approach "provides a useful starting point for understanding the assumptions and manipulations that have been built into the secondary source material which is typically employed by the majority of analysts".

This top-down approach made it possible to compile a consistent database.

2.3. Adjusting and balancing the SAM

The totals of the above-mentioned incomplete NAM were different from the ones calculated from the definitive national accounts (Tables 1, 2 and C.1) and some data were also missing. Therefore, discrepancies and missing data were handled in different ways in keeping with the specifications of the contents, sources and methodology based on the (macro-)SAM blocks of sub-matrices, which are described, respectively, in Chapter 3 (Section 3.2) and Appendix E.

The advice of Stone (1981) was therefore closely heeded: firstly, all the known discrepancies and gaps were identified; secondly, within each block in which something had been identified by this first step, a detailed analysis was carried out in order to review its contents, methodological specifications and all the information provided about the disaggregated values (LEG, 2003), as well as its interdependence with the other parts and totals; thirdly, the gaps were filled in; and finally, the discrepancies were adjusted.

Gaps were identified in the vectors of the compensation of labour from and to the rest of the world and the current transfers of households from and to the rest of the world. Firstly, the balances were deducted from the difference between the (detailed) value added or domestic product and the generated income or national product, in the first case, and from the difference between the (detailed) national and disposable incomes, in the second case. From the structure of these values, the gaps were filled in by working with the totals (for labour and households) of the macro-SAM. Direct purchases abroad by households, considered here together with the current transfers to the rest of the world, were deducted from the difference between the final consumption of the original NAM and the author's estimates of final consumption.

In turn, discrepancies were adjusted using the RAS (Richard A. Stone) method[6].

In accordance with what has been seen so far, the database for the model that is the main subject of this work is a SAM with 34 rows and 34 columns. This has the particularity of being balanced and perfectly consonant with the national accounts when aggregated at the level of 26 rows and columns, which is, in fact, the case of the macro-SAM represented by Table 2. However, as mentioned above, the disaggregation into 34 rows and columns was also performed from credible sources, with the differences from the aggregated level (26 x 26) not being very significant, generally speaking. The correspondence between the two SAMs is shown in Table 3.

---

[6] Significant work using the cross-entropy method was carried out by Sherman Robinson and the author, operating with the support of the former. However, this work will not be adopted here because it does not make it possible both to maintain the definitive blocks of the sub-matrices and to work only with those that need to be adjusted to the definitive totals. This work will, however, be followed in order to make it possible to adjust only parts (sub-matrices) of a matrix.

Table 3 – Association between the accounts of the macro-SAM and the SAM

macro -SAM				SAM		
Account		Description		Account		Description
Nº	symbol			Nº	symbol	
	f	Factors of production			f	Factors of production
1	fle	Labour – employees		1	flel	.. with low education level
				2	flem	.. with medium education level
				3	fleh	.. with high education level
2	foa	Own assets	Labour – employers and/or own-account workers (foal)	4	foall	.. with low education level
				5	floalm	.. with medium education level
				6	floalh	.. with high education level
			Capital	7	foak	..
	a	Activities			*a*	Activities
3	*a*1	agriculture, hunting and forestry; fishing and operation of fish hatcheries and fish farms		8	*a*1	..
4	*a*2	industry, including energy		9	*a*2	..
5	*a*3	construction		10	*a*3	..
6	*a*4	wholesale and retail trade, repair of motor vehicles and household goods, hotels and restaurants; transport and communications		11	*a*4	..
7	*a*5	financial, real-estate, renting and business activities		12	*a*5	..
8	*a*6	other service activities		13	*a*6	..
	p	Products			p	Products
9	p1	products of agriculture, hunting, forestry, fisheries and aquaculture		14	p1	..
10	p2	products from mining and quarrying, manufactured products and energy products		15	p2	..
11	p3	construction work		16	p3	..
12	p4	wholesale and retail trade services, repair services, hotel and restaurant services, transport and communication services		17	p4	..
13	p5	financial intermediation services, real estate, renting and business services		18	p5	..
14	p6	other services		19	p6	..
	dic	Domestic Institutions – Current Account			dic	Domestic Institutions – Current Account
15	dich	Households		20	dich1	.. - employees
				21	dich2	.. - employers and own-account workers
				22	dich3	.. - recipients of pensions
				23	dich4	.. – others

macro -SAM			SAM		
Account		Description	Account		Description
Nº	symbol		Nº	symbol	
16	dicnfc	Non-financial corporations	24	dicnfc	..
17	dicfc	Financial corporations	25	dicfc	..
18	dicg	General government	26	dicg	..
19	dicnp	Non-profit institutions serving households	27	dicnp	..
	dik	Domestic Institutions – Capital Account		dik	Domestic Institutions – Capital Account
20	dikh	Households	28	dikh	..
21	diknf	Non-financial corporations	29	diknf	..
22	dikfc	Financial corporations	30	dikfc	..
23	dikg	General government	31	dikg	..
24	diknp	Non-profit institutions serving households	32	diknp	..
25	dif	Domestic Institutions – Financial Account	33	dif	..
26	rw	Rest of the world	34	rw	..

Key: .. the same description as for the macro-SAM

If we consider T to be the matrix of the SAM transactions, represented by tij, or a payment from column account j to row account i, and y to be the vector of row sums, which equal the vector of column sums x:

$$y_i = \sum_j t_{ij} \tag{2.1}$$

$$x_j = \sum_i t_{ij} \tag{2.2}$$

and

$$y_i = x_j, \text{ when } i = j \tag{2.3}$$

the t_{ij}´s of the macro-SAM (26x26), with the factors of production (fle and foa) and the current account of households (dich) completely aggregated and perfectly consonant with the national accounts and balanced (Table 2), can be considered as the "control" – total of the t_{ij}´s of the SAM (34x34).

Therefore the SAM will have sub-matrices that are disaggregations of cells (the "control" totals) of the macro-SAM, which will occupy the shaded parts of Table 4 and whose initial versions will be considered as Z_{ij}, with typical element z_{ij}.

Table 4 – Portuguese SAM (Social Accounting Matrix) for 1995 (in millions of euros), with only the macro-SAM values

Outlays (expenditures) / Incomes (receipts)		PRODUCTION and TRADE														
		FACTORS											ACTIVITIES			
		Labour (employees)				Own Assets						Total	Agriculture, hunting and foresty; fishing ...	Industry, including energy	Constru-ction	Wholesale and retail trade, repair of .. motor
						Labour (employers and/or own-account work.)				Capital	Total					
		Lower	Medium	Higher	Total	Lower	Medium	Higher	Total							
		1	2	3		4	5	6		7			8	9	10	11
PRODUCTION and TRADE – FACTORS – Labour (employees) – Lower	1	0	0	0	0	0	0	0	0	0	0	0				
Medium	2	0	0	0	0	0	0	0	0	0	0	0				
Higher	3	0	0	0	0	0	0	0	0	0	0	0				
Total		0	0	0	0	0	0	0	0	0	0	0	652	9 258	2 589	8 222
Own Assets – Labour (employers and/or own-account work) – Lower	4	0	0	0	0	0	0	0	0	0	0	0				
Medium	5	0	0	0	0	0	0	0	0	0	0	0				
Higher	6	0	0	0	0	0	0	0	0	0	0	0				
Total		0	0	0	0	0	0	0	0	0	0	0				
Capital	7	0	0	0	0	0	0	0	0	0	0	0				
Total		0	0	0	0	0	0	0	0	0			3 327	8 054	2 303	9 478
Total		0	0	0	0	0	0	0	0	0	0	0	3 979	17 313	4 892	17 700
ACTIVITIES – Agriculture, hunting and foresty..	8	0	0	0	0	0	0	0	0	0	0	0	0	0	0	0
Industry, including energy	9	0	0	0	0	0	0	0	0	0	0	0	0	0	0	0
Construction	10	0	0	0	0	0	0	0	0	0	0	0	0	0	0	0
Wholesale and retail trade, repair ..	11	0	0	0	0	0	0	0	0	0	0	0	0	0	0	0
Financial, real-estate, renting and..	12	0	0	0	0	0	0	0	0	0	0	0	0	0	0	0
Other service activities	13	0	0	0	0	0	0	0	0	0	0	0	0	0	0	0
Total		0	0	0	0	0	0	0	0	0	0	0	0	0	0	0
PRODUCTS – Products of agriculture, hunting ..	14	0	0	0	0	0	0	0	0	0	0	0	606	4 640	0	369
Products from mining and quarry..	15	0	0	0	0	0	0	0	0	0	0	0	1 756	29 158	5 096	6 608
Construction work	16	0	0	0	0	0	0	0	0	0	0	0	30	250	3 394	280
Wholesale & retail trade services..	17	0	0	0	0	0	0	0	0	0	0	0	121	1 198	247	4 193
Financ.intermediation serv, real .	18	0	0	0	0	0	0	0	0	0	0	0	112	3 019	563	3 092
Other services	19	0	0	0	0	0	0	0	0	0	0	0	26	315	38	347
Total		0	0	0	0	0	0	0	0	0	0	0	2 651	38 579	9 337	14 889
INSTITUTIONS – CURRENT ACCOUNT – Households (by main source of income) – employees	20												0	0	0	0
employers and/or o.a. work	21												0	0	0	0
recipients of pensions	22												0	0	0	0
others	23												0	0	0	0
Total					38 620						20 994	59 614	0	0	0	0
Enterprises (non financial corporations)	24	0	0	0	0	0	0	0	0	11 561	11 561	11 561	0	0	0	0
Financial corporations	25	0	0	0	0	0	0	0	0	1 787	1 787	1 787	0	0	0	0
Government	26	0	0	0	0	0	0	0	0	- 2 558	- 2 558	- 2 558	- 135	- 31	- 20	- 96
Non Profit Inst Serv.Househ. (NPISH)	27	0	0	0	0	0	0	0	0	137	137	137	0	0	0	0
Total					38 620						31 922	70 542	- 135	- 31	- 20	- 96
CAPITAL A. – Households	28	0	0	0	0	0	0	0	0	0	0	0	0	0	0	0
Enterprises (non financial corporations)	29	0	0	0	0	0	0	0	0	0	0	0	0	0	0	0
Financial corporations	30	0	0	0	0	0	0	0	0	0	0	0	0	0	0	0
Government	31	0	0	0	0	0	0	0	0	0	0	0	0	0	0	0
Non Profit Inst Serv.Househ. (NPISH)	32	0	0	0	0	0	0	0	0	0	0	0	0	0	0	0
Total		0	0	0	0	0	0	0	0	0	0	0	0	0	0	0
FINANCIAL ACCOUNT	33	0	0	0	0	0	0	0	0	0	0	0	0	0	0	0
REST OF THE WORLD	34				64	0	0	0	0	3 363	3 363	3 426	- 34	- 8	- 5	- 24
TOTAL					38 683						35 285	73 968	6 460	55 852	14 204	32 469

Source: Portuguese National Accounts (Appendix A)

Table 4 – Portuguese SAM (Social Accounting Matrix) for 1995 (in millions of euros), with only the macro-SAM values (continued)

Incomes (receipts) \ Outlays (expenditures)		PRODUCTION and TRADE: ACTIVITIES: Financial, real-estate, renting and busin..activi (12)	Other service activities (13)	Total	PRODUCTS: Products of agriculture, hunting, forest.. (14)	Products from mining and quar-rying (15)	Construction work (16)	Wholesale and retail trade services; (17)	Financial intermediation services, real estate, renting (18)	Other services (19)	Total	INSTITUTIONS: CURRENT ACCOUNT: Households (by main source of income): employees (20)	employers and/or o.a. work (21)	recipients of pens. (22)	others (23)	Total
PRODUCTION and TRADE – FACTORS – Labour (employees) – Lower	1				0	0	0	0	0	0	0	0	0	0	0	0
Medium	2				0	0	0	0	0	0	0	0	0	0	0	0
Higher	3				0	0	0	0	0	0	0	0	0	0	0	0
Total		4 212	13 630	38 563	0	0	0	0	0	0	0	0	0	0	0	0
Own Assets – Labour (employers and/or own-...) – Lower	4				0	0	0	0	0	0	0	0	0	0	0	0
Medium	5				0	0	0	0	0	0	0	0	0	0	0	0
Higher	6				0	0	0	0	0	0	0	0	0	0	0	0
Total					0	0	0	0	0	0	0	0	0	0	0	0
Capital	7				0	0	0	0	0	0	0	0	0	0	0	0
Total		5 583	3 417	32 161	0	0	0	0	0	0	0	0	0	0	0	0
Total		9 794	17 047	70 725	0	0	0	0	0	0	0	0	0	0	0	0
ACTIVITIES – Agriculture, hunting and foresty..	8	0	0	0	6 060	379	2	0	19	0	6 460	0	0	0	0	0
Industry, including energy	9	0	0	0	0	55 321	69	2	413	48	55 852	0	0	0	0	0
Construction	10	0	0	0	0	12	14 191	0	0	0	14 204	0	0	0	0	0
Wholesale and retail trade, repair ..	11	0	0	0	0	25	13	31 749	683	0	32 469	0	0	0	0	0
Financial, real-estate, renting and..	12	0	0	0	0	5	14	0	20 967	0	20 987	0	0	0	0	0
Other service activities	13	0	0	0	3	81	28	78	852	23 379	24 421	0	0	0	0	0
Total		0	0	0	6 064	55 823	14 317	31 829	22 934	23 427	154 394	0	0	0	0	0
PRODUCTS – Products of agriculture, hunting ..	14	0	78	5 693	0	0	0	0	0	0	0					2 546
Products from mining and quarry..	15	1 559	3 346	47 524	0	0	0	0	0	0	0					27 967
Construction work	16	525	128	4 606	0	0	0	0	0	0	0					74
Wholesale & retail trade services..	17	897	896	7 552	1 236	13 886	0	- 15 122	0	0	0					5 467
Financ.intermediation serv, real .	18	7 514	2 365	16 666	0	0	0	0	0	0	0					6 388
Other services	19	713	623	2 062	0	0	0	0	0	0	0					6 136
Total		11 209	7 437	84 102	1 236	13 886	0	- 15 122	0	0	0					48 578
INSTITUTIONS – CURRENT ACCOUNT – Households (by main source of income) – employees	20	0	0	0	0	0	0	0	0	0	0					
employers and/or o.a. work	21	0	0	0	0	0	0	0	0	0	0					
recipients of pensions	22	0	0	0	0	0	0	0	0	0	0					
others	23	0	0	0	0	0	0	0	0	0	0					
Total		0	0	0	0	0	0	0	0	0	0					470
Enterprises (non financial corporations)	24	0	0	0	0	0	0	0	0	0	0					1 339
Financial corporations	25	0	0	0	0	0	0	0	0	0	0					2 125
Government	26	- 13	- 50	- 346	- 1	7 108	405	1 046	1 347	378	10 283					13 883
Non Profit Inst.Serv.Househ. (NPISH)	27	0	0	0	0	0	0	0	0	0	0					323
Total		- 13	- 50	- 346	- 1	7 108	405	1 046	1 347	378	10 283					18 141
CAPITAL A. – Households	28	0	0	0	0	0	0	0	0	0	0	615	6 385	1 071	- 119	7 952
Enterprises (non financial corporations)	29	0	0	0	0	0	0	0	0	0	0	0	0	0	0	0
Financial corporations	30	0	0	0	0	0	0	0	0	0	0	0	0	0	0	0
Government	31	0	0	0	0	0	0	0	0	0	0	0	0	0	0	0
Non Profit Inst.Serv.Househ. (NPISH)	32	0	0	0	0	0	0	0	0	0	0	0	0	0	0	0
Total		0	0	0	0	0	0	0	0	0	0					7 952
FINANCIAL ACCOUNT	33	0	0	0	0	0	0	0	0	0	0	0	0	0	0	0
REST OF THE WORLD	34	- 3	- 13	- 87	1 481	24 689	32	840	1 181	156	28 379	1 126	363	205	49	1 743
TOTAL		20 987	24 421	154 394	8 781	101 506	14 754	18 592	25 462	23 961	193 056					76 413

Source: Portuguese National Accounts (Appendix A)

Table 4 – Portuguese SAM (Social Accounting Matrix) for 1995 (in millions of euros), with only the macro-SAM values (continued)

Incomes (receipts) \ Outlays (expenditures)		INSTITUTIONS – CURRENT ACCOUNT: Enterprises (nonfinancial corporations)	Financial corporations	Govern-ment	Non Profit Institutions Serving Households (NPISH)	Total	INSTITUTIONS – CAPITAL ACCOUNT: Households	Enterprises (nonfinancial corporations)	Financial corporations	Govern-ment	Non Profit Institutions Serving Households (NPISH)	Total	FINANCIAL ACCOUNT	REST OF THE WORLD	TOTAL
		24	25	25	27		28	29	30	31	32		33	34	
PRODUCTION and TRADE – FACTORS – Labour (employees) – Lower	1	0	0	0	0	0	0	0	0	0	0	0	0		
Medium	2	0	0	0	0	0	0	0	0	0	0	0	0		
Higher	3	0	0	0	0	0	0	0	0	0	0	0	0		
Total		0	0	0	0	0	0	0	0	0	0	0	0	120	38 683
Own Assets – Labour (employers and/or own-) – Lower	4	0	0	0	0	0	0	0	0	0	0	0	0	0	
Medium	5	0	0	0	0	0	0	0	0	0	0	0	0	0	
Higher	6	0	0	0	0	0	0	0	0	0	0	0	0	0	
Total		0	0	0	0	0	0	0	0	0	0	0	0	0	
Capital	7	0	0	0	0	0	0	0	0	0	0	0	0	3 123	
Total		0	0	0	0	0	0	0	0	0	0	0	0	3 123	35 285
Total		0	0	0	0	0	0	0	0	0	0	0	0	3 243	73 968
ACTIVITIES – Agriculture, hunting and foresty..	8	0	0	0	0	0	0	0	0	0	0	0	0	0	6 460
Industry, including energy	9	0	0	0	0	0	0	0	0	0	0	0	0	0	55 852
Construction	10	0	0	0	0	0	0	0	0	0	0	0	0	0	14 204
Wholesale and retail trade, repair ..	11	0	0	0	0	0	0	0	0	0	0	0	0	0	32 469
Financial, real-estate, renting and..	12	0	0	0	0	0	0	0	0	0	0	0	0	0	20 987
Other service activities	13	0	0	0	0	0	0	0	0	0	0	0	0	0	24 421
Total		0	0	0	0	0	0	0	0	0	0	0	0	0	154 394
PRODUCTS – Products of agriculture, hunting ..	14	0	0	18	0	2 564	185	130	0	3	0	318	0	205	8 781
Products from mining and quarry..	15	0	0	628	0	28 595	768	5 282	347	452	246	7 095	0	18 292	101 506
Construction work	16	0	0	0	0	74	4 148	2 816	437	2 552	120	10 072	0	1	14 754
Wholesale & retail trade services..	17	0	0	37	0	5 504	91	194	19	1	0	305	0	5 231	18 592
Financ.intermediation serv, real .	18	0	0	77	43	6 508	505	1 049	110	8	0	1 671	0	617	25 462
Other services	19	0	0	14 272	1 245	21 653	58	91	10	1	1	160	0	87	23 961
Total		0	0	15 032	1 288	64 898	5 755	9 562	922	3 018	366	19 623	0	24 433	193 056
INSTITUTIONS – CURRENT ACCOUNT – Households (by main source of income) – employees	20						0	0	0	0	0	0	0	2 353	
employers and/or o.a. work.	21						0	0	0	0	0	0	0	754	
recipients of pensions	22						0	0	0	0	0	0	0	120	
others	23						0	0	0	0	0	0	0	66	
Total		1 349	2 051	9 623	13	13 506	0	0	0	0	0	0	0	3 293	76 413
Enterprises (non financial corporations)	24	58	363	0	0	1 759	0	0	0	0	0	0	0	23	13 344
Financial corporations	25	329	29	4	14	2 501	0	0	0	0	0	0	0	35	4 323
Government	26	2 108	229	6 866	7	23 092	0	0	0	0	0	0	0	609	31 081
Non Profit Inst.Serv.Househ. (NPISH)	27	50	34	878	0	1 286	0	0	0	0	0	0	0	0	1 423
Total		3 894	2 705	17 371	35	42 145	0	0	0	0	0	0	0	3 960	126 583
CAPITAL A. – Households	28	0	0	0	0	7 952	0	0	812	206	0	1 018	- 4 023	147	5 095
Enterprises (non financial corporations)	29	9 342	0	0	0	9 342	0	0	0	707	0	707	- 49	896	10 896
Financial corporations	30	0	1 558	0	0	1 558	0	484	328	2	0	814	- 287	0	2 085
Government	31	0	0	- 1 661	0	- 1 661	63	161	3	1 870	4	2 100	4 423	1 275	6 136
Non Profit Inst.Serv.Househ. (NPISH)	32	0	0	0	100	100	0	0	0	291	0	291	- 23	1	370
Total		9 342	1 558	- 1 661	100	17 291	63	645	1 143	3 075	4	4 930	40	2 320	24 582
FINANCIAL ACCOUNT	33	0	0	0	0	0	0	0	0	0	0	0	35 030	9 257	44 287
REST OF THE WORLD	34	108	60	339	0	2 249	- 723	689	20	43	0	29	9 217	0	43 213
TOTAL		13 344	4 323	31 081	1 423	126 583	5 095	10 896	2 085	6 136	370	24 581	44 287	43 213	

Source: Portuguese National Accounts (Appendix A)

The purpose will be to maintain all the values of Table 4, since all of them are from national accounts, adjusting the values collected for the shaded cells accordingly. Three types of situations can be identified in the values collected for the shaded cells (zij), which are described below.

a) The macro-SAM value is the SAM row-column total.

a.1) The macro-SAM cell (dich, fle) or (15,1), the value of which is 38,620 million euros, represents the compensation of labour (employees) received by Portuguese households in 1995. The disaggregation of that value, in accordance with the education level of the employees and the main source of income of the households, had the following initial values:

Table 5 – Compensation of labour (employees) received by Portuguese households in 1995 (in millions of euros) – initial values

SAM account (see Table 3)		1	2	3	(sub)total
		flel	flem	fleh	
20	dich1	21 062	7 353	8 851	37 266
21	dich2	750	401	136	1 286
22	dich3	287	159	83	530
23	dich4	255	94	58	407
(sub)total		22 354	8 007	9 128	39 489

Source: Table C.2.2.

a.2) The macro-SAM cell (dich, foa) or (15,2), the value of which is 20,994 million euros, represents the compensation of own-account labour and capital received by Portuguese households in 1995. The disaggregation of that value, in accordance with the education level of the employers and own-account employees, capital and the main source of income of the households, had the following initial values:

Table 6 – Compensation of own assets received by Portuguese households in 1995 (in millions of euros) – initial values

SAM account (see Table 3)		4 foall	5 foalm	6 Foalh	7 foak	(sub)total
20	dich1	1 957	517	426	2 459	5 359
21	dich2	6 325	858	302	1 105	8 590
22	dich3	279	104	17	544	945
23	dich4	145	44	8	138	335
(sub)total		8 706	1 523	753	4 247	15 229

Source: Table C.2.2.

a.3) The macro-SAM cell (dich, dich) or (15,15), the value of which is 470 million euros, represents the current transfers taking place within Portuguese households in 1995. The disaggregation of that value in accordance with the main source of income of the households had the following initial values:

Table 7 – Current transfers within Portuguese households in 1995 (in millions of euros) – initial values

SAM account (see Table 3)		20 dich1	21 dich2	22 dich3	23 dich4	(sub)total
20	dich1	127	50	18	16	210
21	dich2	53	21	7	7	88
22	dich3	39	15	5	5	64
23	dich4	72	28	9	9	119
(sub)total		291	114	36	36	481

Source: Table C.2.4.

b) The macro-SAM value is the SAM row total.

b.1) The macro-SAM cell (rw, fle) or (26,1), the value of which is 64 million euros, represents the compensation of labour (employees) sent to the rest of the world in 1995. The disaggregation of that value in accordance with the education level of the employees had the following initial values:

Table 8 – Compensation of labour (employees) sent to the rest of the world in 1995 (in millions of euros) – initial values

SAM account (see Table 3)		1	2	3	(sub)total
		flel	flem	fleh	
34	rw	150	3 868	55	4 073

Source: Tables C.2.2. and C.2.3.

Note: See the considerations made about these values at the beginning of this section.

b.2) The macro-SAM vector (p1-p6, dich) or (9-14, 15), the values of which are shown in the right-hand columns of Table 9, represents the consumption of Portuguese households in 1995 by products. The left-hand side of Table 9 represents the initial values that resulted from the disaggregation of the households in accordance with their main source of income.

Table 9 – Final consumption of Portuguese households in 1995 by products (in millions of euros)

SAM account (see Table 3)		Initial values					macro SAM account (see Table 3)		15
		20	21	22	23	(sub)total			
		dich1	dich2	dich3	dich4				dich
14	p1	1 465	491	533	73	2 563	9	p1	2 546
15	p2	17 395	5 564	4 117	918	27 994	10	P2	27 967
16	p3	41	10	22	3	75	11	p3	74
17	p4	4 436	1 291	702	208	6 637	12	p4	5 467
18	p5	3 711	1 574	861	183	6 329	13	p5	6 388
19	p6	3 986	1 080	874	154	6 094	14	p6	6 136
(sub)total		31 033	10 011	7 109	1 540	49 692	(sub)total		45 578

Source: Tables C.2.1 and 2

b.3) The macro-SAM vector (dicnfc-dicnp, dich) or (16-19, 15), the values of which are shown in the right-hand columns of Table 10, represents the current transfers from Portuguese households to the other institutions in 1995. The left-hand side of Table 10 represents the initial values that resulted from the disaggregation of the households in accordance with their main source of income.

Table 10 – Current transfers from Portuguese households to other institutions in 1995 (in millions of euros)

SAM account (see Table 3)		Initial values					Macro-SAM account (see Table 3)		15
		20	21	22	23	(sub)total			
		dich1	dich2	dich3	Dich4				dich
24	dicnfc	313	125	900	31	1 369	16	dicnfc	1 339
25	dicfc	1 698	221	143	42	2 103	17	dicfc	2 125
26	dicg	12 197	1 094	854	174	14 319	18	dicg	13 883
27	dicnp	220	66	17	28	331	19	dicnp	323
(sub)total		14 428	1 506	1 914	275	18 122	(sub)total		17 670

Source: Table C.2.4 [cell (5,5)] and Table 2

c) The macro-SAM value is the SAM column total.

c.1) The macro-SAM vector (fle, *a*1-*a*6) or (1, 3-8), the values of which are shown in the bottom rows of Table 11, represents the gross added value, at factor cost, of labour (employees), in 1995 by activity. The top rows of Table 11 represent the initial values that resulted from the disaggregation of labour in accordance with the education level of employees.

Table 11 – Gross added value, at factor cost, of labour (employees), by activity in 1995 (in millions of euros)

SAM account (see Table 3)		Initial values						
		8	9	10	11	12	13	(sub)total
		a1	*a2*	*a3*	*a4*	*a5*	*a6*	
1	flel	540	5 421	1 400	3 729	1 291	4 618	17 000
2	flem	171	3 107	84	1 659	1 237	5 366	11 625
3	fleh	22	1 046	120	797	1 116	3 465	6 567
(sub)total		733	9 575	1 604	6 185	3 645	13 450	35 193

macro-SAM account (see Table 3)		3	4	5	6	7	8	(sub)total
		a1	*a2*	*a3*	*a4*	*a5*	*a6*	
1	fle	652	9 258	2 589	8 222	4 212	13 630	38 563

Source: (Portuguese) *Instituto Nacional de Estatística* – Portuguese Pilot–NAM for 1995 (detailed gross value added sub-matrix) and Table 2

c.2) The macro-SAM vector (foa, *a*1-*a*6) or (2, 3-8), the values of which are shown in the bottom rows of Table 12, represents the gross added value, at factor cost, of own-account labour and capital, by activity in 1995. The top rows of Table 12 represent the initial values that resulted from the disaggregation of that value, in accordance with the education level of employers and own-account employees and capital.

Table 12 – Gross added value, at factor cost, of own assets, by activity in 1995 (in millions of euros)

SAM account (see Table 3)		Initial values						
		8	9	10	11	12	13	(sub) total
		a1	*a2*	*a3*	*a4*	*a5*	*a6*	
4	foall	1 422	320	167	1 011	115	549	3 585
5	foalm	836	140	9	406	178	576	2 144
6	foalh	48	70	10	225	140	217	710
7	foak	626	10 280	3 103	9 240	7 006	2 240	32 494
(sub)total		2 932	10 810	3 289	10 882	7 439	3 582	38 933

macro-SAM account (see Table 3)		3	4	5	6	7	8	(sub) total
		a1	*a2*	*a3*	*a4*	*a5*	*a6*	
2	foa	3 327	8 054	2 303	9 478	5 583	3 417	32 161

Source: (Portuguese) *Instituto Nacional de Estatística* – Portuguese Pilot–NAM for 1995 (detailed gross value added sub-matrix) and Table 2

c.3) The macro-SAM vector (dich, dicnfc-dicnp) or (15, 24-27), the values of which are shown in the bottom rows of Table 13, represents the current transfers from other institutions to households in 1995. The top rows of Table 13 represent the initial values that resulted from the disaggregation of the households in accordance with their main source of income.

Table 13 – Current transfers to Portuguese households from other institutions in 1995 (in millions of euros)

SAM account (see Table 3)		Initial values				
		24	25	26	27	(sub)total
		Dicnfc	dicfc	Dicg	dicnp	
20	dich1	319	427	2 288	3	3 037
21	dich2	126	93	905	1	1 126
22	dich3	900	498	6 385	9	7 792
23	dich4	34	295	260	0	588
(sub)total		1 379	1 312	9 838	13	12 543

macro-SAM account (see Table 3)		24	25	26	27	(sub)total
		Dicnfc	dicfc	Dicg	dicnp	
15	dich	1 349	2 051	9 623	13	13 036

Source: Table C.2.4 [cell (5,5)] and Table 2

c.4) The macro-SAM cell (fle, rw) or (1, 26), the value of which is 120 million euros, represents the compensation of labour (employees) received from the rest of the world in 1995. The disaggregation of that value in accordance with the education level of the employees had the following initial values:

Table 14 – Compensation of labour (employees) received from the rest of the world in 1995 (in millions of euros) – initial values

SAM account (see Table 3)		34
		rw
1	flel	5 504
2	flem	250
3	fleh	2 615
(sub)total		8 369

Source: Table E.2.2. and Table E.2.3.

Note: See the considerations made about these values at the beginning of this section.

An adjusted SAM T'_{ij} will be obtained from the adjustment of the sub-matrices Z_{ij}, represented by Tables 5-14. In order to do this, these sub-matrices will be adjusted one by one, using the above-mentioned RAS method.

Therefore, each element, derived from a sub-matrix[7] Z_{ij}, of the adjusted matrix T'_{ij} will be represented by the following equation:

$$t'_{ij} = r_i * z_{ij} * s_j \tag{2.4}$$

$$\text{with, } r_i = \frac{c_i}{\sum_j z_{ij}} \tag{2.5}$$

$$\text{and } s_j = \frac{d_j}{\sum_i z_{ij}} \tag{2.6}$$

where:

t'_{ij} = SAM (adjusted) cell
r^i = row multiplier
c_i = row control total[8]
z_{ij} = typical element of the sub-matrix Z_{ij}
s_j = column multiplier
d_j = column control total[9]
i and j = flel, flem, fleh, foall, foalm, foalh, foak, dich1..dich4

As is made clear by Round (2003), this procedure results from the minimisation of

$$\sum_{ij} t'_{ij} * \ln\left(\frac{t'_{ij}}{z_{ij}}\right) \tag{2.7}$$

[7] Vectors were calculated by applying the structure of the vectors of initial values to the control totals.

[8] In situations type a) and c), except c.4), these vectors were calculated by applying the structure of initial row totals to the corresponding macro-SAM row totals.

[9] In situations type a) and b), except b.1), these vectors were calculated by applying the structure of initial column totals to the corresponding macro-SAM column totals.

$$\text{subject to: } \sum_{ij} t'_{ij} = c_i; \sum_{i} t'_{ij} = d_j; z_{ij} > 0.$$

The calculations were performed iteratively, with the sub--matrices Z_{ij} in the first iteration being those represented in Tables 5-14, and, in the last iteration, in which r_i and s_j are equal to 1, those included in Table 15, corresponding to the shaded parts of Table 4.

Table 15 will be the database of the model to be defined and worked with in the next chapter.

Table 15 – Portuguese SAM (Social Accounting Matrix) for 1995 (in millions of euros)

Incomes (receipts) \ Outlays (expenditures)		PRODUCTION and TRADE														
		FACTORS											ACTIVITIES			
		Labour (employees)				Own Assets						Total	Agriculture, hunting and foresty; fishing ...	Industry, including energy	Construction	Wholesale and retail trade, repair of .. motor
		Lower	Medium	Higher	Total	Labour (employers and/or own-account work.) Lower	Medium	Higher	Total	Capital	Total					
		1	2	3		4	5	6		7			8	9	10	11
PRODUCTION and TRADE – FACTORS – Labour (employees) – Lower	1	0	0	0	0	0	0	0	0	0	0	0	473	5 113	2 244	4 846
Medium	2	0	0	0	0	0	0	0	0	0	0	0	159	3 112	144	2 290
Higher	3	0	0	0	0	0	0	0	0	0	0	0	20	1 034	201	1 086
Total		0	0	0	0	0	0	0	0	0	0	0	652	9 258	2 589	8 222
Own Assets – Labour (employers and/or own-account work) – Lower	4	0	0	0	0	0	0	0	0	0	0	0	1 509	181	89	685
Medium	5	0	0	0	0	0	0	0	0	0	0	0	874	78	5	271
Higher	6	0	0	0	0	0	0	0	0	0	0	0	60	47	7	180
Total		0	0	0	0	0	0	0	0	0	0	0	2 442	305	100	1 136
Capital	7	0	0	0	0	0	0	0	0	0	0	0	884	7 749	2 203	8 342
Total		0	0	0	0	0	0	0	0	0			3 327	8 054	2 303	9 478
Total		0	0	0	0	0	0	0	0	0	0	0	3 979	17 313	4 892	17 700
ACTIVITIES – Agriculture, hunting and foresty..	8	0	0	0	0	0	0	0	0	0	0	0	0	0	0	0
Industry, including energy	9	0	0	0	0	0	0	0	0	0	0	0	0	0	0	0
Construction	10	0	0	0	0	0	0	0	0	0	0	0	0	0	0	0
Wholesale and retail trade, repair ..	11	0	0	0	0	0	0	0	0	0	0	0	0	0	0	0
Financial, real-estate, renting and..	12	0	0	0	0	0	0	0	0	0	0	0	0	0	0	0
Other service activities	13	0	0	0	0	0	0	0	0	0	0	0	0	0	0	0
Total		0	0	0	0	0	0	0	0	0	0	0	0	0	0	0
PRODUCTS – Products of agriculture, hunting ..	14	0	0	0	0	0	0	0	0	0	0	0	606	4 640	0	369
Products from mining and quarry..	15	0	0	0	0	0	0	0	0	0	0	0	1 756	29 158	5 096	6 608
Construction work	16	0	0	0	0	0	0	0	0	0	0	0	30	250	3 394	280
Wholesale & retail trade services..	17	0	0	0	0	0	0	0	0	0	0	0	121	1 198	247	4 193
Financ.intermediation serv, real .	18	0	0	0	0	0	0	0	0	0	0	0	112	3 019	563	3 092
Other services	19	0	0	0	0	0	0	0	0	0	0	0	26	315	38	347
Total		0	0	0	0	0	0	0	0	0	0	0	2 651	38 579	9 337	14 889
INSTITUTIONS – CURRENT ACCOUNT – Households (by main source of income) – employees	20	17 699	11 719	7 029	36 446	313	322	205	840	6 548	7 388	43 834	0	0	0	0
employers and/or o.a. work.	21	576	584	98	1 258	2 586	1 365	371	4 322	7 520	11 842	13 100	0	0	0	0
recipients of pensions	22	223	234	61	518	37	54	7	98	1 205	1 302	1 820	0	0	0	0
others	23	208	145	45	398	25	30	4	59	402	461	859	0	0	0	0
Total		18 705	12 682	7 233	38 620	2 961	1 771	587	5 319	15 675	20 994	59 614	0	0	0	0
Enterprises (non financial corporations)	24	0	0	0	0	0	0	0	0	11 561	11 561	11 561	0	0	0	0
Financial corporations	25	0	0	0	0	0	0	0	0	1 787	1 787	1 787	0	0	0	0
Government	26	0	0	0	0	0	0	0	0	- 2 558	- 2 558	- 2 558	- 135	- 31	- 20	- 96
Non Profit Inst.Serv.Househ. (NPISH)	27	0	0	0	0	0	0	0	0	137	137	137	0	0	0	0
Total		18 705	12 682	7 233	38 620	2 961	1 771	587	5 319	26 603	31 922	70 542	- 135	- 31	- 20	- 96
CAPITAL A. – Households	28	0	0	0	0	0	0	0	0	0	0	0	0	0	0	0
Enterprises (non financial corporations)	29	0	0	0	0	0	0	0	0	0	0	0	0	0	0	0
Financial corporations	30	0	0	0	0	0	0	0	0	0	0	0	0	0	0	0
Government	31	0	0	0	0	0	0	0	0	0	0	0	0	0	0	0
Non Profit Inst.Serv.Househ. (NPISH)	32	0	0	0	0	0	0	0	0	0	0	0	0	0	0	0
Total		0	0	0	0	0	0	0	0	0	0	0	0	0	0	0
FINANCIAL ACCOUNT	33	0	0	0	0	0	0	0	0	0	0	0	0	0	0	0
REST OF THE WORLD	34	2	60	1	64	0	0	0	0	3 363	3 363	3 426	- 34	- 8	- 5	- 24
TOTAL		18 708	12 742	7 234	38 683	2 961	1 771	587	5 319	29 965	35 285	73 968	6 460	55 852	14 204	32 469

Source: Portuguese National Accounts (Appendix A) and Portuguese Pilot – National Accounting Matrix (Appendix B)

Table 15 – Portuguese SAM (Social Accounting Matrix) for 1995 (in millions of euros) (continued)

Incomes (receipts) \ Outlays (expenditures)		PRODUCTION and TRADE – ACTIVITIES: Financial, real-estate, renting and busin. activi	ACTIVITIES: Other service activities	ACTIVITIES: Total	PRODUCTS: Products of agriculture, hunting, forest..	PRODUCTS: Products from mining and quar-rying	PRODUCTS: Construction work	PRODUCTS: Wholesale and retail trade services;	PRODUCTS: Financial intermediation services, real estate, renting	PRODUCTS: Other services	PRODUCTS: Total	INSTITUTIONS – CURRENT ACCOUNT – Households (by main source of income): employees	employers and/or o.a. work	recipients of pens.	others	Total
		12	13		14	15	16	17	18	19		20	21	22	23	
PRODUCTION and TRADE – FACTORS – Labour (employees) – Lower	1	1 441	4 513	18 629	0	0	0	0	0	0	0	0	0	0	0	0
Medium	2	1 466	5 568	12 739	0	0	0	0	0	0	0	0	0	0	0	0
Higher	3	1 305	3 549	7 196	0	0	0	0	0	0	0	0	0	0	0	0
Total		4 212	13 630	38 563	0	0	0	0	0	0	0	0	0	0	0	0
Own Assets – Labour (employers and/or own-) – Lower	4	66	431	2 961	0	0	0	0	0	0	0	0	0	0	0	0
Medium	5	100	445	1 771	0	0	0	0	0	0	0	0	0	0	0	0
Higher	6	94	200	587	0	0	0	0	0	0	0	0	0	0	0	0
Total		259	1 076	5 319	0	0	0	0	0	0	0	0	0	0	0	0
Capital	7	5 323	2 341	26 842	0	0	0	0	0	0	0	0	0	0	0	0
Total		5 583	3 417	32 161	0	0	0	0	0	0	0	0	0	0	0	0
Total		9 794	17 047	70 725	0	0	0	0	0	0	0	0	0	0	0	0
ACTIVITIES – Agriculture, hunting and foresty..	8	0	0	0	6 060	379	2	0	19	0	6 460	0	0	0	0	0
Industry, including energy	9	0	0	0	0	55 321	69	2	413	48	55 852	0	0	0	0	0
Construction	10	0	0	0	0	12	14 191	0	0	0	14 204	0	0	0	0	0
Wholesale and retail trade, repair ..	11	0	0	0	0	25	13	31 749	683	0	32 469	0	0	0	0	0
Financial, real-estate, renting and..	12	0	0	0	0	5	14	0	20 967	0	20 987	0	0	0	0	0
Other service activities	13	0	0	0	3	81	28	78	852	23 379	24 421	0	0	0	0	0
Total		0	0	0	6 064	55 823	14 317	31 829	22 934	23 427	154 394	0	0	0	0	0
PRODUCTS – Products of agriculture, hunting ..	14	0	78	5 693	0	0	0	0	0	0	0	1 459	488	527	73	2 546
Products from mining and quarry..	15	1 559	3 346	47 524	0	0	0	0	0	0	0	17 408	5 553	4 088	918	27 967
Construction work	16	525	128	4 606	0	0	0	0	0	0	0	40	10	21	3	74
Wholesale & retail trade services..	17	897	896	7 552	1 236	13 886	0	- 15 122	0	0	0	3 659	1 062	574	172	5 467
Financ.intermediation serv, real ..	18	7 514	2 365	16 666	0	0	0	0	0	0	0	3 752	1 588	864	185	6 388
Other services	19	713	623	2 062	0	0	0	0	0	0	0	4 020	1 087	874	155	6 136
Total		11 209	7 437	84 102	1 236	13 886	0	- 15 122	0	0	0	30 337	9 787	6 949	1 505	48 578
INSTITUTIONS – CURRENT ACCOUNT – Households (by main source of income) – employees	20	0	0	0	0	0	0	0	0	0	0	124	49	17	15	206
employers and/or o.a. work.	21	0	0	0	0	0	0	0	0	0	0	52	20	7	6	86
recipients of pensions	22	0	0	0	0	0	0	0	0	0	0	38	15	5	5	62
others	23	0	0	0	0	0	0	0	0	0	0	70	28	10	9	116
Total		0	0	0	0	0	0	0	0	0	0	285	112	39	35	470
Enterprises (non financial corporations)	24	0	0	0	0	0	0	0	0	0	0	307	122	880	30	1 339
Financial corporations	25	0	0	0	0	0	0	0	0	0	0	1 715	223	144	43	2 125
Government	26	- 13	- 50	- 346	- 1	7 108	405	1 046	1 347	378	10 283	11 825	1 061	828	169	13 883
Non Profit Inst.Serv.Househ. (NPISH)	27	0	0	0	0	0	0	0	0	0	0	215	65	17	27	323
Total		- 13	- 50	- 346	- 1	7 108	405	1 046	1 347	378	10 283	14 346	1 582	1 908	304	18 141
CAPITAL A. – Households	28	0	0	0	0	0	0	0	0	0	0	615	6 385	1 071	- 119	7 952
Enterprises (non financial corporations)	29	0	0	0	0	0	0	0	0	0	0	0	0	0	0	0
Financial corporations	30	0	0	0	0	0	0	0	0	0	0	0	0	0	0	0
Government	31	0	0	0	0	0	0	0	0	0	0	0	0	0	0	0
Non Profit Inst.Serv.Househ. (NPISH)	32	0	0	0	0	0	0	0	0	0	0	0	0	0	0	0
Total		0	0	0	0	0	0	0	0	0	0					7 952
FINANCIAL ACCOUNT	33	0	0	0	0	0	0	0	0	0	0	0	0	0	0	0
REST OF THE WORLD	34	- 3	- 13	- 87	1 481	24 689	32	840	1 181	156	28 379	1 126	363	205	49	1 743
TOTAL		20 987	24 421	154 394	8 781	101 506	14 754	18 592	25 462	23 961	193 056	46 424	18 117	10 133	1 740	76 413

Source: Portuguese National Accounts (Appendix A) and Portuguese Pilot – National Accounting Matrix (Appendix B)

Table 15 – Portuguese SAM (Social Accounting Matrix) for 1995 (in millions of euros) (continued)

Incomes (receipts) \ Outlays (expenditures)					INSTITUTIONS – CURRENT ACCOUNT: Enterprises (nonfinancial corporations)	Financial corporations	Govern-ment	Non Profit Institutions Serving Households (NPISH)	Total	INSTITUTIONS – CAPITAL ACCOUNT: Households	Enterprises (nonfinancial corporations)	Financial corporations	Govern-ment	Non Profit Institutions Serving Households (NPISH)	Total	FINANCIAL ACCOUNT	REST OF THE WORLD	TOTAL
					24	25	25	27		28	29	30	31	32		33	34	
PRODUCTION and TRADE	FACTORS	Labour (employees)	Lower	1	0	0	0	0	0	0	0	0	0	0	0	0	79	18 708
			Medium	2	0	0	0	0	0	0	0	0	0	0	0	0	4	12 742
			Higher	3	0	0	0	0	0	0	0	0	0	0	0	0	37	7 234
			Total		0	0	0	0	0	0	0	0	0	0	0	0	120	38 683
		Own Assets – Labour (employers and/or own-)	Lower	4	0	0	0	0	0	0	0	0	0	0	0	0	0	2 961
			Medium	5	0	0	0	0	0	0	0	0	0	0	0	0	0	1 771
			Higher	6	0	0	0	0	0	0	0	0	0	0	0	0	0	587
			Total		0	0	0	0	0	0	0	0	0	0	0	0	0	5 319
		Own Assets	Capital	7	0	0	0	0	0	0	0	0	0	0	0	0	3 123	29 965
			Total		0	0	0	0	0	0	0	0	0	0	0	0	3 123	35 285
		Total			0	0	0	0	0	0	0	0	0	0	0	0	3 243	73 968
	ACTIVITIES	Agriculture, hunting and foresty..		8	0	0	0	0	0	0	0	0	0	0	0	0	0	6 460
		Industry, including energy		9	0	0	0	0	0	0	0	0	0	0	0	0	0	55 852
		Construction		10	0	0	0	0	0	0	0	0	0	0	0	0	0	14 204
		Wholesale and retail trade, repair ..		11	0	0	0	0	0	0	0	0	0	0	0	0	0	32 469
		Financial, real-estate, renting and..		12	0	0	0	0	0	0	0	0	0	0	0	0	0	20 987
		Other service activities		13	0	0	0	0	0	0	0	0	0	0	0	0	0	24 421
		Total			0	0	0	0	0	0	0	0	0	0	0	0	0	154 394
	PRODUCTS	Products of agriculture, hunting ..		14	0	0	18	0	2 564	185	130	0	3	0	318	0	205	8 781
		Products from mining and quarry..		15	0	0	628	0	28 595	768	5 282	347	452	246	7 095	0	18 292	101 506
		Construction work		16	0	0	0	0	74	4 148	2 816	437	2 552	120	10 072	0	1	14 754
		Wholesale & retail trade services..		17	0	0	37	0	5 504	91	194	19	1	0	305	0	5 231	18 592
		Financ.intermediation serv, real ..		18	0	0	77	43	6 508	505	1 049	110	8	0	1 671	0	617	25 462
		Other services		19	0	0	14 272	1 245	21 653	58	91	10	1	1	160	0	87	23 961
		Total			0	0	15 032	1 288	64 898	5 755	9 562	922	3 018	366	19 623	0	24 433	193 056
INSTITUTIONS	CURRENT ACCOUNT	Households (by main source of income)	employees	20	312	667	2 238	3	3 426	0	0	0	0	0	0	0	2 353	49 613
			employers and/or o.a. work.	21	124	145	885	1	1 242	0	0	0	0	0	0	0	754	15 096
			recipients of pensions	22	881	778	6 245	9	7 975	0	0	0	0	0	0	0	120	9 915
			others	23	33	460	254	0	864	0	0	0	0	0	0	0	66	1 789
			Total		1 349	2 051	9 623	13	13 506	0	0	0	0	0	0	0	3 293	76 413
		Enterprises (non financial corporations)		24	58	363	0	0	1 759	0	0	0	0	0	0	0	23	13 344
		Financial corporations		25	329	29	4	14	2 501	0	0	0	0	0	0	0	35	4 323
		Government		26	2 108	229	6 866	7	23 092	0	0	0	0	0	0	0	609	31 081
		Non Profit Inst.Serv.Househ. (NPISH)		27	50	34	878	0	1 286	0	0	0	0	0	0	0	0	1 423
		Total			3 894	2 705	17 371	35	42 145	0	0	0	0	0	0	0	3 960	126 583
	CAPITAL A.	Households		28	0	0	0	0	7 952	0	0	812	206	0	1 018	- 4 023	147	5 095
		Enterprises (non financial corporations)		29	9 342	0	0	0	9 342	0	0	0	707	0	707	- 49	896	10 896
		Financial corporations		30	0	1 558	0	0	1 558	0	484	328	2	0	814	- 287	0	2 085
		Government		31	0	0	- 1 661	0	- 1 661	63	161	3	1 870	4	2 100	4 423	1 275	6 136
		Non Profit Inst.Serv.Househ. (NPISH)		32	0	0	0	100	100	0	0	0	291	0	291	- 23	1	370
		Total			9 342	1 558	- 1 661	100	17 291	63	645	1 143	3 075	4	4 930	40	2 320	24 582
	FINANCIAL ACCOUNT			33	0	0	0	0	0	0	0	0	0	0	0	35 030	9 257	44 287
REST OF THE WORLD				34	108	60	339	0	2 249	- 723	689	20	43	0	29	9 217	0	43 213
TOTAL					13 344	4 323	31 081	1 423	126 583	5 095	10 896	2 085	6 136	370	24 581	44 287	43 213	

Source: Portuguese National Accounts (Appendix A) and Portuguese Pilot – National Accounting Matrix (Appendix B)

3.

The Model

3.1. Framework and assumptions

Now that all the details inherent in the SAM that will serve as the database for the model to be designed below have been specified, the starting idea will be the one outlined in the article "Macroeconomic Modelling Based on Social-Accounting Principles" and expressed in the following words:

> "A dictum usually attributed to Lord Keynes posits that every economic model has a corresponding accounting framework. For macroeconomic models, this accounting framework must be complete in the sense that every receipt must be offset by a corresponding expenditure. One consequence is that all the transactions in a model can be expressed within a SAM framework. The values assumed by all the different types of transactions can therefore be set out as the elements of a SAM" (Drud et al., 1986: 112).

Therefore, a static model will be defined and conceived as a starting point for both a comparative static and a dynamic approach. On the other hand, since it will not be possible to calculate and work with price and volume indexes, only a valuation system will be defined, which will serve as the basis for the price system to be defined later on. For the time being, a fixed-price model will be designed. Linear equations will be worked with, avoiding elasticities, marginal propensities and other parameters. These are necessarily estimated from an empirical base, which is not available.

Thus, the main concern will be to capture (to begin with in a very simple way) all the national accounting transactions considered in the numerical version of the SAM (the database for this model), and, after its calibration, to conduct some experiments and define some scenarios for the aspects that the author intends to study.

The process of calibration will involve determining the parameters and exogenous variables that are to be specified, so that, after processing the model, the base SAM (presented in Chapter 2) is exactly replicated. The software used to process the model was the GAMS (General Algebraic Modelling System) and the quantification of the whole process took into consideration all the available information, involving the values calculated using the information contained in that same base SAM, further supplemented by additional data, as described in Appendix E. These values will be assumed as valid for the "experiments and scenarios with the distributional impact of government policies", which are to be outlined in Chapter 6, except for those which will be subject to shocks.

Since the purpose of this model is to study income distribution, some usual specifications for the model will not be considered. These specifications include the ones that are also constructed within a general equilibrium framework, usually to study trade issues, such as the distinction between domestically produced and imported products, while external trade will be considered exogenous in this version of the model.

For the purposes of simplification, it will be assumed that all domestically produced output is market output, and therefore any output produced for own final use and other non-market output will be considered as non-existent[10].

---

[10] In the year of this study, these two components together account for almost 13% of total output. However, considering that this model is the

On the other hand, it will be assumed that there is sufficient production capability available in the economy to enable domestic output to respond to aggregate demand. Such a response will be considered exclusive, since (for the time being) imports are exogenous.

Many fixed parameters will be adopted and some variables will be calculated from exogenous parameters and other variables, in order to enable future experiments to be carried out with their changes.

This model is considered to be a step forward in comparison with the ones that the author has previously worked with, and, at the same time, a (necessary) stage along a path that she would like to pursue in SAM modelling. From her own experience, the author feels that SAM modelling does have a convenient path. Thus, on the one hand, when working on SAM modelling or with SAM-based models, some knowledge of SAM construction is considered to be a necessary, although not a sufficient, condition. On the other hand, underlying SAM modelling is a process of gradual maturation, which should begin with the construction and decomposition of accounting and fixed-price multipliers and the conducting of experiments with them. That is what the author has done, based essentially on the works of Pyatt, 1988; Pyatt and Roe, 1977; and Pyatt and Round, 1985. For an illustration of this work, see Santos, 1999; 2001; 2003; 2003a; 2004; 2004a; 2005a; and 2007.

This work is the materialisation of the step after multipliers.

Both before and during the development of this work, research was undertaken into SAM-based models (excluding multipliers), notably into Computable General Equilibrium (CGE) models. Some of the works studied proved important for the formation of the basic ideas used in this one, although none of them had developed any identical model. Some of them, however,

---

preliminary version of a model that will be progressively improved, they will not be considered at this stage.

were at more advanced stages of the above-mentioned modelling process. Included in this group are the following: Braber et al. (1996); Breuss and Tesche (1993); Dervis et al. (1982); Devarajan et al. (1991, 1996); Khan (1996); Lofgren et al. (2001); Norton et al. (1986); Reinert and Roland-Holst (1996); Roberts and Zolkiewski (1996); Robinson (1989); Stifel and Thorbecke (2003); Thorbecke (2000); Taylor (1990). Other works that were studied were not considered, since they represented a more advanced stage in the modelling process than the point at which this work is[11].

3.2. Specification by SAM blocks of sub-matrices

As this model is supported by a SAM database, constructed in perfect consonance with the national accounts, its specifications will either obey or be derived from the SNA, as described below.

The sources of information and the method of calculation used in the construction of the numerical (macro-)SAM (only in the case of those sub-matrices that are not calculated either

[11] Namely Blonigen B. et al. (1996), Sector-Focused General Equilibrium Modelling, in François J., Reinert K. (eds.) *Applied Methods for Trade Policy Analysis*, Cambridge University Press, Cambridge (UK), 189-230; Bourguignon F. et al. (1983) "Short-run rigidities and long-run adjustments in a CGE model of income distribution and development", *Journal of Development Economics* 13: 21-43; Capros P. et al. (1990) "An Empirical Assessment of Macroeconometric and CGE Approaches to Modeling", *Journal of Policy Modeling* 12:557-585; Coxhead I. and Warr P. (1991) "Technical Change, Land Quality, and Income Distribution: A General Equilibrium Analysis", *American Journal of Agricultural Economics* 73: 345-359; Dixon P. et al. (1992), *Notes and Problems in Applied General Equilibrium Economics*, Elsevier Science Publishers, Amsterdam (Netherlands), 392p.; Dixon P. et al. (2002), CGE models for practical policy analysis. The Australian experience, in Fossati A. and Wiegard, W. (eds.) *Policy Evaluation with Computable General Equilibrium Models*, Routledge, London and New York, 56-32; Melo J. (1988) "Computable General Equilibrium Models for Trade Policy Analysis in Developing Countries: A Survey" *Journal of Policy Modeling* 10: 469-503.

directly from the sources or whenever there are details that justify a reference to them) may also be consulted in Appendix E.

In order to make the following exposition more comprehensible, the symbols used in the description of the model will be described after the equations, which will obviously involve some repetition; however, they will be listed alphabetically and without any indices, according to their type (endogenous or exogenous variables and parameters), in Appendix F.

By convention, the parameters will be stated in lower case and the variables in upper case (at least the first letter). Endogenous variables will be written in normal letters, whereas exogenous variables, as well as the parameters, will be written in italics. The indices of each variable and parameter (the sets in Appendix F; see also the symbols with their corresponding descriptions in Table 3) – identified in lower-case subscripts – describe the SAM accounts, the first index representing the row and the second one the column, each of which is separated by commas.

In Appendix D, all the additional data will be found that are needed to calculate parameters or to establish the exogenous variables (besides those data that are contained in Appendix A and Appendix C or that can be directly collected from the SAM database).

The entire model will be worked upon in gross terms, so that the consumption of fixed capital will therefore not be considered.

The SAM blocks, identified in Table 17, are sub-matrices or sets of sub-matrices (as seen in the Basic SAM – Table 1) with common characteristics. The specification of these blocks will be carried out below and involves, on the one hand, an identification of the transactions of the National Accounts that are considered in the calculation of these in the numerical SAM and, on the other hand, a definition and specification of the equation, or system of equations, to be considered in the algebraic SAM or SAM-based model.

Table 17 – Basic SAM by blocks

Incomes (receipts) \ Outlays (expenditures)		Production and Trade			Institutions			Rest of the World (rw)
		Factors (f)	Activities (*a*)	Products (p)	Current A. (dic)	Capital A. (dik)	Financial A. (dif)	
Production and Trade	Factors (f)	0		0	0	0	0	
	Activities (*a*)	0	0	Production	0	0	0	0
	Products (p)	0		Trade and Transport Margins			0	
Institutions	Current A. (dic)					0	0	
	Capital A. (dik)	0	0	0	Gross Saving		(-) Net lending/ borrowing	
	Financial A. (dif)	0	0	0	0	0		
Rest of the World (rw)								X

Blocks with more than one sub-matrix:

- Compensation of the factors of production
- Domestic Trade
- External Trade
- Net Indirect Taxes
- Current Transfers
- Capital Transfers
- Financial Transactions

3.2.1. *Compensation of the factors of production*

This block consists of the income of the institutional sectors originating from the compensation of the services provided through their real and financial assets to the activities of production and to the rest of the world, namely:

- Compensation of employees (transaction D1 of the National Accounts), which is the total remuneration, in cash or in kind, payable by an employer to an employee in return for work done by the latter during the accounting period. Compensation of employees is broken down into wages and salaries (in cash or in kind; transaction D11) and employers' social contributions (actual and imputed social contributions; transaction D12) (SNA 93, paragraphs 7.21-7.47; ESA 95, paragraphs 4.02-4.13).
- Compensation of own-account assets, i.e. all the above-mentioned income that is not derived from the compensation of employees, including the compensation of employers and/or own-account workers, and of capital, namely property income (transaction D4 of the National Accounts). This is the income that is receivable by the owner of a financial asset or a tangible non-produced asset in return for providing funds to, or putting the tangible non-produced asset at the disposal of, another institutional unit. Property income is composed of interest, the distributed income of corporations, dividends, withdrawals from the income of quasi-corporations, reinvested earnings from direct foreign investment, property income attributed to insurance policy holders and rents (SNA 93, paragraphs 7.87-7.133; ESA 95, paragraphs 4.41-4.76).

3.2.1.1. *Gross Added Value*

Considering the framework and the assumptions described in Section 3.1, the gross added value of each group of activities will be an exogenous proportion (β_a) of its value of production, which is defined in Section 3.2.2. In turn, this gross added value will be distributed among types of labour in constant proportions ($d1s_{fle,a}$ for employees and $b3s_{foal,a}$ for employers and/or own-account workers), while the share attributed to the capital will also be a constant proportion ($b2gp_{foak,a}$), but in this case of the part of the gross added value attributed to labour. From the later and exogenously defined coefficients of wages and salaries ($w_{fle,a}$) and employers' social contributions ($esc_{fle,a}$), on the one hand, and gross mixed income ($b3gc_{foal,a}$), on the other hand, it is possible to calculate, respectively, the number of employees (LE) and of employers and/or own-account workers (LOA). It will then be possible to calculate the unemployment rate (Ur) of a given active population (*AP*).

$$\mathrm{GAV}_a = \beta_a * \mathrm{VP}_a \quad (3.1)$$
$$\mathrm{GAV}_{fle,a} = d1s_{fle,a} * \mathrm{GAV}_a \quad (3.2)$$
$$\mathrm{LE}_{fle,a} = \mathrm{GAV}_{fle,a} \,/\, (w_{fle,a} + esc_{fle,a}) \quad (3.3)$$
$$\mathrm{LE} = \Sigma_{fle}\, \Sigma_a\, \mathrm{LE}_{fle,a} \quad (3.4)$$
$$\mathrm{D1}_a = \Sigma_{fle}\, \mathrm{GAV}_{fle,a} \quad (3.5)$$
$$\mathrm{GAV}_{fle} = \Sigma_a\, \mathrm{GAV}_{fle,a} \quad (3.6)$$
$$\mathrm{GAV}_{foal,a} = b3s_{foal,a} * \mathrm{GAV}_a \quad (3.7)$$
$$\mathrm{LOA}_{foal,a} = \mathrm{GAV}_{foal,a} / \, b3gc_{foal,a} \quad (3.8)$$
$$\mathrm{LOA} = \Sigma_{foal}\, \Sigma_a\, \mathrm{LOA}_{foal,a} \quad (3.9)$$
$$\mathrm{B3g}_a = \Sigma_{foal}\, \mathrm{GAV}_{foal,a} \quad (3.10)$$
$$\mathrm{GAV}_{foal} = \Sigma_a\, \mathrm{GAV}_{foal,a} \quad (3.11)$$
$$\mathrm{E} = \mathrm{LE} + \mathrm{LOA} \quad (3.12)$$
$$\mathrm{Ur} = 1 - (\mathrm{E}/\, AP)*100 \quad (3.13)$$
$$\mathrm{GAV}_{foak,a} = b2gp_{foak,a} * (\mathrm{D1}_a + \mathrm{B3g}_a) \quad (3.14)$$
$$\mathrm{B2g}_a = \Sigma_{foak}\, \mathrm{GAV}_{foaka} \quad (3.15)$$
$$\mathrm{GAV}_{foak} = \Sigma_a\, \mathrm{GAV}_{foak,a} \quad (3.16)$$
$$\mathrm{GAV}_a = \mathrm{D1}_a + \mathrm{B3g}_a + \mathrm{B2g}_a \quad (3.17)$$

Where:

GAV_a = gross added value (at factor cost) of activities *a*

β_a = proportion of gross added value in the value of production of activities *a*

VP_a = value of production of activities *a*, in accordance with (3.29)

$GAV_{fle,a}$ = gross added value (at factor cost) of activities *a* generated by employees

$d1s_{fle,a}$ = share of compensation of employees in the gross added value of activities *a*

$LE_{fle,a}$ = employees of activities *a*

$w_{fle,a}$ = wages and salary (in cash or in kind) coefficient: amount of wages/salary (transaction D11 of the National Accounts) paid by activities *a* to each employee

$esc_{fle,a}$ = employers' social contributions (actual and imputed social contributions) coefficient: amount of social contributions (transaction D12 of the National Accounts) paid by the employers of activities *a* to the government per employee

LE = labour – employees (total)

$D1_a$ = compensation of employees paid by activities *a*

GAV_{fle} = gross added value (at factor cost) generated by employees (total)

$GAV_{foal,a}$ = gross added value (at factor cost) of activities *a* generated by employers and/or own-account workers

$b3s_{foal,a}$ = share of compensation of employers and/or own-account workers (gross mixed income) in the gross added value of activities *a*

$LOA_{foal,a}$ = employers and/or own-account workers of activities *a*

$b3gc_{foal,a}$ = gross mixed income coefficient: amount of gross mixed income of activities *a* per employer and/or own-account worker

LOA = labour – employers and/or own-account workers (total)

$B3g_a$ = gross mixed income of activities *a*

GAV_{foal} = gross added value (at factor cost) generated by employers and/or own-account workers (total)

E = employed population

Ur = unemployment rate

AP = active population

$GAV_{foak,a}$ = gross added value (at factor cost) of activities a generated by capital

$b2gp_{foak,a}$ = proportion of capital compensation (gross operating surplus) in labour compensation of activities a

$B2g_a$ = gross operating surplus of activities a

GAV_{foak} = gross added value (at factor cost) generated by capital (total)

3.2.1.2. *Compensation of factors from the rest of the world*

All this part will be considered as exogenous.

$$CFR_{fle,rw} = D1RW_{fle}$$

$$CFR_{foak,rw} = D4RW$$

Where:

$CFR_{fle,rw} = D1RW_{fle}$ = compensation of employees received from the rest of the world

$CFR_{foak,rw} = D4RW$ = property income received from the rest of the world

3.2.1.3. *Gross National Income*

The gross national income attributed to the factors of production will be obtained by excluding from the gross added value at factor cost generated in the domestic economy the compensation (of the factors of production) sent to the rest of the world, and by including the compensation (of the factors of production) received from the rest of the world. The part relating to labour (employees – GNI_{fle} and employers and/or own-account workers – GNI_{foal}) will be distributed among each group of households according to fixed coefficients of their main source of income ($ce_{dic,fle}$ for employees and $coa_{dic,foal}$ for employers and/or own-account workers). In turn, the compensation of capital will be distributed among the domestic institutions through exogenously defined shares ($sk_{dic,foak}$).

$$\mathrm{GNI}_{fle} = \mathrm{GAV}_{fle} + CFR_{fle,rw} - \mathrm{CFS}_{rw,fle} \quad (3.18)$$

$$\mathrm{GNI}_{dic,fle} = ce_{dic,fle} * \mathrm{GNI}_{fle} \quad (3.19)$$

$$\mathrm{GNI}_{foal} = \mathrm{GAV}_{foal} \quad (3.20)$$

$$\mathrm{GNI}_{dic,foal} = coa_{dic,foal} * \mathrm{GNI}_{foal} \quad (3.21)$$

$$\mathrm{GNI}_{foak} = \mathrm{GAV}_{foak} + CFR_{foak,rw} - CFS_{rw,foak} \quad (3.22)$$

$$\mathrm{GNI}_{dic,foak} = sk_{dic,foak} * \mathrm{GNI}_{foak} \quad (3.23)$$

$$\mathrm{GNI}_{dic} = \Sigma_{fle}\, \mathrm{GNI}_{dic,fle} + \Sigma_{foal}\, \mathrm{GNI}_{dic,foal} + \mathrm{GNI}_{dic,foak} \quad (3.24)$$

$$\mathrm{GNI} = \Sigma_{dic}\, \mathrm{GNI}_{dic} \quad (3.25)$$

Where:

GNI_{fle} = gross national income (at factor cost) generated by employees

GAV_{fle} = gross added value (at factor cost) generated by employees, in accordance with (3.6)

$CFR_{fle,rw}$ = compensation of employees received from the rest of the world (see Section 3.2.1.2.)

$\mathrm{CFS}_{rw,fle}$ = compensation of employees sent to the rest of the world, in accordance with (3.26)

$\mathrm{GNI}_{dic,fle}$ = gross national income (at factor cost) of domestic institutions (households – dich) generated by employees

$ce_{dic,fle}$ = coefficient of main source of income of domestic institutions (households – dich) that are recipients of compensation of employees

GNI_{foal} = gross national income (at factor cost) generated by employers and/or own-account workers

GAV_{foal} = gross added value (at factor cost) generated by employers and/or own-account workers, in accordance with (3.11)

$\mathrm{GNI}_{dic,foal}$ = gross national income (at factor cost) of domestic institutions (households-dich) generated by employers and/or own-account workers

$coa_{dic,foal}$ = coefficient of main source of income of domestic institutions (households – dich) that are recipients of compensation of employers and/or own-account workers

GNI_{foak} = gross national income (at factor cost) generated by capital

GAV_{foalk} = gross added value (at factor cost) generated by capital, in accordance with (3.16)

$CFR_{foak,rw}$ = property income received from the rest of the world (see Section 3.2.1.2.)

$CFS_{rw,foak}$ = property income sent to the rest of the world (see Section 3.2.1.4.)

$GNI_{dic,foak}$ = gross national income (at factor cost) of domestic institutions generated by capital

$sk_{dic,foak}$ = share of compensation of capital received by domestic institutions (dic)

GNI_{dic} = (total) national income (at factor cost) of domestic institutions (dic)

GNI = gross national income (at factor cost) – total

3.2.1.4. *Compensation of factors to the rest of the world*

The only part of this vector that will be defined by the model is the one relating to the compensation of employees (sent to the rest of the world), which will be considered as a fixed share ($clr_{rw,fle}$) of the gross added value (at factor cost) generated by them.

$$CFS_{rw,fle} = clr_{rw,fle} * GAV_{fle} \qquad (3.26)$$

$$CFS_{rw,foak} = D4PRW$$

Where:

$CFS_{rw,fle}$ = compensation of employees sent to the rest of the world

$clr_{rw,fle}$ = share of the compensation of employees paid by activities and sent to the rest of the world

GAV_{fle} = gross added value (at factor cost) generated by employees, in accordance with (3.6)

$CFS_{rw,foak} = D4PRW$ = property income sent to the rest of the world

3.2.2. *Production*

This matrix/block represents the output of goods and services (transaction P1 of the National Accounts) and consists of the products created during the accounting period. It is subdivided into market output, output produced for own final use and other non-market output (SNA 93, paragraphs 6.38-6.51; ESA 95, paragraphs 3.14-3.68).

As assumed in section 3.1, all output will be considered as market output, which will respond exclusively to aggregate demand, since there is sufficient production capability available in the economy.

In order to identify and calculate the various components of the valuation system underlying the prices implicit in these values, the production value of products will be broken down into basic price components: factor cost (Cfe, Cfoa, Cfk), intermediate consumption (Cic) and net taxes on production (Cnta). On the other hand, a fixed share of the production of each group of activities will be considered in the value of production of each group of products ($\alpha_{a,p}$).

$$VP_p = AD_p\text{-}TMT_p\text{-}NTP_p\text{-}IM_p \quad (3.27)$$
$$VP_{a,p} = VP_p{}^*\alpha_{a,p} \quad (3.28)$$
$$VP_a = \Sigma_p \; VP_{a,p} \quad (3.29)$$
$$VP = \Sigma_p \; \Sigma_a \; VP_{a,p} \quad (3.30)$$
$$Cfe_p = VP_{p,a}{}^*(D1_a \,/VCT_a) \quad (3.31)$$
$$Cfoa_p = VP_{p,a}{}^*(B3g_a \,/VCT_a) \quad (3.32)$$
$$Cfk_p = VP_{p,a}{}^*(B2g_a \,/VCTa) \quad (3.33)$$
$$Cic_p = VP_{p,a}{}^*(VIC_a \,/VCT_a) \quad (3.34)$$
$$Cnta_p = VP_{p,a}{}^*(NTAA_a \,/VCT_a) \quad (3.35)$$
$$VP_p = Cfe_p\text{+}Cfoa_p\text{+}Cfk_p\text{+}Cic_p\text{+}Cnta_p \quad (3.36)$$

Where:

VP_p = value of production (domestic output, at basic prices) of products p

AD_p = value of aggregate demand of products p, in accordance with (3.105)

TMT_p = trade and transport margins on domestically transacted products p with correction, in accordance with (3.51)

NTP_p = net taxes on domestically transacted products p, in accordance with (3.43)

IM_p = value of imports of products p (see Section 3.2.3.)

$VP_{a,p}$ = value of production (domestic output, at basic prices) of products p by activities *a*

$\alpha_{a,p}$ = share of the production of activities *a* in the value of production of products p

VP_a = value of production (domestic output, at basic prices) of activities *a*

VP = value of production (domestic output, at basic prices) (total)

Cfe_p = factor cost component – labour (employees): amount relating to the compensation of employees in the value of production of products p

$D1_a$ = compensation of employees paid by activities *a*, in accordance with (3.5)

VCT_a = value of total costs of activity *a*, in accordance with (3.113)

$Cfoa_p$ = factor cost component – labour (employers and/or own-account workers): amount relating to the compensation of employers and/or own-account workers in the value of production of products p

$B3g_a$ = gross mixed income of activities *a*, in accordance with (3.10)

Cfk_p = factor cost component – capital: amount relating to the compensation of capital in the value of production of products p

$B2g_a$ = gross operating surplus of activities *a*, in accordance with (3.15)

Cic_p = intermediate consumption component: amount relating to intermediate consumption in the value of production of products p

VIC_a = value of intermediate consumption of activities *a*, in accordance with (3.57)

$Cnta_p$ = net taxes on production component: amount relating to net taxes on production in the value of production of products p

$NTAA_a$ = net taxes on production paid by activities *a* (see Section 3.2.4.1.)

3.2.3. *External Trade*

This block represents the transactions in goods and services (purchases, barter, gifts or grants) from non-residents to residents, or imports (transaction P7 of the National Accounts – $IM_{rw,p}$), and from residents to non-residents, or exports (transaction P6 of the National Accounts – $EX_{p,rw}$) (ESA 95, paragraphs 3.128-3.146[12]).

Although the National Accounts consider direct purchases abroad by residents ($FC_{rw,dic}$) as an import, in this model they will be considered as a current transfer from households to the rest of the world, considering that they will not be traded in the domestic market.

Imports are valued at c.i.f. (cost-insurance-freight included) prices (at the border of the importing country), whereas exports are valued at f.o.b. (free on board) prices (at the border of the exporting country) (ESA 95, paragraph 3.138). Therefore, both levels of valuation can be considered equivalent to the basic price level.

In this (preliminary) version of the model external trade will be considered to be exogenous, as assumed in section 3.1.

[12] The SNA 93 does not deal directly with these transactions, which are dealt with in all the other transactions with the rest of the world in its section XIV – The Rest of the World Account (external transactions account).

3.2.4. *Net Indirect Taxes or net taxes on production and imports*

Net indirect taxes or the net taxes on production and imports have two main components: net taxes on production and net taxes on products, which will be treated separately in the model. On the other hand, the amount of each component will represent a receipt not only of the Portuguese general government, through the domestic institutions' current account (dicg), but also of the European Union institutions, through the rest of the world account (rw), which will also be treated separately in the model.

3.2.4.1. *Net Taxes on Production*

This part represents the (other) taxes on production (transaction D29 of the National Accounts) minus the (other) subsidies to production (transaction D39 of the National Accounts). The former consists of all the taxes that enterprises incur as a result of engaging in production, regardless of the quantity or value of the goods and services produced or sold (SNA 93, paragraph 7.70; ESA 95, paragraphs 4.22-4.24), while the latter consists of subsidies, except those subsidies to products which resident producer units may receive as a consequence of engaging in production (SNA 93, paragraph 7.79; ESA 95, paragraphs 4.36-4.40).

Therefore, the net taxes on production paid by each group of activities ($NTAA_a$) will be considered as exogenous, its distribution among domestic (Portuguese general government – dicg) and foreign (European Union institutions – rw) receivers being carried out through fixed shares ($ntag_{\mathrm{dic},a}$ and $ntarw_{\mathrm{rw},a}$, respectively).

$$\mathrm{NTA}_{\mathrm{dic},a} = ntag_{\mathrm{dic},a} * NTAA_a \qquad (3.37)$$

$$\mathrm{NTA}_{\mathrm{rw},a} = ntarw_{\mathrm{rw},a} * NTAA_a \qquad (3.38)$$

$$\mathrm{NTA}_{\mathrm{dic}} = \Sigma_a \mathrm{NTA}_{\mathrm{dic},a} \qquad (3.39)$$

$$\mathrm{NTA}_a = \Sigma_{\mathrm{dic}} \mathrm{NTA}_{\mathrm{dic},a} \qquad (3.40)$$

$$NTA_{rw} = \Sigma_a NTA_{rw,a} \quad (3.41)$$
$$NTA = \Sigma_{dic} NTA_{dic} + NTA_{rw} \quad (3.42)$$

Where:

$NTAA_a$ = (total) net taxes on production paid by activities a

$NTA_{dic,a}$= net taxes on production paid by activities a and received by domestic institutions (Portuguese general government – dicg)

$ntag_{dic,a}$ = share of net taxes on production paid by activities a and received by domestic institutions (Portuguese general government – dicg)

$NTA_{rw,a}$ = net taxes on production paid by activities a and received by the rest of the world (European Union institutions)

$ntarw_{rw,a}$ = share of net taxes on production paid by activities a and received by the rest of the world (European Union institutions)

NTA_{dic} = net taxes on production received by domestic institutions (Portuguese general government – dicg), from all activities

NTA_a = (total) net taxes on production paid by activities a to (all) domestic institutions

NTA_{rw} = net taxes on production received by the rest of the world (European Union institutions), from all activities

NTA = net taxes on production (total)

3.2.4.2. *Net Taxes on Products*

This part represents the taxes on products (transaction D21 of the National Accounts) minus the subsidies on products (transaction D31 of the National Accounts). The former consists of taxes that are payable per unit of a good or service produced or transacted (SNA 93, paragraphs 7.62-7.69; ESA 95, paragraphs 4.16-4.21), while the latter consists of subsidies payable per unit of a good or service produced or imported (SNA 93, paragraphs 7.73-7.78; ESA 95, paragraphs 4.33-4.35).

Therefore, the net taxes on products will be a function of those products that are produced domestically and not exported (at basic prices) and imported products (at c.i.f. prices) – i.e. domestically transacted products (at basic/c.i.f. prices) (DT_p) – as well as a rate (tp_p) that is exogenously fixed. Like the net taxes on production, its distribution among domestic (Portuguese general government – dicg) and foreign (European Union institutions – rw) receivers will be carried out through fixed shares ($ntpg_{dic,p}$ and $ntprw_{rw,p}$, respectively)

$$NTP_p = tp_p * DT_p \tag{3.43}$$
$$NTP_{dic,p} = ntpg_{dic,p} * NTP_p \tag{3.44}$$
$$NTP_{rw,p} = ntprw_{rw,p} * NTP_p \tag{3.45}$$
$$NTP_{dic} = \Sigma_p NTP_{dic,p} \tag{3.46}$$
$$NTP_{rw} = \Sigma_p NTP_{rw,p} \tag{3.47}$$
$$NTP = \Sigma_{dic} NTP_{dic} + NTP_{rw} \tag{3.48}$$

Where:

NTP_p = net taxes on domestically transacted products p

tp_p = (net) tax rate on products p: amount of (net) taxes on products per unit of value of domestically transacted products p

DT_p = value of domestically transacted products p, at basic-c.i.f. prices, in accordance with (3.53)

$NTP_{dic,p}$ = net taxes on domestically transacted products p received by domestic institutions (Portuguese general government – dicg)

$ntpg_{dic,p}$ = share of net taxes on products p received by domestic institutions (Portuguese general government – dicg)

$NTP_{rw,p}$ = net taxes on domestically transacted products p received by the rest of the world (European Union institutions)

$ntprw_{rw,p}$ = share of net taxes on products p received by the rest of the world (European Union institutions)

NTP_{dic} = net taxes on (all) domestically transacted products received by domestic institutions (Portuguese general government – dicg)

NTP_{rw} = net taxes on (all) domestically transacted products received by the rest of the world (European Union institutions)

NTP = net taxes on domestically transacted products (total)

3.2.5. *Trade and transport margins*

Trade and transport margins are realised on goods purchased for resale. They are a part of the production of wholesale trade services, retail trade services and the repair services of motor vehicles, motorcycles and personal and household goods. They are recorded as part of the trade in products and are therefore included under the various components of aggregate demand. They amount to zero, since they are negative in relation to the three above mentioned activities (because the corresponding value has already been recorded in the production sub-matrix), but are positive and have the same amount in relation to all the other ones (SNA 93, paragraphs 6.110-6.114, 15.40-15.44; ESA 95, paragraphs 3.60, 9.38-9.41).

Being realised on goods purchased for resale, and therefore excluding services (p3-p6 – SAM accounts 11-14), trade and transport margins will be considered as a function of the value of domestically transacted goods (imported and domestically produced and not exported, at c.i.f./basic prices), based on an exogenously fixed rate (*tm*).

On the other hand, being a part of the production of wholesale trade services, retail trade services and the repair services of motor vehicles, motorcycles and personal and household goods (p4 and SAM account 12), which is considered in the production sub-matrix, the trade and transport margins sub-matrix will have only one non-zero row (p4 and SAM account 12).

This is the one relating to the products that result from the above-mentioned resale activity, which, with the addition of a value of correction (TMc), will amount to zero, since the positive entries for the columns relating to the resale of goods (p1-p2 and

SAM accounts 9-10) will be cancelled out by a negative entry introduced (in column p4 – SAM account 12) to avoid the double entry of the production of these activities, as referred to above.

$$TM_{p,p} = tm_{p,p}*DT_{p} \quad (3.49)$$
$$TMc_{p,p} = tmc_{p,p}*DT_{p} \quad (3.50)$$
$$TMT_{p} = \Sigma_{p} (TM_{p,p} + TMc_{p,p}) \text{ (column sum)} \quad (3.51)$$

Where:

$TM_{p,p}$ = trade and transport margins (without correction) on domestically transacted products p

$tm_{p,p}$ = rate of trade and transport margins on domestically transacted products p: amount of trade and transport margins per unit of value of domestically transacted products p

$TMc_{p,p}$ = trade and transport margins on domestically transacted products p – correction

$tmc_{p,p}$ = trade and transport margins coefficient of correction

TMT_{p} = trade and transport margins on domestically transacted products p with correction

DT_{p} = value of domestically transacted products p, at basic-c.i.f. prices, in accordance with (3.53)

3.2.6. *Domestic Trade*

Domestic trade is represented by the value of domestically transacted products, either domestically produced or imported. It is represented by the sub-matrices of intermediate and final consumption, as well as gross capital formation – transactions are valued at market or purchasers' prices, i.e. having added the trade and transport margins and the net taxes on products to the basic prices of domestically produced products or to the c.i.f. prices of imported products.

As in the case of the basic price level of the value of production, the values of the submatrices of this block will be decomposed into market price components – basic-c.i.f., trade margins and the taxes on products – through the proportions: basic-c.i.f. (Pbcif); trade and transport margins (Ptm); and net taxes on products (Pntp).

$$DTmp_p = VIC_p + FC_p + GCF_p \quad (3.52)$$
$$DT_p = DTmp_p - TMT_p - NTP_p \quad (3.53)$$
$$Ptm_p = TMT_p \;/\; DTmp_p \quad (3.54)$$
$$Pntp_p = NTP_p \;/\; DTmp_p \quad (3.55)$$
$$Pbcif_p = DT_p \;/\; DTmp_p \quad (3.56)$$

Where:

$DTmp_p$ = value of domestically transacted products p, at market prices

VIC_p = value of intermediate consumption (at market prices) of products p, in accordance with (3.59)

FC_p = value of final consumption (at market prices) of products p, in accordance with (3.68)

GCF_p = value of gross capital formation (at market prices) in products p, in accordance with (3.77)

DT_p = value of domestically transacted products p, at basic--c.i.f. prices

TMT_p = trade and transport margins on domestically transacted products p with correction, in accordance with (3.51)

NTP_p = net taxes on domestically transacted products p, in accordance with (3.43)

Ptm_p = proportion of trade and transport margins in the value of domestically transacted products p (at market prices)

$Pntp_p$ = proportion of net taxes on products in the value of domestically transacted products p (at market prices)

$Pbcif_p$ = proportion of basic-c.i.f. component in the value of domestically transacted products p (at market prices)

3.2.6.1. *Intermediate consumption*

The intermediate consumption (transaction P2 of the National Accounts) matrix/block consists of the value of the goods and services consumed as inputs by a process of production, excluding those fixed assets whose consumption is recorded as consumption of fixed capital.

The goods and services may be either transformed or used up by the production process (SNA 93, paragraphs 6.147-6.178; ESA 95, paragraphs 3.69-3.73).

It will be accepted that the total intermediate consumption value of each group of activities will be a proportion (γ_a) of their value of production, while the consumption of (domestically produced or imported) products that are used as inputs in its process of production will, in turn, be a constant proportion ($icp_{p,a}$) of that total.

$$VIC_a = \gamma_a * VP_a \tag{3.57}$$
$$VIC_{p,a} = icp_{p,a} * VIC_a \tag{3.58}$$
$$VIC_p = \Sigma_a VIC_{p,a} \tag{3.59}$$
$$VIC = \Sigma_p \Sigma_a VIC_{p,a} \tag{3.60}$$
$$Cvictm_p = VIC_p * Ptm_p \tag{3.61}$$
$$Cvicntp_p{}^{13} = VIC_p * Pntp_p \tag{3.62}$$
$$Cvicbcif_p = VIC_p * Pbcif_p \tag{3.63}$$
$$VIC_p = Cvictm_p + Cvicnt_p + Cvicbcif_p \tag{3.64}$$

Where:

VIC_a = value of intermediate consumption (at market prices) of activities *a*

γ_a = proportion of intermediate consumption in the value of production of activities *a*

[13] Since VAT (value added type tax, transaction D211 of the National Accounts) is recorded net, in the sense that it is recorded only by those purchasers who are not able to deduct it, i.e. by final (and not intermediate) users (ESA 95, paragraph 4.17), it is not included here.

VP_a = value of production of activities *a*, in accordance with (3.29)

$VIC_{p,a}$ = value of intermediate consumption (at market prices) of products p by activities *a*

$icp_{p,a}$ = coefficient of the intermediate consumption of products p: proportion of intermediate consumption of products p per unit of intermediate consumption of activities *a*

VIC_p = value of intermediate consumption (at market prices) of products p

VIC = value of intermediate consumption (at market prices) (total)

$Cvictm_p$ = trade and transport margins component of the value of intermediate consumption of products p

Ptm_p = proportion of trade and transport margins in the value of domestically transacted products p (at market prices), in accordance with (3.54)

$Cvicntp_p$ = net taxes on products component of the value of intermediate consumption of products p

$Pntp_p$ = proportion of net taxes on products in the value of domestically transacted products p (at market prices), in accordance with (3.55)

$Cvicbcif_p$ = basic-c.i.f. component of the value of intermediate consumption of products p

$Pbcif_p$ = proportion of basic-c.i.f. component in the value of domestically transacted products p (at market prices), in accordance with (3.56)

3.2.6.2. *Final Consumption*

Final consumption (transaction P3 of the National Accounts) consists of the expenditure incurred by resident institutional units on those goods or services that are used for the direct satisfaction of individual needs or wants or of the collective needs of members of the community. Such consumption takes place within the domestic territory or abroad. (SNA 93, paragraphs 9.45-9.71; ESA 95, paragraphs 3.75-3.80).

Direct purchases abroad by residents ($FC_{rw,dic}$) will be defined here, but will be included in the current transfers to the rest of the world (the current transfers block).

Direct purchases by non-residents in the domestic market are included in exports (the external trade block).

Domestic institutions will be considered to purchase products for final consumption in accordance with an exogenous average propensity to spend their disposable income (apc_{dic}).

Consumption by products within the domestic territory or abroad will be determined by applying fixed proportions of expenditure to the total final consumption expenditure of institutions ($fcs_{p,dic}$ and $fcsrw_{rw,dic}$, respectively).

$$FC_{dic} = apc_{dic} * DI_{dic} \quad (3.65)$$
$$FC_{p,dic} = fcs_{p,dic} * FC_{dic} \quad (3.66)$$
$$FC_{rw,dic} = fcsrw_{rw,dic} * FC_{dic} \quad (3.67)$$
$$FC_p = \Sigma_{dic} FC_{p,dic} \quad (3.68)$$

$$Cfctm_p = FC_p * Ptm_p \quad (3.69)$$
$$Cfcntp_p = FC_p * Pntp_p \quad (3.70)$$
$$Cfcbcif_p = FC_p * Pbcif_p \quad (3.71)$$
$$FC_p = Cfctm_p + Cfcntp_p + Cfcbcif_p \quad (3.72)$$

Where:

FC_{dic} = value of final consumption (at market prices) of domestic institutions (dic)

apc_{dic} = average propensity to consume: amount of final consumption of domestic institutions (dic) per unit of (gross) disposable income

DI_{dic} = (gross) disposable income of domestic institutions (dic), in accordance with (4.4)

$FC_{p,dic}$ = value of final consumption (at market prices) of products p by domestic institutions (dic)

$fcs_{p,dic}$ = proportion of expenditure on final consumption of products p in the total value of the final consumption of domestic institutions (dic)

$FC_{rw,dic}$ = direct purchases abroad by residents

$fcsrw_{rw,dic}$ = proportion of expenditure on final consumption in the rest of the world in the total value of the final consumption of domestic institutions (dic)

FC_p = (total) value of final consumption (at market prices) of products p

$Cfctm_p$ = trade and transport margins component of the final consumption value of products p

Ptm_p = proportion of trade and transport margins in the value of domestically transacted products p (at market prices), in accordance with (3.54)

$Cfcnt_p$ = net taxes on products component of the final consumption value of products p

$Pntp_p$ = proportion of net taxes on products in the value of domestically transacted products p (at market prices), in accordance with (3.55)

$Cfcbcif_p$ = basic-c.i.f. component of the final consumption value of products p

$Pbcif_p$ = proportion of basic-c.i.f. component in the value of domestically transacted products p (at market prices), in accordance with (3.56)

3.2.6.3. *Gross Capital Formation*

The gross capital formation (transaction P5 of the National Accounts) matrix/block consists of gross fixed capital formation (transaction P51), changes in inventories (transaction P52), and acquisitions minus disposals of valuables (transaction P53) (SNA 93, paragraphs 10.32-10.130; ESA 95, paragraphs 3.100-3.127).

The gross fixed capital formation of domestic institutions ($P51_{dik}$) will be considered as exogenous, following the approach of Taylor and Arnim: "this view follows Keynesian theory in which entrepreneurs decide about the investment projects according to long-term expectations and *animal spirits* rather than automatically channelling available savings flows into physical investment" (Taylor and Arnim, 2006: 32). Its distribution among each group of products will respect fixed shares ($gfcf_{p,dik}$).

The total changes in inventories of each group of products ($P52_p$) will be defined from a fixed coefficient ($chinvc_p$) of the aggregate supply (AS_p) that, in turn, will be shared by domestic institutions in fixed proportions ($chinv_{p,dik}$).

The acquisitions less disposals of valuables of domestic institutions ($P53_{dik}$) will be considered as a fixed coefficient ($advc_{dik}$) of its gross saving (S_{dik}) that, in turn, will be shared by each group of products in fixed proportions ($adv_{p,dik}$).

$$GCF_{p,dik} = gfcf_{p,dik} * P51_{dik} + P52_p * chinv_{p,dik} + adv_{p,dik} * P53_{dik} \quad (3.73)$$
$$P52_p = chinvc_p * AS_p \quad (3.74)$$
$$P53_{dik} = advc_{dik} * S_{dik} \quad (3.75)$$
$$GCF_{dik} = \Sigma_p GCF_{pdik} \quad (3.76)$$
$$GCF_p = \Sigma_{dik} GCF_{pdik} \quad (3.77)$$
$$Cgfctm_p = GCF_p * Ptm_p \quad (3.78)$$
$$Cgfcntp_p = GCF_p * Pntp_p \quad (3.79)$$
$$Cgfcbcif_p = GCF_p * Pbcif_p \quad (3.80)$$
$$GCF_p = Cgfctm_p + Cgfcntp_p + Cgfcbcif_p \quad (3.81)$$

Where:

$GCF_{p,dik}$ = value of gross capital formation (at market prices) in products p by domestic institutions (dik)

$gfcf_{p,dik}$ = share of the value of gross fixed capital formation in products p by domestic institutions (dik) in the total value of gross fixed capital formation by these institutions

$P51_{dik}$ = (total) value of gross fixed capital formation of domestic institutions (dik)

$P52_p$ = (total) value of changes in inventories of products p

$chinv_{p,dik}$ = share of the value of changes in inventories of products p by domestic institutions (dik) in the total value of changes in inventories of that group of products

$adv_{p,dik}$ = share of the value of acquisitions less disposals of valuables of products p by domestic institutions (dik) in the total value of acquisitions less disposals of valuables by these institutions

$P53_{dik}$ = (total) value of acquisitions less disposals of valuables by domestic institutions (dik)

$chinvc_p$ = coefficient of changes in inventories of products p: amount of changes in inventories of products p per unit of supply

AS_p = value of aggregate supply of products p, in accordance with (3.114)

$advc_{dik}$ = coefficient of acquisitions less disposals of valuables by domestic institutions (dik): amount expended by domestic institutions (dik) on acquisitions less disposals of valuables per unit of gross saving

S_{dik} = gross saving of domestic institutions (dik), in accordance with (3.97)

GCF_{dik} = value of gross capital formation (at market prices) by domestic institutions (dik)

GCF_p = value of gross capital formation (at market prices) in products p

$Cgfctm_p$ = trade and transport margins component of the value of gross capital formation in products p

Ptm_p = proportion of trade and transport margins in the value of domestically transacted products p (at market prices), in accordance with (3.54)

$Cgfcntp_p$ = net taxes on products component of the value of gross capital formation in products p

$Pntp_p$ = proportion of net taxes on products in the value of domestically transacted products p (at market prices), in accordance with (3.55)

$Cgfcbcif_p$ = basic-c.i.f. component of the value of gross capital formation in products p

$Pbcif_p$ = proportion of basic-c.i.f. component in the value of domestically transacted products p (at market prices), in accordance with (3.56)

3.2.7. *Current Transfers*

This block includes:

- Current taxes on income, wealth, etc. (transaction D5 of the National Accounts), which cover all compulsory, unrequited payments, in cash or in kind, levied periodically by general government and by the rest of the world on the income and wealth of institutional units, as well as some periodic taxes which are levied on neither income nor wealth (SNA 93, paragraphs 8.43-8.54; ESA 95, paragraphs 4.77-4.82).
- Social benefits and contributions (transaction D6 of the National Accounts). Social benefits are transfers to households, in cash (transaction D62) or in kind (transaction D63), intended to relieve them of the financial burden of a number of risks or needs, made either through collectively organised schemes or outside such schemes by government units and non-profit institutions serving households; they include payments from general government to producers which individually benefit households and which are made in the context of social risks or needs. Social contributions (transaction D61) include (employers' and employees') actual social contributions transferred to general government (SNA 93, paragraphs 8.67-8.83 and 8.99-8.106; ESA 95, paragraphs 4.83-4.108). Because the amount of social transfers in kind represents a final consumption expenditure of the government and the non-profit institutions serving households, it is not considered here, since it is included in the final consumption block.
- Other current transfers (transaction D7 of the National Accounts), which consist of net non-life insurance premiums, non-life insurance claims, current transfers within general government, current international co-operation and miscellaneous current transfers (SNA 93, paragraphs 8.84-8.98; ESA 95, paragraphs 4.109-4.140).

- Adjustment made for the change in the net equity of households in pension fund reserves (transaction D8 of the National Accounts), which represents the adjustment needed in order to cause to appear in the saving of households the change in the actuarial reserves on which households have a definite claim and which are fed by premiums and contributions recorded in the secondary distribution of income account as social contributions (SNA 93, paragraphs 9.14-9.20; ESA 95, paragraphs 4.141--4.144).

The current taxes on income, wealth, etc. paid by domestic institutions ($D5_{dic}$) will be defined from the application of an exogenous tax rate (ti_{dic}) on their aggregate income (AI_{dic}), with the payments being allocated to the due receivers through fixed shares ($d5s_{dic,dic}$).

The social contributions paid by domestic institutions ($D61_{dic}$) will be defined through the application of an exogenous rate (sc_{dic}) to the income generated by these, both within and outside the economy (GNI_{dic}), with the payments (once again) being allocated to the due receivers through fixed shares ($d61s_{dic,dic}$).

The social benefits other than social transfers in kind ($D62P_{dic}$) as well as the other current transfers ($D7P_{dic}$) paid by domestic institutions will be defined exogenously and their distribution among domestic and foreign receivers will be defined through fixed shares ($d62s_{dic,dic}$ and $d62rws_{rw,dic}$ in the case of the social benefits other than social transfers in kind; $d7_{dic,dic}$ and $d7rws_{rw,dic}$ in the case of the other current transfers). The same benefits and transfers received from the rest of the world ($D62RW_{dic,rw}$ and $D7RW_{dic,rw}$) will also be defined exogenously.

The adjustment made for the change in the net equity of households in pension fund reserves paid by households to financial corporations ($D8_{dic,dic}$) will also be defined exogenously.

As already mentioned and specified above, in the section on final consumption, direct purchases abroad by residents ($FC_{rw,dic}$)

will be added to the current transfers from households to the rest of the world.

$$CT_{dic,dic} = d5s_{dic,dic}*D5_{dic} + d61s_{dic,dic}*D61_{dic} + d62s_{dic,dic}*D62Pdic + + d7_{dic,dic}*D7P_{dic} + D8_{dic,dic} \quad (3.82)$$
$$D5_{dic} = ti_{dic}*AI_{dic} \quad (3.83)$$
$$D61_{dic} = sc_{dic}*GNI_{dic} \quad (3.84)$$
$$CT_{rw,dic} = d62rws_{rw,dic}*D62P_{dic} + d7rws_{rw,dic*}D7P_{dic} \quad (3.85)$$
$$CT_{dic,rw} = D62RW_{dic,rw} + D7RW_{dic,rw} \quad (3.86)$$
$$CTR_{dic} = \Sigma_{dic}\ CT_{dic,dic} \text{ (row sum)} \quad (3.87)$$
$$CTP_{dic} = \Sigma_{dic}\ CT_{dic,dic} \text{ (column sum)} \quad (3.88)$$

Where:

$CT_{dic,dic}$ = current transfers within domestic institutions (dic)

$d5s_{dic,dic}$ = share of current tax on income, wealth, etc. paid by domestic institutions (dic) to domestic institutions (Portuguese general government – dicg), in the total of current tax on income, wealth, etc. paid by the former

$D5_{dic}$ = (total) current taxes on income, wealth, etc. paid by domestic institutions (dic)

$d61s_{dic,dic}$ = share of social contributions paid by domestic institutions (dic) to domestic institutions (dic), in the total of social contributions paid by the former

$D61_{dic}$ = (total) social contributions paid by domestic institutions (dic)

$d62s_{dic,dic}$ = share of social benefits other than social transfers in kind paid by domestic institutions (dic) to domestic institutions (dic), in the total of social benefits other than social transfers in kind paid by the former

$D62P_{dic}$ = (total) social benefits other than social transfers in kind paid by domestic institutions (dic)

$d7_{dic,dic}$ = share of other current transfers paid by domestic institutions (dic) to domestic institutions (dic), in the total of other current transfers paid by the former

$D7P_{dic}$ = other current transfers paid by domestic institutions (dic)

$D8_{dic,dic}$ = adjustment made for the change in the net equity of households in pension fund reserves paid by domestic institutions (households – dich) to domestic institutions (financial corporations – dicfc)

ti_{dic} = direct tax rate paid by domestic institutions (dic): current taxes on income, wealth, etc. paid by domestic institutions (dic), per unit of received aggregate income

AI_{dic} = aggregate income received by domestic institutions (dic), in accordance with (3.106)

sc_{dic} = social contribution rate paid by domestic institutions (households – dich): social contributions paid by domestic institutions (households – dich), per unit of received gross national income

GNI_{dic} = (total) national income (at factor cost) of domestic institutions (dic), in accordance with (3.24)

$\mathrm{CT}_{rw,dic}$ = current transfers to the rest of the world from domestic institutions (dic)

$d62rws_{rw,dic}$ = share of social benefits other than social transfers in kind paid by domestic institutions (dic) to the rest of the world, in the total of social benefits other than social transfers in kind paid by the former

$d7rws_{rw,dic}$ = share of other current transfers paid by domestic institutions (dic) to the rest of the world, in the total of other current transfers paid by the former

$\mathrm{CT}_{dic,rw}$ = current transfers to domestic institutions (dic) from the rest of the world

$D62RW_{dic,rw}$ = social benefits other than social transfers in kind received by domestic institutions (dic) from the rest of the world

$D7RW_{dic,rw}$ = other current transfers received by domestic institutions (dic) from the rest of the world

CTR_{dic} = (total) current transfers received by domestic institutions (dic) from (all) domestic institutions

CTP_{dic} = (total) current transfers paid by domestic institutions (dic) to (all) domestic institutions

3.2.8. *Capital Transfers*

Capital transfers[14] (transaction D9 of the National Accounts) cover capital taxes (transaction D91), investment grants (transaction D92) and other capital transfers (transaction D99) (SNA 93, paragraphs 10.131-10.141; ESA 95, paragraphs 4.146-4.167). Acquisitions less disposals of non-financial non-produced assets (transaction K2 of the National Accounts) – nonfinancial non-produced assets consist of land and other tangible non-produced assets that may be used in the production of goods and services, as well as intangible non-produced assets (SNA 93, paragraphs 10.120-10.130; ESA 95, paragraphs 6.06-6.13) – are also covered.

The capital taxes paid by domestic institutions ($D91P_{dik}$) – more precisely by the households – will be defined through the application of an exogenous tax (tk_{dik}) on the other capital transfers received by these ($D99R_{dik}$), with the corresponding payments being allocated to their due receivers through fixed shares ($d91_{dik,dik}$).

Investment grants will be received by domestic institutions ($D92R_{dik}$) in accordance with the application of an exogenous rate of coverage ($cgfcf_{dik}$) to the corresponding amount of gross fixed capital formation ($P51_{dik}$) and their distribution among domestic and foreign payers will be defined through fixed shares ($d92_{dik,dik}$

---

[14] Capital transfers are different from current transfers because they involve the acquisition or disposal of an asset, or assets, by at least one of the parties to the transaction. Whether made in cash or in kind, such transfers should result in a commensurate change in the financial, or non-financial, assets shown in the balance sheets of one or both parties to the transaction (ESA 95, paragraphs 4.145).

and $d92rw_{dik,rw}$). The same item paid by domestic institutions – more precisely by the government – to the rest of the world ($D92P_{rw,dik}$) will be defined exogenously.

The other capital transfers received by domestic institutions ($D99R_{dik}$) will be defined exogenously and the distribution of these among domestic and foreign payers will be defined through fixed shares ($d99_{dik,dik}$ and $d99rw_{dik,rw}$). The same transfers paid to the rest of the world ($D99P_{rw,dik}$) will also be defined exogenously, as will the acquisitions less disposals of non-financial non-produced assets ($K2_{rw,dik}$).

$$\mathrm{KT}_{dik,dik} = d91_{dik,dik}{*}\mathrm{D91P}_{dik} + \mathrm{D92R}_{dik}{*}d92_{dik,dik} + D99R_{dik}{*}d99_{dik,dik} \qquad (3.89)$$

$$\mathrm{D91P}_{dik} = tk_{dik}{*}D99R_{dik} \qquad (3.90)$$

$$\mathrm{D92R}_{dik} = cgfcf_{dik}{*}P51_{dik} \qquad (3.91)$$

$$\mathrm{KT}_{rw,dik} = D92P_{rw,dik} + D99P_{rw,dik} + K2_{rw,dik} \qquad (3.92)$$

$$\mathrm{KT}_{dik,rw} = \mathrm{D92R}_{dik}{*}d92rw_{dik,rw} + D99R_{dik}{*}d99rw_{dik,rw} \qquad (3.93)$$

$$\mathrm{KTR}_{dik} = \Sigma_{dik}\ \mathrm{KT}_{dik,dik} \text{ (row sum)} \qquad (3.94)$$

$$\mathrm{KTP}_{dik} = \Sigma_{dik}\ \mathrm{KT}_{dik,dik} \text{ (column sum)} \qquad (3.95)$$

Where:

$\mathrm{KT}_{dik,dik}$ = capital transfers within domestic institutions (dik)

$d91_{dik,dik}$ = share of capital taxes paid by domestic institutions (households – dikh) to domestic institutions (Portuguese general government – dikg), in the total of capital taxes paid by the former

$\mathrm{D91P}_{dik}$ = capital taxes paid by domestic institutions (households – dikh)

$\mathrm{D92R}_{dik}$ = investment grants received by domestic institutions (dik)

$d92_{dik,dik}$ = share of investment grants paid by domestic institutions (Portuguese general government – dikg) to domestic institutions (dik) in the total of investment grants received by the latter

$D99R_{dik}$ = other capital transfers received by domestic institutions (dik)

$d99_{dik,dik}$ = share of other capital transfers paid by domestic institutions (dik) to domestic institutions (dik) in the total of other capital transfers received by the latter

tk_{dik} = rate of capital tax levied on other capital transfers received by domestic institutions (dik)

$cgfcf_{dik}$ = rate of coverage of gross fixed capital formation of domestic institutions (dik) by investment grants received by these institutions

$P51_{dik}$ = (total) value of gross fixed capital formation of domestic institutions (dik) (see Section 3.2.6.3.)

$\mathrm{KT}_{rw,dik}$ = capital transfers to the rest of the world from domestic institutions (dik)

$D92P_{rw,dik}$ = investment grants paid by domestic institutions (Portuguese general government – dikg) to the rest of the world

$D99P_{rw,dik}$ = other capital transfers paid by domestic institutions (dik) to the rest of the world

$K2_{rw,dik}$ = acquisitions less disposals of non-financial non--produced assets paid by domestic institutions (dik) to the rest of the world

$\mathrm{KT}_{dik,rw}$ = capital transfers to domestic institutions (dik) from the rest of the world

$d92rw_{dik,rw}$ = share of investment grants paid by the rest of the world to domestic institutions (dik) in the total of investment grants received by the latter

$d99rw_{dik,rw}$ = share of other capital transfers paid by the rest of the world to domestic institutions (dik) in the total of other capital transfers received by the latter

KTR_{dik} = (total) capital transfers received by domestic institutions (dik) from (all) domestic institutions

KTP_{dik} = (total) capital transfers paid by domestic institutions (dik) to (all) domestic institutions

3.2.9. *Gross Saving*

Gross saving measures the portion of aggregate income that is not used for final consumption expenditure and current transfers to Portuguese institutions or to the rest of the world (saving: SNA 93, paragraphs 9.17-9.20; ESA 95, paragraph 8.96).

Savings will therefore be the part of the disposable income that is not consumed and represent the current budget balance of domestic institutions.

$$S_{dic} = (1\text{-}apc_{dic}) * DI_{dic} \tag{3.96}$$
$$S_{dik,dic} = si_{dik,dic} {}^*S_{dic} \tag{3.97}$$
$$S_{dik} = \Sigma_{dik} S_{dik,dic} \tag{3.97}$$

Where:

S_{dic} or $S_{dik,dic}$ or S_{dik} = gross saving of domestic institutions (dic or dik)

apc_{dic} = average propensity to consume of domestic institutions (dic): amount of final consumption per unit of (gross) disposable income

DI_{dic} = (gross) disposable income of domestic institutions (dic), in accordance with (4.4)

$si_{dik,dic}$ = saving identity special[15]

3.2.10. *Financial Transactions*

Financial transactions (F1-7 of the National Accounts) are transactions in financial assets and liabilities between institutional units ($FT_{dif,dif}$), and between these and the rest of the world ($FTRW_{dif,rw}$ and $FT_{rw,dif}$). They are classified as monetary gold and special drawing rights; currency and deposits; securities other than shares; loans; shares and other equity; insurance technical reserves; and other accounts receivable/payable.

---

[15] In order to make the saving matrix diagonal.

The outlays (expenditures) side of the (financial) account records changes in the assets, i.e. acquisitions less disposals of financial assets. The incomes (receipts) side of the same account records changes in liabilities and net worth, i.e. the incurrence of liabilities minus their repayment. The balancing item of the financial account, i.e. the net acquisition of financial assets minus the net incurrence of liabilities, is net lending (+)/net borrowing (-) (SNA 93, paragraphs 11.1-11.111; ESA 95, paragraphs 5.01-5.151) – this will be the only endogenous part of this block in this version of the model.

$$FTRW_{dif,rw} = FT_{rw,dif} + NLB_{dif} \tag{3.98}$$

Where:

$FTRW_{dif,rw}$ = financial transactions received by domestic institutions (dif) from the rest of the world

$FT_{rw,dif}$ = financial transactions from domestic institutions (dif) to the rest of the world

NLB_{dif} = net lending/borrowing of the economy, in accordance with (3.100)

3.3. *Closure – Net lending/borrowing*

The net lending (+) or borrowing (-) of the total economy is the sum of the net lending or borrowing of the institutional sectors. It represents the net resources that the total economy makes available to the rest of the world (if it is positive) or receives from the rest of the world (if it is negative). The net lending (+) or borrowing (-) of the total economy is equal (but with an opposite mathematical sign) to the net borrowing (-) or lending (+) of the rest of the world (ESA 95, paragraph 8.98).

Here, those amounts that fall short of (+) or exceed (-) the investment funds used to cover aggregate investment are registered in the capital and financial accounts, since they are financial transactions from (in the case of net borrowing) or to (in the case of net lending) the rest of the world – this is why the mathematical signs defined in the first paragraph of this item (ESA 95, paragraph 8.98) were exchanged.

The net borrowing/lending represents the total budget balance of domestic institutions – a deficit in the case of net borrowing and a surplus in the case of net lending.

$$NLB_{dik,dif} = AINV_{dik} - (S_{dik} + KTR_{dik} + KT_{dik,rw}) \quad (3.99)$$
$$NLB_{dif} = \Sigma_{dik} NLB_{dik,dif} \quad (3.100)$$

Where:

$NLB_{dik,dif}$ = net lending/borrowing of domestic institutions (dik)

$AINV_{dik}$ = aggregate investment of domestic institutions (dik), in accordance with (3.116)

S_{dik} = gross saving of domestic institutions (dik), in accordance with (3.97)

KTR_{dik} = (total) capital transfers received by domestic institutions (dik) from (all) domestic institutions, in accordance with (3.94)

$KT_{dik,rw}$ = capital transfers to domestic institutions (dik) from the rest of the world, in accordance with (3.93)

NLB_{dif} = net lending/borrowing of the economy

3.4. Clearing

3.4.1. *Row totals*

Aggregate factors income (received):

$$AFIR_{fle} = GAV_{fle} + CFR_{fle,rw} \quad (3.101)$$
$$AFIR_{foal} = GAV_{foal} \quad (3.102)$$
$$AFIR_{foak} = GAV_{foak} + CFR_{floak,rw} \quad (3.103)$$

Where:

$AFIR_{fle}$ = aggregate factors income of employees (received)

GAV_{fle} = gross added value (at factor cost) generated by employees (total), in accordance with (3.6)

$CFR_{fle,rw}$ = compensation of employees received from the rest of the world (see Section 3.2.1.2.)

$AFIR_{foal}$ = GAV_{foal} = aggregate factors income of employers and/or own-account workers (received) = gross added value (at factor cost) generated by employers and/or own-account workers (total), in accordance with (3.11)

$AFIR_{foak}$ = aggregate factors income of capital (received)

GAV_{foak} = gross added value (at factor cost) generated by capital (total), in accordance with (3.16)

$CFR_{foak,rw}$ = property income received from the rest of the world (see Section 3.2.1.2.)

Production value: $VPT_a = \Sigma_p VP_{a,p}$ (3.104)

Where:

VPT_a = total production value (at basic prices) of activities a

$VP_{a,p}$ = value of production (domestic output, at basic prices) of products p by activities a, in accordance with (3.28)

Aggregate demand:

$AD_p = VIC_p + FC_p + GCF_p + EX_{p,rw}$ (3.105)

Where:

AD_p = value of aggregate demand (at market prices) of products p

VIC_p = value of intermediate consumption (at market prices) of products p, in accordance with (3.59)

FC_p = value of final consumption (at market prices) of products p, in accordance with (3.68)

GCF_p = value of gross capital formation (at market prices) in products p, in accordance with (3.77)

$EX_{p,rw}$ = value of exports (at f.o.b. prices) of products p (see Section 3.2.3.)

Aggregate income:

$$AI_{dic} = GNI_{dic} + NTA_{dic} + NTP_{dic} + CTR_{dic} + CT_{dic,rw} \qquad (3.106)$$

Where:

AI_{dic} = aggregate income of domestic institutions (dic) (received)

GNI_{dic} = national income (at factor cost) of domestic institutions (dic), in accordance with (3.24)

NTA_{dic} = (total) net taxes on production received by domestic institutions (Portuguese general government – dicg), in accordance with (3.39)

NTP_{dic} = net taxes on (all) domestically transacted products received by domestic institutions (Portuguese general government – dicg), in accordance with (3.46)

CTR_{dic} = current transfers received by domestic institutions (dic) from (all) domestic institutions, in accordance with (3.87)

$CT_{dic,rw}$ = current transfers to domestic institutions (dic) from the rest of the world, in accordance with (3.86)

Investment funds:

$$INVF_{dik} = S_{dik} + KTR_{dik} + NLB_{dik,dif} + KT_{dik,rw} \qquad (3.107)$$

Where:

$INVF_{dik}$ = investment funds of domestic institutions (dik)

S_{dik} = gross saving of domestic institutions (dik), in accordance with (3.97)

KTR_{dik} = capital transfers received by domestic institutions (dik) from (all) domestic institutions, in accordance with (3.94)

$NLB_{dik,dif}$ = net lending/borrowing of domestic institutions (dik), in accordance with (3.99)

$KT_{dik,rw}$ = capital transfers to domestic institutions (dik) from the rest of the world, in accordance with (3.93)

Total financial transactions:

$$TFTR_{dif} = FT_{dif,dif} + FTRW_{dif,rw} \tag{3.108}$$

Where:

$TFTR_{dif}$ = total financial transactions of domestic institutions (dif) (received)

$FT_{dif,dif}$ = financial transactions within domestic institutions (dif) (see Section 3.2.10.)

$FTRW_{dif,rw}$ = financial transactions received by domestic institutions (dif) from the rest of the world, in accordance with (3.98)

Value of transactions to the rest of the world:

$$TVRWP_{rw} = \Sigma_{fle} CFS_{rw,fle} + CFS_{rw,foak} + \Sigma_{a} NTA_{rw,a} + \Sigma_{p}(NTP_{rw,p} + IM_{rw,p}) + \Sigma_{dic} (CTr_{w,dic} + FC_{rw,dic}) + \Sigma_{dik} KT_{rw,dik} + FT_{rw,dif} \tag{3.109}$$

Where:

$TVRWP_{rw}$ = value of transactions (from domestic institutions) to the rest of the world

$CFS_{rw,fle}$ = compensation of employees sent to the rest of the world, in accordance with (3.26)

$CFS_{rw,foak}$ = property income sent to the rest of the world (see Section 3.2.1.4.)

$NTA_{rw,a}$ = net taxes on production paid by activities *a* to the rest of the world (European Union institutions), in accordance with (3.38)

$NTP_{rw,p}$ = net taxes on domestically transacted products p received by the rest of the world (European Union institutions), in accordance with (3.45)

$IM_{rw,p}$ = value of imports of products p (see Section 3.2.3.)

$CT_{rw,dic}$ = current transfers to the rest of the world from domestic institutions (dic), in accordance with (3.85)

$FC_{rw,dic}$ = direct purchases abroad by residents, in accordance with (3.67)

$KT_{rw,dik}$ = capital transfers to the rest of the world from domestic institutions (dik), in accordance with (3.92)

$FT_{rw,dif}$ = financial transactions from domestic institutions (dif) to the rest of the world (see Section 3.2.10.)

3.4.2. *Column totals*

Aggregate factors income (paid):

$$AFIP_{fle} = GNI_{fle} + CFS_{rw,fle} \quad (3.110)$$

$$AFIP_{foal} = GNI_{foal} \quad (3.111)$$

$$AFIP_{foak} = GNI_{foak} + CFS_{rw,foak} \quad (3.112)$$

Where:

$AFIP_{fle}$ = aggregate factors income of employees (paid)

GNI_{fle} = gross national income (at factor cost) generated by employees, in accordance with (3.18)

$CFS_{rw,fle}$ = compensation of employees sent to the rest of the world, in accordance with (3.26)

$AFIP_{foal}$ = GNI_{foal} = aggregate factors income of employers and/or own-account workers (paid) = gross national income (at factor cost) generated by employers and/or own-account workers, in accordance with (3.20)

$AFIP_{foak}$ = aggregate factors income of capital (paid)

$CFS_{rw,foak}$ = property income sent to the rest of the world (see Section 3.2.1.4.)

Total Costs:

$$VCT_a = GAV_a + VIC_a + NTA_a + NTA_{rw,a} \quad (3.113)$$

Where:

VCT_a = value of total costs (at basic prices) of activities *a*

GAV_a = gross added value (at factor cost) of activities *a*, in accordance with (3.1)

VIC_a = value of intermediate consumption (at market prices) of activities *a*, in accordance with (3.57)

NTA_a = net taxes on production paid by activities *a* to (all) domestic institutions (Portuguese general government – dicg), in accordance with (3.40)

$NTA_{rw,a}$ = net taxes on production paid by activities *a* and received by the rest of the world (European Union institutions), in accordance with (3.38)

Aggregate supply:

$$AS_p = VP_p + TMT_p + NTP_p + IM_{rw,p} \quad (3.114)$$

Where:

AS_p = value of aggregate supply (at market prices) of products p

VP_p = value of production (domestic output, at basic prices) of products p, in accordance with (3.27)

TMT_p = trade and transport margins on domestically transacted products p with correction, in accordance with (3.51)

NTP_p = net taxes on domestically transacted products p, in accordance with (3.43)

$IM_{rw,p}$ = value of imports (at c.i.f. prices) of products p (see Section 3.2.3.)

Aggregate income:

$$AIP_{dic} = FC_{dic} + CTP_{dic} + S_{dic} + (CT_{rw,dic} + FC_{rw,dic}) \quad (3.115)$$

Where:

AIP_{dic} = aggregate income of domestic institutions (dic) (paid)

FC_{dic} = value of final consumption (at market prices) of domestic institutions (dic), in accordance with (3.65)

CTP_{dic} = (total) current transfers paid by domestic institutions (dic) to (all) domestic institutions, in accordance with (3.88)

S_{dic} = gross saving of domestic institutions (dic), in accordance with (3.96)

$CT_{rw,dic}$ = current transfers to the rest of the world from domestic institutions (dic), in accordance with (3.85)

$FC_{rw,dic}$ = direct purchases abroad by residents, in accordance with (3.67)

Aggregate investment:

$$AINV_{dik} = GCF_{dik} + KTP_{dik} + KT_{rw,dik} \tag{3.116}$$

Where:

$AINV_{dik}$ = aggregate investment of domestic institutions (dik)

GCF_{dik} = value of gross capital formation (at market prices) by domestic institutions (dik), in accordance with (3.76)

KTP_{dik} = (total) capital transfers paid by domestic institutions (dik) to (all) domestic institutions, in accordance with (3.95)

$KT_{rw,dik}$ = capital transfers to the rest of the world from domestic institutions (dik), in accordance with (3.92)

Total financial transactions:

$$TFTP_{dif} = NLB_{dif} + FT_{dif,dif} + FT_{rw,dif} \tag{3.117}$$

Where:

$TFTP_{dif}$ = total financial transactions of domestic institutions (dif) (paid)

NLB_{dif} = net lending/borrowing of the economy, in accordance with (3.100)

$FT_{dif,dif}$ = financial transactions within domestic institutions (dif) (see Section 3.2.10.)

$FT_{rw,dif}$ = financial transactions from domestic institutions (dif) to the rest of the world (see Section 3.2.10.)

Value of transactions from the rest of the world:

$$TVRWR_{rw} = \Sigma_{fle}\, CFR_{fle,rw} + CFR_{foak,rw} + \Sigma_{p}\, EX_{p,rw} + \Sigma_{dic} CT_{dic,rw} + + \Sigma dik\ KT_{dik,rw} + FTRW_{dif,rw} \tag{3.118}$$

Where:

$TVRWR_{rw}$ = value of transactions from the rest of the world (to domestic institutions)

$CFR_{fle,rw}$ = compensation of employees received from the rest of the world (see Section 3.2.1.2.)

$CFR_{foak,rw}$ = property income received from the rest of the world (see Section 3.2.1.2.)

$EX_{p,rw}$ = value of exports of products p (see Section 3.2.3.)

$CT_{dic,rw}$ = current transfers to domestic institutions (dic) from the rest of the world , in accordance with (3.86)

$KT_{dik,rw}$ = capital transfers to domestic institutions (dik) from the rest of the world, in accordance with (3.93)

$FTRW_{dif,rw}$ = financial transactions received by domestic institutions (dif) from the rest of the world, in accordance with (3.98)

3.4.3. *Row totals = column totals*

$$AFIR_{fle} = AFIP_{fle} \quad (3.119)$$
$$AFIR_{foal} = AFIP_{foal} \quad (3.120)$$
$$AFIR_{foak} = AFIP_{foak} \quad (3.121)$$
$$VPT_{a} = VCT_{a} \quad (3.122)$$
$$AD_{p} = AS_{p} \quad (3.123)$$
$$AI_{dic} = AIP_{dic} \quad (3.124)$$
$$INVF_{dik} = AINV_{dik} \quad (3.125)$$
$$TFTR_{dif} = TFTP_{dif} \quad (3.126)$$
$$TVRWP_{rw} = TVRWR_{rw} \quad (3.127)$$

Where:

$AFIR_{fle}$ = aggregate factors income of employees (received), in accordance with (3.101)

$AFIP_{fle}$ = aggregate factors income of employees (paid), in accordance with (3.110)

$AFIR_{foal}$ = aggregate factors income of employers and/or own--account workers (received), in accordance with (3.102)

$AFIP_{foal}$ = aggregate factors income of employers and/or own-account workers (paid), in accordance with (3.111)

$AFIR_{foak}$ = aggregate factors income of capital (received), in accordance with (3.103)

$AFIP_{foak}$ = aggregate factors income of capital (paid), in accordance with (3.112)

VPT_a = total production value (at basic prices) of activities *a*, in accordance with (3.104)

VCT_a = value of total costs (at basic prices) of activities *a*, in accordance with (3.113)

AD_p = value of aggregate demand (at market prices) of products p, in accordance with (3.105)

AS_p = value of aggregate supply (at market prices) of products p, in accordance with (3.114)

AI_{dic} = aggregate income of domestic institutions (dic) (received), in accordance with (3.106)

AIP_{dic} = aggregate income of domestic institutions (dic) (paid), in accordance with (3.115)

$INVF_{dik}$ = investment funds of domestic institutions (dik), in accordance with (3.107)

$AINV_{dik}$ = aggregate investment of domestic institutions (dik), in accordance with (3.116)

$TFTR_{dif}$ = total financial transactions of domestic institutions (dif) (received), in accordance with (3.108)

$TFTP_{dif}$ = total financial transactions of domestic institutions (dif) (paid), in accordance with (3.117)

$TVRWP_{rw}$ = value of transactions (from domestic institutions) to the rest of the world, in accordance with (3.109)

$TVRWR_{rw}$ = value of transactions from the rest of the world (to domestic institutions), in accordance with (3.118)

4.

Macroeconomic aggregates and balances

From the two versions of the SAM already defined, it is possible to deduce macroeconomic aggregates, such as the ones described below.

Gross domestic product, at market prices:

$$GDP = \Sigma_a GAV_a + NTP + NTA \quad (4.1)$$

Where:

GDP = gross domestic product, at market prices

GAV_a = gross added value (at factor cost) of activities *a*, in accordance with (3.1)

NTP = net taxes on domestically transacted products (total), in accordance with (3.48)

NTA = net taxes on production (total), in accordance with (3.42).

GDP = 80,827 million euros, from the numerical version.

Gross national income, at market prices:

$$GNIMP = GNI + \Sigma_{dic} NTP_{dic} + \Sigma_{dic} NTA_{dic} \quad (4.2)$$

Where:

GNIMP = gross national income, at market prices

GNI = gross national income (at factor cost) – total, in accordance with (3.25)

NTP_{dic} = net taxes on (all) domestically transacted products received by domestic institutions (Portuguese general government – dicg), in accordance with (3.46)

NTA_{dic} = net taxes on production received by domestic institutions (Portuguese general government – dicg), from all activities, in accordance with (3.39)

GNIMP = 80,479 million euros, from the numerical version.

Gross disposable income:

$$DI = \Sigma_{dic}\, DI_{dic} \qquad (4.3)$$

$$DI_{dic} = GNI_{dic} + NTA_{dic} + NTP_{dic} + CTR_{dic} + CT_{dic,rw} - \\ - CTPdic - CT_{rw,dic} \qquad (4.4)$$

Where:

DI = (gross) disposable income – total

DI_{dic} = (gross) disposable income of domestic institutions (dic)

GNI_{dic} = (total) national income (at factor cost) of domestic institutions (dic), in accordance with (3.24)

NTA_{dic} = net taxes on production received by domestic institutions (Portuguese general government – dicg), from all activities, in accordance with (3.39)

NTP_{dic} = net taxes on (all) domestically transacted products received by domestic institutions (Portuguese general government – dicg), in accordance with (3.46)

CTR_{dic} = (total) current transfers received by domestic institutions (dic) from (all) domestic institutions, in accordance with (3.87)

$CT_{dic,rw}$ = current transfers to domestic institutions (dic) from the rest of the world, in accordance with (3.86)

CTP_{dic} = (total) current transfers paid by domestic institutions (dic) to (all) domestic institutions, in accordance with (3.88)

$CT_{rw,dic}$ = current transfers to the rest of the world from domestic institutions (dic), in accordance with (3.85)

DI = 83,517 million euros, from the numerical version.

Gross saving:

$$S = \Sigma_{dic} S_{dic} \quad (4.5)$$

Where:

S_{dic} = gross saving of domestic institutions (dic), in accordance with (3.96)

S = 17,291 million euros, from the numerical version.

Net lending/borrowing (of the economy): NLB_{dif}

From the numerical version, the Portuguese economy had a net borrowing of 40 million euros (0.05% of GDP).

In turn, from the rest of the world SAM account, one can also calculate the main items of the balance of payments, as follows:

Balance of Payments – Current Account – Goods and Services:

$$GSB = \Sigma_p EX_{p,rw} - (\Sigma_p IM_{rw,p} + \Sigma_{dic} FC_{rw,dic}) \quad (4.6)$$

Where:

GSB = goods and services balance

$EX_{p,rw}$ = value of exports of products p (see Section 3.2.3.)

$IM_{rw,p}$ = value of imports of products p (see Section 3.2.3.)

$FC_{rw,dic}$ = direct purchases abroad by residents, in accordance with (3.67).

Balance of Payments – Current Account – Income:

$$IB = (\Sigma_{fle} CFR_{fle,rw} + \Sigma_{foak} CFR_{foak,rw}) - (\Sigma_{fle} CFS_{rw,fle} + \\ + \Sigma_{foak} CFS_{rw,foak}) \quad (4.7)$$

Where:

IB = income balance

$CFR_{fle,rw}$ = compensation of employees received from the rest of the world (see Section 3.2.1.2.)

$CFR_{foak,rw}$ = property income received from the rest of the world (see Section 3.2.1.2.)

$CFS_{rw,fle}$ = compensation of employees sent to the rest of the world, in accordance with (3.26)

$CFS_{rw,foak}$ = property income sent to the rest of the world (see Section 3.2.1.4.)

Balance of Payments – Current Account – current transfers:

$$CTB = \Sigma_{dic} CT_{dic,rw} - (\Sigma_{dic} CT_{rw,dic} + NTA_{rw} + NTP_{rw}) \qquad (4.8)$$

Where:

CTB = current transfers balance

$CT_{dic,rw}$ = current transfers to domestic institutions (dic) from the rest of the world, in accordance with (3.86)

$CT_{rw,dic}$ = current transfers to the rest of the world from domestic institutions (dic), in accordance with (3.85)

NTA_{rw} = net taxes on production received by the rest of the world (European Union institutions), from all activities, in accordance with (3.41)

NTP_{rw} = net taxes on (all) domestically transacted products received by the rest of the world (European Union institutions), in accordance with (3.47).

Balance of Payments – Current Account – Total:

$$CB = GSB + IB + CTB \qquad (4.9)$$

Where:

CB = current balance

GSB = goods and services balance, in accordance with (4.6)

IB = income balance, in accordance with (4.7)

CTB = current transfers balance, in accordance with (4.8).

Balance of Payments – Capital Account:

$$KB = \Sigma_{dik} KT_{dik,rw} - \Sigma_{dik} KT_{rw,dik} \qquad (4.10)$$

Where:

KB = capital balance

$KT_{dik,rw}$ = capital transfers to domestic institutions (dik) from the rest of the world, in accordance with (3.93)

$KT_{rw,dik}$ = capital transfers to the rest of the world from domestic institutions (dik), in accordance with (3.92).

Balance of Payments – Financial Account (+ Errors and Omissions):

$$FB = FTRW_{dif,rw} - FT_{rw,dif} \quad (4.11)$$

Where:

FB = financial balance

$FTRW_{dif,rw}$ = financial transactions received by domestic institutions (dif) from the rest of the world, in accordance with (3.98)

$FT_{rw,dif}$ = financial transactions from domestic institutions (dif) to the rest of the world (see Section 3.2.10).

The following table was constructed from the numerical version of the SAM:

Table 18 – The Balance of Payments in the Portuguese SAM for 1995 (in millions of euros)

	Resources (row)		Uses (column)		Balance
1. Current Account		31 636		33 967	- 2331
- Goods & Services	Exports	24 433	Imports (28127) + direct purchases abroad by residents (1327)	29 454	- 5 021
- Income	Compensation of factors from the RW	3 243	Compensation of factors to the RW	3 426	- 183
- Current Transfers	Current transfers from the RW	3 960	Current transfers to the RW (922) + net taxes on production to the RW (-87)+ net taxes on production to the RW (252)	1 087	2 873
2. Capital Account	Capital transfers from the RW	2 320	Capital transfers to the RW	29	2 291
3 = 1 + 2 (Balance = Net borrowing)		33 956		33 996	- 40
4. Financial Account	Financial transfers from the RW	9 257	Financial transfers to the RW	9 217	40
5 = 3 + 4 = Total		43 213		43 213	0

Source: Tables 1, 2 or 15 (rest of the world row/column totals)

These are approximate values, since the Portuguese balance of payments is calculated from the National Accounts and other sources of information, being published by the Portuguese Central Bank (*Banco de Portugal*) and not by the Portuguese Institute of Statistics (*Instituto Nacional de Estatística*), with the two values being relatively different.

In accordance with Chapter 2 (Section 2.2), these values can also be disaggregated into the European Union (member states and institutions) and non-member countries and international organisations – as Santos (2003) does for 1997.

On the other hand, the main items in the budget of all institutions, namely of the government, can be calculated from the respective accounts. Thus: the total budget balance is the respective net lending/borrowing – $NLB_{dik,dif.}$; the current budget balance is the respective gross saving – S_{dik}; and the capital budget balance is the difference between the first and the second.

From the numerical version, Table 19 was constructed for the government and households – the same procedure could also be carried out for the other institutions.

From that table, as well as from Table 15 – cells: (28,33) – (32,33), it can be seen that the net borrowing of the government is almost completely covered by the net lending of households, although all the other institutions have a relatively small amount of net lending. In other words, the government is the institution that has a total budget balance with a deficit, which is almost completely covered by the other institutions, with households being in a highly significant position, which is, however, not sufficient to avoid a net borrowing for the economy of 40 million euros (0.05% of GDP). In terms of the current balance, or gross saving (see also Table 15 – cells: (28,20) – (32,27)), the government is again the institution that has a deficit, although, within households, the group labelled as "others" (those whose main source of income is not wages and salaries, mixed income including property income or income in connection with old age) also has a deficit. Therefore, with the exception of the government, all the institutions covered their needs in terms of investment funds, as well as a substantial part of those of the government.

From Table 19, it is easy to see how current transfers from Portuguese institutions and net taxes on products are the main sources of the government's receipts, while current transfers to Portuguese institutions and final consumption are the main sources of its expenditure. In the case of households, the income generated by these (or gross national income) and final consumption are, respectively, the main sources of receipts and expenditure.

Despite its not being a macroeconomic aggregate or balance, the unemployment rate not only provides important information about the macroeconomic situation, but it also has an important role to play in any study about income distribution. In the algebraic version of the SAM, this rate is calculated in the block of the compensation of the factors of production – submatrix "Gross Added Value" (see Section 3.2.1.1.), although it cannot be calculated from its numerical version, except with the use of additional data (Table D.3). Thus, the unemployment rate in Portugal in 1995 was 5.29%.

Table 19 – The Government and Households Budget in the Portuguese SAM for 1995 (in millions of euros)

	Resources or Receipts (row)			Uses or Expenditure (column)			Balance	
		Government	Households		Government	Households	Government	Households
1. Current Account (a)		31 081	76 413		32 742	68 461	- 1661	7 952
	Gross National Income at factor cost (a)	- 2558	59 614	Final Consumption	15 032	49 905		
	Net taxes on production	- 346	-	Current transfers to Portuguese institutions	17 371	18 141		
	Net taxes on products	10 283	-	Current transfers to the RW	339	416		
	Current transfers from Portuguese institutions	23 092	13 506					
	Current transfers from the RW	609	3 293					
2. Capital Account		3 375	1 166		6 136	5 095	- 2 761	- 3929
	Capital transfers from Portuguese institutions	2 100	1 018	Gross Capital Formation	3 018	5 755		
	Capital transfers from the RW	1 275	147	Capital transfers to Portuguese institutions	3 075	63		
				Capital transfers to the RW	43	- 723		
3 = 1 + 2 (b)		34 456	77 579		38 878	73 556	- 4 423	4 023

Source: Table 2 (rows/columns 18 and 23)

(a) Balance = Gross saving (Sd_{ikg} for government; S_{dikg} for households).
(b) Balance = Net lending (+)/borrowing (-) ($NLB_{dikg,dif}$ for government; $NLB_{dikh,dif}$ for households).

5.

The structural indicators of the distribution and use of income

Considering that the distributional relationships across production sectors or activities and social groups are determined by the macro behaviour, which, in turn, is determined by the behaviour of individuals within and on behalf of institutions, this means that if we are to study the distributional impact of exogenous shocks resulting from any policy, as proposed in the Introduction (Chapter 1) and exemplified in Chapter 6, it is important to have some indicators that, in addition to the macroeconomic aggregates and balances, synthesise that impact as much as possible. Therefore, two aspects will be considered: the distribution of generated income and the distribution and use of disposable income.

Due to a lack of information about the total number of persons by groups of households, the structures of the distribution and use of income will be considered here in order to identify inequality, although, in the case of generated income, some *per capita* (worker) information will also be worked with. These structures and the possible *per capita* information can be deduced as follows from the two versions of the SAM that have already been defined.

A. Distribution of generated income

A.1. *Among factors of production and activities*

The functional distribution of income can be studied here from an analysis of the division of gross added value at factor cost (excluding indirect taxes) between labour and capital, disaggregated by activity. It is also important to distinguish between types of labour (Dervis et al., 1982) – in this case by the level of education of workers.

$$Digav_{fle,a} = (D1_a \;/\; GAV_a)*100 \quad (5.1)$$
$$Digav_{foal,a} = (B3g_a \;/\; GAV_a)*100 \quad (5.2)$$
$$Digav_{foak,a} = (B2g_a \;/\; GAV_a)*100 \quad (5.3)$$
$$Digav_{fle} = (\Sigma_a D1_a \;/\; \Sigma_a GAV_a)*100 \quad (5.4)$$
$$Digav_{foal} = (\Sigma_a B3g_a \;/\; \Sigma_a GAV_a)*100 \quad (5.5)$$
$$Digav_{foak} = (\Sigma_a B2g_a \;/\; \Sigma_a GAV_a)*100 \quad (5.6)$$
$$Digavfle_{fle,a} = (GAV_{fle,a} \;/\; D1_a)*100 \quad (5.7)$$
$$Digavfoal_{foal,a} = (GAV_{foal,a} \;/\; B3g_a)*100 \quad (5.8)$$
$$Digavfle_{fle} = (GAV_{fle} \;/\; \Sigma_a D1_a)*100 \quad (5.9)$$
$$Digavfoal_{foal} = (GAV_{foal} \;/\; \Sigma_a B3g_a)*100 \quad (5.10)$$
$$Wgav_{fle,a} = GAV_{fle,a}*1000 \;/\; LE_{fle,a} \quad (5.11)$$
$$Wgavfle_a = D1_a*1000 \;/\; \Sigma_{fle} LE_{fle,a} \quad (5.12)$$
$$Wgav_{foal,a} = GAV_{foal,a}*1000 \;/\; LOA_{foal,a} \quad (5.13)$$
$$Wgavfoal_a = B3g_a*1000 \;/\; \Sigma_{foal} LOA_{foal,a} \quad (5.14)$$
$$Wgavfle_{fle} = GAV_{fle}*1000 \;/\; \Sigma_{fle} LE_{fle,a} \quad (5.15)$$
$$Wgavfoal_{foal} = GAV_{foal}*1000 \;/\; \Sigma_{foal} LOA_{foal,a} \quad (5.16)$$

Where:

$Digav_{fle,a}$ = percentage of income generated by employees in activities *a*

$D1_a$ = compensation of employees paid by activities *a*, in accordance with (3.5)

GAV_a = gross added value (at factor cost) of activities *a*, in accordance with (3.1)

$Digav_{foal,a}$ = percentage of income generated by employers and/or own-account workers in activities *a*

$B3g_a$ = gross mixed income of activities *a*, in accordance with (3.10)

$Digav_{foak,a}$ = percentage of income generated by capital in activities *a*

$B2g_a$ = gross operating surplus of activities *a*, in accordance with (3.15)

$Digav_{fle}$ = percentage of income generated by employees in the whole economy

$Digav_{foal}$ = percentage of income generated by employers and/or own-account workers in the whole economy

$Digav_{foak}$ = percentage of income generated by capital in the whole economy

$Digavfle_{fle,a}$ = percentage of income generated by employees in activities *a*, by level of education

$GAV_{fle,a}$ = gross added value (at factor cost) of activities *a* generated by employees, in accordance with (3.2)

$Digavfoal_{foal,a}$ = percentage of income generated by employers and/or own-account workers in activities *a*, by level of education

$GAV_{foal,a}$ = gross added value (at factor cost) of activities *a* generated by employers and/or own-account workers, in accordance with (3.7)

$Digavfle_{fle}$ = percentage of income generated by employees in the whole economy, by level of education

GAV_{fle} = gross added value (at factor cost) generated by employees (total), in accordance with (3.6)

$Digavfoal_{foal}$ = percentage of income generated by employers and/or own-account workers in the whole economy, by level of education

GAV_{foal} = gross added value (at factor cost) generated by employers and/or ownaccount workers (total), in accordance with (3.11)

$Wgav_{fle,a}$ = amount of income generated by employee in activities *a*, by level of education

$LE_{fle,a}$ = employees (by level of education) of activities *a*, in accordance with (3.3)

$Wgavfle_a$ = amount of income generated by employee in activities *a*

$Wgav_{foal,a}$ = amount of income generated by employer and/or own-account worker in activities *a*, by level of education

$LOA_{foal,a}$ = employers and/or own-account workers (by level of education) of activities *a*, in accordance with (3.8)

$Wgavfoal_a$ = amount of income generated by employer and/or own-account worker in activities *a*

$Wgavfle_{fle}$ = amount of income generated by employee in the whole economy

$Wgavfoal_{foal}$ = amount of income generated by employer and/or own-account worker in the whole economy

The following tables were constructed from the numerical version of the SAM, as well as from additional data in the case of Table 22 – the links to the algebraic version are shown between brackets.

Table 20 – Distribution of gross added value, at factor cost, among factors of production and activity, in the Portuguese SAM for 1995 (in percentage terms)

		a1	*a2*	*a3*	*a4*	*a5*	*a6*	Total
Labour – employees ($Digav_{fle,a}$; $Digav_{fle}$, for Total)		16.4	53.5	52.9	46.5	43.0	80.0	54.5
Own assets	Labour - employers and/or own-account workers ($Digav_{foal,a}$; $Digav_{foal}$, for Total)	61.4	1.8	2.0	6.4	2.6	6.3	7.5
	Capital ($Digav_{foak,a}$;$Digav_{foak}$, for Total)	22.2	44.8	45.0	47.1	54.4	13.7	38.0
Total		100.0	100.0	100.0	100.0	100.0	100.0	100.0

Source: Table 15.

Key to activities:

a1 – agriculture, hunting and forestry; fishing and operation of fish hatcheries and fish farms;

a2 – industry, including energy;
a3 – construction;
a4 – wholesale and retail trade, repair of motor vehicles and household goods, hotels and restaurants; transport and communications;
a5 – financial, real estate, renting and business activities;
a6 – other service activities.

Table 21 – Distribution of gross added value, at factor cost, generated by labour by level of education of the workers and activity, in the Portuguese SAM for 1995 (in percentage terms)

		a1	*a2*	*a3*	*a4*	*a5*	*a6*	Total
Employees with ($Digavfle_{fle,a}$; $Digavfle_{fle}$, for (row) Total)	low education level	72.5	55.2	86.7	58.9	34.2	33.1	48.3
	medium education level	24.4	33.6	5.6	27.9	34.8	40.9	33.0
	high education level	3.1	11.2	7.8	13.2	31.0	26.0	18.7
	Total	100.0	100.0	100.0	100.0	100.0	100.0	100.0
Employers and/or own-account workers with ($Digavfoal_{foal,a}$; $Digavfoal_{foal}$, for (row) Total)	low education level	61.8	59.3	89.0	60.3	25.3	40.1	55.7
	medium education level	35.8	25.5	4.5	23.8	38.5	41.3	33.3
	high education level	2.5	15.2	6.5	15.8	36.2	18.6	11.0
	Total	100.0	100.0	100.0	100.0	100.0	100.0	100.0

Source: Table 15.

See key to activities in Table 20.

Table 22 – Gross added value, at factor cost, generated *per worker*, by level of education and activity, in the Portuguese SAM for 1995 (in thousands of euros *per worker*)

		a1	*a2*	*a3*	*a4*	*a5*	*a6*	Total
Employees with ($Wgav_{fle,a}$; $Wgavfle_{fle}$, for (row) Total)	low education level	6.3	7.3	10.9	8.6	7.8	6.0	7.5
	medium education level	9.7	20.3	3.2	18.5	36.1	33.6	23.4
	high education level	2.2	11.7	7.7	15.1	55.5	37.0	22.8
	Total ($Wgavfle_a$)	6.5	9.8	9.4	10.8	16.9	13.4	11.5
Employers and/or own-account workers with ($Wgav_{foal,a}$; $Wgavfoal_{foal}$, for (row) Total)	low education level	3.8	3.0	0.9	3.1	0.6	3.9	3.0
	medium education level	26.2	15.2	0.5	14.4	10.2	47.7	20.9
	high education level	3.0	15.1	1.3	15.8	15.9	35.5	11.5
	Total ($Wgavfoal_a$)	5.5	4.5	0.9	4.5	2.0	8.6	4.7

Source: Tables 15, D.1, D.2 and D.3.

See key to activities in Table 20.

Thus, from Tables 20 and 21, it can be concluded that wages and salaries, or the compensation of labour received by employees, represent 54.5% of generated income, whereas the compensation of labour received by the employers and/or own-account workers represents 7.5%. Within these two parts of generated income, almost half (48.3%), in the first case and more than half (55.7%), in the second case, is received by workers with a low education level while, in both cases, workers with a medium education level receive 33.3% and those with a high education level receive the remainder. Capital, therefore, represents 38% of generated income. This general structure is the result of a relative heterogeneity in the distributions (of generated income) among activities. The group of activities of "agriculture, hunting and forestry; fishing and operation of fish hatcheries and fish farms" (*a*1) is the one that contributes most to that heterogeneity, with wages and salaries representing only 16.4% and the compensation of labour received by employers and/or own-account workers representing 61.4% – resulting in one of the lowest shares for the compensation of capital (22.2%, after the other service activities – group *a*6 – with 13.7%). This group of activities also has one of the highest shares of workers with a low education level (employees – 72.5% – and employers and/or own-account workers – 61.8%, after construction – group *a*3 – with 86.9% and 89%, respectively).

On the other hand, albeit in greater number, the workers that have a low education level are those who generate less income *per worker*, except in the case of the groups of activities of "agriculture, hunting and forestry; fishing and operation of fish hatcheries and fish farms" (*a*1) and "construction" (*a*3), as can be seen in Table 22. Workers with a medium education level (employees and employers and/or own-account workers) represent, on average, the group that generates most income *per worker*, although the heterogeneity among activities is, also significant here: "financial, real estate, renting and business activities" (*a*5) and the "other service activities" (*a*6) underline the strong position of the income generated *per worker* with medium and high educational levels, especially employees.

A.2. *Among institutions and socioeconomic groups, within households*

The institutional distribution of the generated income can be studied through the division of gross national income among domestic institutions.

$$Digni_{dic} = (GNI_{dic} / GNI) *100 \qquad (5.17)$$

Where:

$Digni_{dic}$ = percentage of generated income received by domestic institutions (dic)

GNI_{dic} = (total) national income (at factor cost) of domestic institutions (dic), in accordance with (3.24)

GNI = gross national income (at factor cost) – total, in accordance with (3.25)

The following table was constructed from the numerical version of the SAM:

Table 23 – Distribution of gross national income, at factor cost, among institutions and socioeconomic groups, within households, in the Portuguese SAM for 1995 (in percentage terms)

Group of households (in accordance with the main source of income)		Other Institutions	
Employees	62.1 %	Non-financial corporations	16.4 %
Employers (including own account workers)	18.6 %	Financial corporations	2.5 %
Recipients of pensions	2.6 %	General government	-3.6 %
Others	1.2 %	Non-profit institutions serving households	0.2 %
Total (households)	84.5 %	Total (all Institutions)	100.0 %

Source: Table 15.

As a result of what was seen with regard to the position of the compensation of labour in generated income, households receive 84.5% of gross national income, with 62.1% corresponding to the group whose main source of income is wages and salaries (employees).

Non-financial corporations receive 16.4%, with the remainder being distributed amongst the other institutions and with the general government recording a negative share.

B. Distribution and use of disposable income, among institutions and socioeconomic groups, within households.

By excluding from gross national income the current transfers paid to other institutions and to the rest of the world, and by including the current transfers received from the other institutions and the rest of the world and, in the case of the government, the net indirect taxes (in accordance with equation (4.4)), the institutional distribution of gross disposable income can be studied. In turn, the use made of gross disposable income is divided into final consumption and saving, although non-financial and financial corporations do not have any final consumption.

The available data only allow for a calculation of the total value of income, final consumption and saving *per capita*.

$$Didi_{dic} = (DI_{dic} \;/\; DI) *100 \qquad (5.18)$$
$$UdiFC_{dic} = (FC_{dic} \;/\; DI_{dic}) *100 \qquad (5.19)$$
$$UdiS_{dic} = (S_{dic} \;/\; DI_{dic}) *100 = 100 - UdiFC_{dic} \qquad (5.20)$$
$$PcDI = \Sigma_{dic} DI_{dic} *10^6 / \; P \qquad (5.21)$$
$$PcFC = \Sigma_{dic} FC_{dic} *10^6 / \; P \qquad (5.22)$$
$$PcS = \Sigma_{dic} S_{dic} *10^6 / \; P \qquad (5.22)$$

Where:

$Didi_{dic}$ = percentage of gross disposable income received by domestic institutions (dic)

DI_{dic} = (gross) disposable income of domestic institutions (dic), in accordance with (4.4)

DI = (gross) disposable income – total, in accordance with (4.3)

$UdiFC_{dic}$ = percentage of gross disposable income used in final consumption by domestic institutions (dic)

FC_{dic} = value of final consumption (at market prices) of domestic institutions (dic), in accordance with (3.65)

$UdiS_{dic}$ = percentage of gross disposable income used in (gross) saving by domestic institutions (dic)

S_{dic} = gross saving of domestic institutions (dic), in accordance with (3.96)

PcDI = gross disposable income *per capita* (in euros)

PcFC = final consumption *per capita* (in euros)

PcS = saving *per capita* (in euros)

P = total population

The following table was constructed from the numerical version of the SAM – the links to the algebraic version are shown between brackets.

Table 24 – Distribution and use of disposable income, among institutions and socioeconomic groups, within households, in the Portuguese SAM for 1995 (in percentage terms)

		Distribution of Disposable Income (Didi$_{dic}$)	Use of Disposable Income	
			Final Consumption (UdiFC$_{dic}$)	Saving (UdiS$_{dic}$)
Group of households (in accordance with the main source of income)	Employees	41.9	98.2	1.8
	Employers (including own account workers)	16.1	52.4	47.6
	Recipients of pensions	9.6	86.6	13.4
	Others	1.8	108.0	- 8.0
	Total (households)	69.3	86.3	13.7
Non-financial corporations		11.2	0.0	100.0
Financial corporations		1.9	0.0	100.0
General government		16.0	112.4	-12.4
Non-profit institutions serving households		1.7	92.8	7.2
Total		100.0	79.3	20.7

Source: Table 15.

Therefore, households have 69.3% of disposable income, with the group whose main source of income is wages and salaries (employees) having 41.9%. The general government has a share of 16% (similar to the group of households whose main source of income is the compensation of labour received by employers, including own account workers), while the share of non-financial corporations is 11.2%; the other shares are less significant. Except in the case of the non-financial and financial corporations, final consumption absorbs the most significant part of disposable income, even exceeding it in the case of both the general government and the group "others" amongst the households (those whose main source of income is not wages and salaries, mixed income including property income or income in connection with old age).

From the numerical version, it also can be seen that the values of income, final consumption and saving *per capita* in 1995 were respectively: 5,832 (PcDI); 5,030 (PcFC) and 802 (PcS) euros.

More specific and exact conclusions would require specification of the households' composition – number of workers by household, size, age composition, dependency ratios, etc. (Dervis et al., 1982).

6.

Experiments and scenarios with the distributional impact of budget policies

Considering the framework, assumptions and purposes of this version of the algebraic SAM, two experiments were carried out involving current transfers from/to households.

Because the intention was to study the distributional impacts of government policies, two scenarios were defined. The first scenario – scenario A – considered a 1% reduction in the direct tax rate (*ti*) paid by households to the government, while scenario B was based on a 1% increase in social benefits other than social transfers in kind (*D62P*) paid by the government to households.

With the help of Table 19 (and 15), it can be seen that in scenario A, the reduction in the current taxes on income, wealth, etc. will involve a leakage from the government's main source of receipts (current transfers from households) and an injection (of receipts, resulting from the reduction in expenditure) into one item of the expenditure of households (current transfers to the government), although not the most important one. In turn, the increase in social benefits other than social transfers in kind, occurring in scenario B, will involve an injection into one source of the receipts of households (current transfers from government), although not the most important one, and a leakage (of receipts, resulting from the increase in expenditure) from the main item of government expenditure (current transfers to households).

The immediate purpose of these two experiments is to improve the financial situation of households.

Table 25 shows the base values and the corresponding relative importance of the flows that were subjected to the above-mentioned shocks.

Table 25 – Current taxes on income, wealth, etc. paid by households to the government and social benefits other than social transfers in kind paid by the government to households, in Portugal in 1995.

Group of households (in accordance with the main source of income)	Current taxes on income, wealth, etc.[(a)]		Social benefits other than social transfers in kind[(c)]	
	millions of euros	direct tax rate[(b)] (%)	millions of euros	% of DI[(d)]
Employees	4 201	8.5	2 206	6.3
Employers (including own account workers)	377	2.5	873	6.5
Recipients of pensions	294	3.0	6 156	77.0
Others	60	3.4	250	16.9
Total (households)	4 932	6.5	9 485	16.4

Source: Tables A.2.2a and b.

Notes:

(a) Transaction D5 of the National Accounts. See Section 2.3. for the methodology used in adjusting the total value to the values of the groups of households.

(b) Current taxes on income, wealth, etc. paid by households to the government, per unit of received aggregate income (*ti*).

(c) Transaction D62 of the National Accounts (*D62P*). See Section 2.3. for the methodology used in adjusting the total value to the values of the groups of households.

(d) Social benefits other than social transfers in kind paid by the government to households, per unit of disposable income of households.

The framework within which scenario A will be defined and the first experiment performed shows that the direct taxes, or the current taxes on income, wealth, etc. paid by households, represent 6.5% of their aggregate income (households pay 68.9% of the direct taxes paid by all the institutions). Employees pay 8.5% of their aggregate income, which is the highest direct rate within the groups of households (they also pay 58.7% of the direct taxes paid by all the institutions and 85.2% of those paid by households). Employers and own account workers pay the lowest rate: 2.5%.

Scenario B will be defined within a framework in which social benefits other than social transfers in kind represent 16.4% of the disposable income of households, with the recipients of pensions having the largest share in the case of this item, with such benefits being responsible for 77% of their disposable income (the corresponding amount is 25% higher than the direct taxes paid by households).

At the level of macroeconomic aggregates and balances, as defined in Chapter 4, the main impacts of the two scenarios can be seen in Table 26.

Table 26 – Impacts (percentage change) on the macroeconomic aggregates of a reduction (of 1%) in the direct tax rate paid by households to the government – scenario A, and of an increase (of 1%) in the social benefits other than social transfers in kind received by households from the government – scenario B.

Macroeconomic Aggregates			Scenario A	Scenario B
Gross domestic product at market prices (GDP)			- 1.47 %	- 0.19 %
Gross national income (at market prices) (GNIMP)			- 1.47 %	- 0.19 %
Gross Disposable Income (DI), of:	Group of households (in accordance with the main source of income)	Employees	- 0.24 %	- 0.15 %
		Employers (including own account workers)	+ 0.07 %	- 0.07 %
		Recipients of pensions	+ 1.13 %	+ 0.73 %
		Others	+ 0.54 %	+ 0.08 %
		Total (households)	+ 0.04 %	0.00 %
	Non-financial corporations		- 1.18 %	- 0.17 %
	Financial corporations		- 2.73 %	- 0,35 %
	General government		- 7.90 %	- 0.97 %
	Non-profit institutions serving households		- 0.11 %	- 0.01 %
	Total		-1.42 %	- 0.18 %
Gross Saving (S)			- 0.04 %	- 0.01 %
Net Borrowing of the economy (NLB)			+ 6.29 %	+ 4.63 %

Source: Table 15 and Appendixes A, C and D were used for the calculation of the parameters used in the model defined in Chapter 3 (from which the values shown in this table were derived).

Therefore, in scenario A, a reduction of 1% in the direct tax rate paid by households to the government resulted in a decrease of 1.47% in the gross domestic product at market prices (GDP), as well as, in the gross national income at market prices (GNIMP). The disposable income (DI) of households only increased by 0.04% and, curiously, employees, who pay the major share of direct taxes, are the only group of households that shows a decrease, due to the importance of generated income (gross national income, which decreased by 1.47%) in their disposable income. The other institutions showed a generalized decrease in their DI, particularly the government, with a decrease of 7.9%, which had a consequent negative impact on both demand and production. This situation is proved by the decreases in GDP and GNIMP, as mentioned above, as well as in the gross saving and net borrowing of the economy, the latter showing a significant increase of 6.29%.

The impacts in scenario B were not so significant, although the percentage changes almost always have the same mathematical sign. Thus, the increase of 1% in the social benefits other than social transfers in kind received by households from the government resulted in decreases of 0.19% in GDP and GNIMP, with the DI of households being maintained – resulting from decreases in employees (-0.15%) and employers (-0.07%) and increases in recipients of pensions (+0.73%) and others (+0.08%) – and a generalized decrease in the DI of the other institutions, with the highest value (-0.97%) being recorded by the government.

The explanation for this process is identical to the one provided for scenario A, although in this case the effects on GDP and GNIMP (-0.19%) and on gross saving (+0.01%) were smaller, as well as on the net borrowing of the economy, which increased by 4.63%.

The dependence of final consumption on the gross disposable income of all domestic institutions, including the government, as well as the relationship between aggregate demand and production, are certainly the main causes of these results.

Without taking into account the balance of payments (since external trade was considered exogenous) at the level of the balances, i.e. at the level of the institutions' budgets, the impacts on current balances, expressed by gross saving, or on the total balances, expressed by the net lending/borrowing, are shown in Table 27.

Table 27 – Impacts (percentage change) on the budget balances of the institutions of a reduction (of 1%) in the direct tax rate paid by households to the government – scenario A – and of an increase (of 1%) in the social benefits other than social transfers in kind received by households from the government – scenario B.

Budget Balances of the institutions			Scenario A	Scenario B
Current balance of:	Group of households (in accordance with the main source of income)	Employees	- 0.24 %	- 0.15 %
		Employers (including own account workers)	+ 0.07 %	- 0.07 %
		Recipients of pensions	+ 1.13 %	+ 0.73 %
		Others	+ 0.54 %	+ 0.08 %
		Total (households)	+ 0.18 %	+ 0.03 %
	Non-financial corporations		- 1.18 %	- 0.17 %
	Financial corporations		- 2.73 %	- 0.35 %
	General government		- 7.90 %	- 0.97 %
	Non-profit institutions serving households		- 0.11 %	- 0.01 %
	Total		- 0.04 %	- 0.01%
Capital balance of:	Households		- 0.02 %	0.00 %
	Non-financial corporations		- 0.03 %	0.00 %
	Financial corporations		- 0.01 %	0.00 %
	General government		0.00 %	0.00 %
	Non-profit institutions serving households		- 0.09 %	- 0.07 %
	Total		- 0.02 %	0.00 %
Total balance of:	Households		+ 0.38 %	+ 0.06 %
	Non-financial corporations		- 215.73 %	- 30.40 %
	Financial corporations		- 14.74 %	- 1.89 %
	General government		- 2.97 %	- 0.36 %
	Non-profit institutions serving households		- 0.19 %	+ 0.18 %
	Total		+ 6.29 %	+ 4.63 %

Source: see Table 26.

As seen in Chapter 4, with the analysis that was made of Table 19, the government was the only institution with both current and total budget deficits (the group labelled as "others" within the group of households also recorded a current deficit, but without this having any significant repercussions on the total current balance of households).

The mathematical signs of the percentage changes, representative of the impacts occurring in both scenarios, continue, in almost all cases, to be equal, albeit with smaller values in scenario B.

Therefore, reflecting the situation defined in Table 26, in scenario A the budget balances of the institutions show a generalized decrease, except in the case of the current balance of those households that do not belong to the group of employees. The current balance of the general government was the one that suffered the greatest impact, with a reduction in the current deficit resulting mainly from the impact of the reduction in disposable income on final consumption. The impacts at the level of the capital balance were not significant – which was expected, because the experiment was conducted with the flows of the current account. In terms of the total balance, the net lending of households recorded a slight improvement (0.38%), whereas that of financial corporations and non-profit institutions serving households worsened – the former significantly (– 14.74%) and the latter slightly (– 0.19%). In turn, the net lending of non-financial corporations was converted into net borrowing, although the net borrowing of the general government recorded a decrease of 2.97% – reflecting the decrease observed in the current deficit. All these fluctuations in the total budget balances resulted in an increase in the net borrowing of the economy of 6.29 %, as seen above.

Scenario B shows almost the same impacts, but with smaller values. In terms of the total budget balance, non-financial corporations maintain their net lending, although at a lower level, while the net borrowing of the general government records a slight decrease (– 0.36%) and the net lending of non-profit institutions serving households records a slight increase (+0.18%). The final result is again an increase in the net borrowing of the economy (4.63%), although not so significant as in scenario A.

In turn, the unemployment rate (5.291% in 1995) increased by 1.517 percentage points in scenario A (6.808 %) and by 0.190 percent points in scenario B (5.481%).

Because the two experiments were performed using a version of the algebraic SAM with too many fixed parameters and exogenous variables, the structural changes were certainly not significant. Let us, however, look at the results.

Tables 20 and 21 showed that the compensation of labour received by employees represented 54.5%, whereas the compensation of labour received by employers and/or own-account workers represented 7.5% and the compensation of capital represented 38% of generated income. From Table 28, a slight improvement can be seen in the positions of the latter two factors of production in detriment to the first – again with less significant impacts in scenario B, as seen before. Workers with high and medium education levels were worse affected than workers with a low education level.

Table 28 – Impacts (percentage change) on the distribution of gross added value, at factor cost, among factors of production of a reduction (of 1%) in the direct tax rate paid by households to the government – scenario A – and of an increase (of 1%) in social benefits other than social transfers in kind received by households from the government – scenario B.

			Scenario A	Scenario B
Labour – employees, with:		low education level	0.0 %	0.0 %
		medium education level	- 0.9 %	- 0.1 %
		high education level	- 1.1 %	- 0.1 %
		Total	- 0.5 %	- 0.1 %
Own assets	Labour - employers and/or own-account workers, with:	low education level	+ 0.4 %	+ 0.1 %
		medium education level	+ 0.0 %	0.0 %
		high education level	- 0.4 %	- 0.1 %
		Total	+ 0.2 %	0.0 %
	Capital		+ 0,6 %	+ 0.1 %

Source: see Table 26.

Table 23 showed that households received 84.5% of gross national income, with 62.1% corresponding to the group whose main source of income was wages and salaries (employees). Non-financial corporations received 16.4%, with the remainder being distributed within the other institutions and with the general government recording a negative share.

From Table 29, one can conclude that the two experiments generated scenarios in which the position of the institutions either did not change or registered a slight improvement – except, in scenario A, in the case of the households in general and of the group whose main source of income is wages and salaries (employees) in particular, and, in both scenarios, in the case of the general government, which recorded an increase in its negative position.

Table 29 – Impacts (percentage change) on the distribution of gross national income, at factor cost, among institutions and socioeconomic groups of a reduction (of 1%) in the direct tax rate paid by households to the government – scenario A – and of an increase (of 1%) in the social benefits other than social transfers in kind received by households from the government – scenario B.

		Scenario A	Scenario B
Group of households (in accordance with the main source of income)	Employees	- 0.3 %	0.0 %
	Employers (including own account workers)	+ 0.4 %	0.1 %
	Recipients of pensions	+ 0.3 %	0.0 %
	Others	+ 0.1 %	0.0 %
	Total (households)	- 0.1 %	0.0 %
Non-financial corporations		+ 0.6 %	+ 0.1 %
Financial corporations		+ 0.6 %	+ 0.1 %
General government		+ 0.6 %	+ 0.1 %
Non-profit institutions serving households		+ 0.6 %	+ 0.1 %

Source: see Table 26.

In turn, Table 24 showed that households had 69.3% of disposable income, with the group whose main source of income is wages and salaries (employees) having 41.9%; the general government had a share of 16% (similar to the group of households whose main source of income is the compensation of labour received by employers, including own account workers) and the non-financial corporations had a share of 11.2%, the others being less significant.

The scenarios that resulted from the two experiments undertaken represent the impacts shown in Table 30. In fact, once again, both scenarios reveal similar impacts, albeit less significant in the case of scenario B, which improved the relative positions of households, non-financial corporations and non-profit institutions serving households in detriment to the other two, with special emphasis being given to the case of the general government. Mention should also be made of the positive impact that was noted in the relative position of the group of households whose main source of income is connected with old age (recipients of pensions).

Table 30 – Impacts (percentage change) on the distribution of the disposable income of the institutions of a reduction (of 1%) in the direct tax rate paid by households to the government – scenario A – and of an increase (of 1%) in the social benefits other than social transfers in kind received by households from the government – scenario B.

		Scenario A	Scenario B
Group of households (in accordance with the main source of income)	Employees	+ 1.20 %	+ 0.03 %
	Employers (including own account workers)	+ 1.51 %	+ 0.11 %
	Recipients of pensions	+ 2.59 %	+ 0.92 %
	Others	+ 1.99 %	+ 0.26 %
	Total (households)	+ 1.48 %	+ 0.18 %
non-financial corporations		+ 0.25%	+ 0.02 %
financial corporations		- 1.32 %	- 0.17 %
general government		- 6.58 %	- 0.79 %
non-profit institutions serving households		+ 1.33 %	+ 0.17 %

Source: see Table 26.

Thus, in this first approach to the question, the two experiments were conducted with the purpose of improving the financial situation of households; however, the scenarios that were generated show that not only did the situation of both households and the general government worsen, but so did the situation of the whole economy.

7.

Summary and concluding remarks

Numerical and algebraic versions of a SAM have been presented in this work, with an application to Portugal. In the former version, each cell assumed a specific numerical value, with the sums of the rows being equal to the sums of the columns. In the latter version, each cell was represented by algebraic expressions that, together with those of all the other cells, represent a SAM-based model, the calibration of which involved a replication of the former version.

The underlying idea was that of Pyatt (1991) in the following text:

> "... a SAM is a framework both for models of how the economy works as well as for data which monitor its workings. Recognition of this duality is of basic importance for quantitative analysis. It implies, *inter alia*, that the accounting identities which are captured by a SAM are not to be regarded simply as consistency requirements which must be imposed on a model, but rather they should be seen as a logical consequence of the paradigms which economists have adopted for analyzing society".

A study was undertaken at a macroeconomic level using the national accounts, within an ESA (95) framework, as the basic source of information.

Using the flexibility of the numerical version, through a top-down approach, additional sources were used to disaggregate the macro-SAM, with the RAS method having been used to adjust them to those of the basic source. In this way, therefore, the consistency of the whole system was not lost. This disaggregation was carried out by considering, on the one hand, the aim of studying the impacts of government policies on the distribution of income and, on the other hand, the data available for this purpose.

The definition of the algebraic version involved an identification of the national accounting transactions and their inclusion, with all possible details, in the characterising equations of each cell. This version, which should only be considered as a starting point, includes a valuation system whose potentialities will be better explored in the future; the equations that have been defined will be tested and the parameters econometrically estimated, from time series of the national accounts transactions. Underlying paradigms should also be revised.

Macroeconomic aggregates and balances, as well as structural indicators of the distribution and use of income, were also calculated and formalised from both versions of the SAM, thereby providing an improved knowledge of the quantifiable side of the studied economy. A number of aspects were identified, such as the following:

- the government is the institution that has a total budget balance with a deficit (represented by its net borrowing), which is almost completely covered by the other institutions, with households having an important share, although this was, however, insufficient to avoid a net borrowing for the economy of 40 million euros (0.05% of GDP);
- current transfers from Portuguese institutions and net taxes on products are the main sources of receipts for the general government, whereas current transfers to Portuguese institutions and final consumption (a substantial

part of this is transformed into transfers to households in kind) are its main items of expenditure;

- the income generated by households (or gross national income) and their final consumptionre the main sources of receipts and expenditure, respectively;
- the compensation of labour received by employees represents 54.5% of generated income, whereas the compensation of labour received by employers and/or own-account workers represents 7.5% – a large proportion of these workers have a low educational level and they can therefore only be attributed with the lower level of income generated *per worker*;
- the above-mentioned functional distribution of income also contributes with a share of 38% to the capital;
- households receive 84.5% of generated income and have 69.3% of disposable income; the group whose main source of income is wages and salaries (employees) is the most representative;
- final consumption absorbs the most significant part of the disposable income of institutions, except for the non-financial and financial corporations, even exceeding it in the case of the general government and of the group "others" amongst the households (those whose main source of income is not wages and salaries, mixed income including property income or income in connection with old age).

With the initial aim of improving the financial situation of households, two scenarios were defined and two experiments were performed in order to measure and identify impacts: a reduction of 1% in the direct tax rate paid by households to the government – scenario A; an increase of 1% in the social benefits other than social transfers in kind paid by the government to households – scenario B. Both of the impacts generated had similar mathematical signs, although the effects of scenario B were smaller. The direct effect of the two above-mentioned shocks on the (reduction of the) receipts of the general government had direct consequences for its final consumption, which, in turn, had obvious repercussions on both final demand and supply. The gross domestic product and gross national income (at market prices) then decreased, with consequences at the level of disposable income, consumption and saving (the current budget balance), as well as at the level of net lending/borrowing (the total budget balance). Particular emphasis is laid on the net borrowing of the economy, which increased by 6.29% in scenario A and by 4.63% in scenario B, as well as on the unemployment rate, which increased by 1.517 percentage points in scenario A and by 0.190 percentage points in scenario B. Therefore, from the algebraic version of the SAM that was defined, the two experiments showed that the intention of improving the financial situation of households resulted in a worse overall situation, not only for the households themselves, but also for the economy in general and for all the other institutions, especially the general government.

Details were specified in order to provide the information needed not only to perform a similar exercise in other applications, but also to easily detect all the underlying failures, inconsistencies, errors, etc. The choice of experiments whose results can be compared with reality (which is not this case) is also very important. In the author's view, this is the way in which a work such as this one can be developed and improved upon.

Modelling techniques can be considered as a support of (socio-)economic theory, so that better and more stable empirical evidence can help in the (re-)evaluation of this theory or even in the (re-)orientation of the way in which reality has traditionally been defined and conceptualised. The SAM, in both its versions, can be a valuable working instrument to be used for these purposes.

At the same time, by using a working instrument such as the SAM, the policy design can be based on a more positive and less normative analysis.

The potentialities and possibilities for further study provided by the SAM were emphasised, and, in this context, the author would like to encourage the authorities to include the teaching of its methodology in the curricula of courses in secondary and higher education, in the areas related with the social sciences.

References

ABBINK G. et al. (1995), "A SAM-CGE demonstration model for Indonesia: static and dynamic specifications and experiments", *International Economic Journal* 9: 15-33.

BRABER M. et al. (1996), "Policy Modeling under Fixed and Flexible Price Regimes: SAMCGE Transitional Applications to Poland and Hungary", *Journal of Policy Modeling* 18: 495-529.

BREUSS F. and TESCHE J. (1993), "Hungary in Transition: A Computable General Equilibrium Model Comparison with Austria", *Journal of Policy Modeling* 15: 581-623.

DERVIS K. et al. (1982), *General Equilibrium Models for Development Policy*, Cambridge University Press, Cambridge (UK), 526 pp.

DEVARAJAN S. et al. (1991), "From Stylized to Applied Models: Building Multisector CGE Models for Policy Analysis", Working Paper No. 616, Department of Agricultural and Resource Economics, University of California at Berkeley, 57 pp.

DEVARAJAN S. et al. (1996), Simple General Equilibrium Modeling, in François J. and Reinert K. (eds.) *Applied Methods for Trade Policy Analysis*, Cambridge University Press, Cambridge (UK), 156-185.

DRUD A. et al. (1986), "Macroeconomic Modelling Based on Social Accounting Principles", *Journal of Policy Modeling* 8: 111-145.

EUROSTAT (1996), *European System of Accounts* (ESA 95). Eurostat, Luxembourg.

ISWG – INTER-SECRETARIAT WORKING GROUP (1993), *System of National Accounts* (SNA 93). Commission of the European Communities – Eurostat, Brussels/Luxembourg; International Monetary Fund, Washington, DC; Organization for Economic Co-operation and Development, Paris; United Nations, Statistical Office, New York; World Bank, Washington DC.

KEUNING S. (1996), *Accounting for Economic Development and Social Change,* IOS Press, Amsterdam (Netherlands), 233 pp.

KEUNING S. and RUIJTER W. (1988), "Guidelines to the construction of a Social Accounting Matrix", *Review of Income and Wealth* 34: 71-100.

KHAN F (1996), Household Disaggregation, in: François J. and Reinert K. (eds.) *Applied Methods for Trade Policy Analysis,* Cambridge University Press, Cambridge (UK), 300-327.

LEG – LEADERSHIP GROUP ON SAM (2003), "Handbook on Social Accounting Matrices and Labour Accounts" Eurostat Working Papers, Theme – Population and Social Conditions 3/2003/E/N 23, Luxembourg, 190 pp.

LOFGREN H. et al. (2001), "A Standard Computable General Equilibrium (CGE) Model in GAMS", TMD (Trade and Macroeconomics Division) Discussion Paper No. 75, IFPRI (International Food Policy Research Institute), Washington, DC, 69 pp.

NORTON R. et al. (1986), "Portugal's Entry Into the EEC: Aggregate and Distributional Effects Determined by Means of a General Equilibrium Model", *Journal of Policy Modeling* 8: 149-180.

PYATT G. (1988), "A SAM Approach to Modeling", *Journal of Policy Modeling* 10: 327-352.

PYATT G. (1991), "Fundamentals of Social Accounting", *Economic Systems Research* 3: 315-341.

PYATT G. and ROE A. (1977), *Social Accounting for Development Planning with special reference to Sri Lanka,* Cambridge University Press, Cambridge, 190 pp.

PYATT G. and ROUND J. (1985), Accounting and Fixed Price Multipliers in a Social Accounting Matrix Framework, in Pyatt G. and Round, J. (eds.) *Social Accounting Matrices. A Basis for Planning.* A World Bank Symposium, The World Bank, Washington, DC 186-206; also in *Economic Journal* 89 (356): 850-873, 1979.

REINERT K. and ROLAND-HOLST D. (1996), Social Accounting Matrices, in François J. and

REINERT K. (eds.) *Applied Methods for Trade Policy Analysis,* Cambridge University Press, Cambridge (UK), 94-121.

ROBERTS B. and ZOLKIEWSKI Z. (1996), "Modelling income distribution in countries in transition: A computable general equilibrium analysis for Poland", *Economic Modelling* 13: 67-90.

ROBINSON S. (1989), "Computable General Equilibrium Models of Developing Countries: Stretching the Neoclassical Paradigm", Working

Paper No. 513, Department of Agricultural and Resource Economics, University of California, Berkeley (USA), 41 pp.

Round J. (2003), "Constructing SAMs for Development Policy Analysis: Lessons Learned and Challenges Ahead", *Economic Systems Research* 15: 161-183.

Santos S. (1999), "The Social Accounting Matrix as a working instrument for defining economic policy. Its application to Portugal during the period 1986-90, with emphasis on the agro-industrial sector", PhD dissertation, ISEG-TULisboa, Lisbon, 309 pp. (only available in Portuguese).

Santos S. (2001), "The importance of the Social Accounting Matrix. Its application to Portugal during the period 1990-95", ISEG-TU Lisboa – Department of Economics' Seminar, Lisbon. 66 pp.

Santos S. (2003), "Quantitative analysis of the economic flows between Portugal and the other European Union Member States and Institutions in 1997", Working Paper No. 2/2003, Centre of Research on European and International Economics – ISEG-TU Lisboa, Lisbon, 44 pp.

Santos S. (2003a), "Social Accounting Matrices for Portugal in 1998-99. Modelling the effects of changes in government receipts and expenditure", Working Paper No. 7/2003/Department of Economics/ Research Unit on Complexity and Economics – ISEG-TU Lisboa, Lisbon, 51 pp.

Santos S. (2004), "Portuguese net borrowing and the government budget balance. A SAM approach", *Journal of Policy Modeling* 26: 703-717.

Santos S. (2004a), "Distribution of aggregate income in Portugal from 1995 to 2000 within a SAM framework. Modelling the household sector", Working Paper No. 12/2004/Department of Economics/ Research Unit on Complexity and Economics – ISEG-TU Lisboa, Lisbon, 33 pp.

Santos S. (2005), "Social Accounting Matrix and the System of National Accounts: An Application", Higher Institute of Economics and Business Administration. Working Paper No. 14/2005/ Department of Economics/Research Unit on Complexity and Economics – ISEG-TU Lisboa, 41 pp.

Santos S. (2005a), "Effects of changes in flows of funds between Government and households. A SAM approach to Portugal".

EconWPA-GE (Working Paper Archive in Economics – General Equilibrium) 0507002, 40 pp.

SANTOS S. (2006), "Constructing a Database for Economic Modelling from the System of National Accounts: a Social Accounting Matrix for Portugal". Working Paper Series – SSRN (Social Science Research Network) abstract=916089, 76 pp.

SANTOS S. (2006a), "Better policy analysis with better data. Constructing a Social Accounting Matrix from the European System of National Accounts", Working Paper No. 22/2006/Department of Economics/Research Unit on Complexity and Economics – ISEG-TU Lisboa, 14 pp.

SANTOS S. (2007), "Modelling Economic Circuit Flows in a Social Accounting Matrix Framework. An Application to Portugal". *Applied Economics* 39: 1753-1771.

SANTOS S. (2007a), "Macro-SAMs for Modelling Purposes. An Application to Portugal in 2003", Working Paper No. 17/2007/ Department of Economics/Research Unit on Complexity and Economics – ISEG-TU Lisboa, 17 pp.

STIFEL D. and THORBECKE E. (2003), "A dual-dual CGE model of an archetype African economy: trade reform, migration and poverty", *Journal of Policy Modeling* 25: 207-235.

STONE R. (1981), *Aspects of Economic and Social Modelling*. Libraire Droz, Geneva, 159 pp.

TAYLOR L. (1990), Structuralist CGE Models, in Taylor L. (ed.) *Socially Relevant Policy Analysis. Structuralist Computable General Equilibrium Models for the Developing World,* The MIT Press, Cambridge, Massachusetts, London, England, 1-70.

TAYLOR L. and ARNIM R. (2006), "Modelling the Impact of Trade Liberalisation. A Critique of Computable General Equilibrium Models", Oxfam International Research Report, New School for Social Research, New York, 61 pp.

THORBECKE, E. (2000), "The use of social accounting matrices in modelling", Paper prepared for the 26th General Conference of the International Association for Research in Income and Wealth, Krakow, Poland, 47 pp.

THORBECKE E. (2001), "The Social Accounting Matrix: Deterministic or Stochastic Concept?", Paper prepared for a conference in honour of Graham Pyatt's retirement, at the Institute of Social Studies, The Hague, Netherlands, 15 pp.

Thorbecke E. (2003), "Towards a stochastic Social Accounting Matrix for Modelling", *Economic Systems Research* 15(2): 185-196.

Yao S., Liu A. (2000), "Policy Analysis in a General Equilibrium Framework", *Journal of Policy Modeling* 22: 589-610.

Appendix A

Portuguese National Accounts for 1995 (SNA Tables)

Table A.1a. Integrated Economic Accounts (in millions of euros) – Uses

Current accounts
Uses

			S.2	S.1	S.15	S.14	S.13	S.12	S.11		
Accounts	**Total**	Goods and Services Account (Resources)	Rest of the World Account	Total of the Economy	NPISHs	Households	General Government	Financial Corporations	Non-Financial Corporations	Code	**Transactions and other flows, stocks and balancing items**
I. Production / external account of goods and services	29 454	29 454								P.7	Imports of goods and services
	24 433		24 433							P.6	Exports of goods and services
	154 394	154 394								P.1	Output of goods and services
	84 102			84 102	1 527	9 294	3 003	1 631	64 959	P.2	Intermediate consumption
	10 535	10 535								D.21-D.31	Net taxes on products
	80 827			**80 827**	**1 190**	**16 966**	**12 386**	**4 333**	**39 105**	**B.1g/B.1*g**	**Gross added value/gross domestic product**
	13 457			13 457	279	3 715	1 526	733	7 204	K.1	Consumption of fixed capital
	67 369			**67 369**	**911**	**13 251**	**10 860**	**3 600**	**31 900**	**B.1n/B.1*n**	**Value added, net/Net domestic product**
	5 021		**5 021**							B.11	**External balance of goods and services**
II.1.1. Generation of income account	38 683		120	38 563	1 126	2 111	10 990	2 309	22 027	D.1	Compensation of employees
	10 102			10 102	- 14	- 118	- 56	- 4	- 241	D.2-D.3	Net taxes on production and imports
	10 535			10 535						D.21-D.31	Net taxes on products
	- 433			- 433	- 14	- 118	- 56	- 4	- 241	D.29-D.39	Net taxes on production
	17 189			**17 189**	**78**		**1 452**	**2 028**	**17 319**	B.2g	**Gross operating surplus**
	14 973			**14 973**		**14 973**				B.3g	**Gross mixed income**
	7 446			**7 446**	**- 201**		**- 74**	**1 295**	**10 115**	B.2n	**Net operating surplus**
	11 258			**11 258**		**11 258**				B.3n	**Net mixed income**
II.1.2. Allocation of primary income account	31 314		3 123	28 191	38	2 976	5 066	12 175	7 936	D.4	Property income
										P.119	Adjustment to the FISIM (Financial Intermediation Services Indirectly Measured)
	80 479			**80 479**	**137**	**59 614**	**7 379**	**1 787**	**11 561**	B.5g	**Gross national income/ Gross balance of primary incomes**
	67 022			**67 022**	**- 142**	**55 899**	**5 853**	**1 054**	**4 357**	B.5n	**Net national income/ Net balance of primary incomes**
II.2. Secondary distribution income account	7 161			7 161	2	4 932		226	2 000	D.5	Current taxes on income, wealth, etc
	11 718			11 718		11 718				D.61	Social contributions
	11 659		29	11 630	13	42	9 515	720	1 339	D.62	Social benefits other than social transfers in kind
	15 737		3 931	11 807	19	1 865	8 194	1 066	663	D.7	Other current transfers
	83 517			**83 517**	**1 388**	**57 105**	**13 371**	**2 311**	**9 342**	B.6g	**Gross disposable income**
	70 059			**70 059**	**1 109**	**53 390**	**11 845**	**1 578**	**2 138**	B.6n	**Net disposable income**
II.3. Redistribution of income in kind account	10 177			10 177	1 288		8 889			D.63	Social transfers in kind
	83 517			**83 517**	**100**	**67 282**	**4 482**	**2 311**	**9 342**	B.7g	**Gross adjusted disposable income**
	70 059			**70 059**	**- 178**	**63 566**	**2 956**	**1 578**	**2 138**	B.7n	**Net adjusted disposable income**
II.4. Use of income account	**83 517**			**83 517**	**1 388**	**57 105**	**13 371**	**2 311**	**9 342**	B.6g	**Gross disposable income**
	70 059			**70 059**	**1 109**	**53 390**	**11 845**	**1 578**	**2 138**	B.6n	**Net disposable income**
	66 225			66 225		60 082	6 143			P.4	Actual Final Consumption
	66 225			66 225	1 288	49 905	15 032			P.3	Final consumption expenditure
	752			752				752		D.8	Adjustment for the change in the net equity of households in pension funds reserves
	17 291			**17 291**	**100**	**7 952**	**- 1 661**	**1 558**	**9 342**	B.8g	**Gross saving**
	3 834			**3 834**	**- 178**	**4 237**	**- 3 187**	**825**	**2 138**	B.8n	**Net saving**
	2 331		**2 331**							B.12	**Current external balance**

Accumulation accounts
Changes in Assets

III.1.1. Change in net worth due to saving and capital transfers account										B.8g	**Gross saving**
										B.8n	**Net saving**
										B.12	**Current external balance**
										D.9	Capital transfers, receivable
										D.9	Capital transfers, payable (-)
	6 165		**40**	**6 125**	**110**	**5 324**	**- 2 902**	**496**	**3 096**	B.10.1	**Changes in net worth due to saving and capital transfers**
III.1.2 Acquisitions of non-financial assets account	18 457			18 457	359	5 383	3 018	918	8 781	P.51	Gross fixed capital formation
	- 13 457			- 13 457	- 279	- 3 715	- 1 526	- 733	- 7 204	K.1	Consumption of fixed capital (-)
	1 026			1 026	1	255			769	P.52	Changes in inventories
	140			140	6	117		4	12	P.53	Acquisitions less disposals of valuables
			0	0		- 738	29	20	689	K.2	Acquisitions less disposals of non-produced non-financial assets
			40	**- 40**	**23**	**4 023**	**- 4 423**	**287**	**49**	B.9	**Net lending (+) /borrowing (-)**

			S.2	S.1	S.15 + S.14		S.13	S.12	S.11		
III.2 Financial account	44 247		9 257	34 990	9 771		1 282	18 231	5 706		Net acquisition of financial assets\
											Net incurrence of liabilities
			- 13	13				13		F.1	Monetary gold and SDRs
	17 287		6 604	10 683	5 860		1 794	2 883	147	F.2	Currency and deposits
	6 379		1 679	4 699	1 320		- 15	2 838	557	F.3	Securities other than shares
	8 745		912	7 833	451		96	7 193	94	F.4	Loans
	4 175		48	4 127	- 86		- 420	3 162	1 471	F.5	Shares and other equity
	3 400		6	3 394	3 260		1	37	96	F.6	Insurance technical reserves
	4 260		20	4 240	- 1 033		- 173	2 105	3 342	F.7	Other accounts receivable/payable
			40	**- 40**	**4 332**		**- 4 422**	**187**	**- 137**	B.9 F	**Net lending (+) /borrowing (-)**
					287			- 100	- 187		Statistical discrepancy

Source: Instituto Nacional de Estatística

Table A.1b. Integrated Economic Accounts (in millions of euros) – Resources

Code	Transactions and other flows, stocks and balancing items	S.11 Non-Financial Corporations	S.12 Financial Corporations	S.13 General Government	S.14 Households	S.15 NPISHs	S.1 Total of the Economy	S.2 Rest of the World Account	Goods and Services Account (Uses)	Total	Accounts
											Current accounts Resources
P.7	Imports of goods and services							29 454		29 454	I. Production / external account of goods and services
P.6	Exports of goods and services								24 433	24 433	
P.1	Output of goods and services	104 064	5 964	15 389	26 260	2 717	154 394			154 394	
P.2	Intermediate consumption								84 102	84 102	
D.21-D.31	Net taxes on products						10 535			10 535	
B.1g/B.1*g	**Gross added value/gross domestic product**	**39 105**	**4 333**	**12 386**	**16 966**	**1 190**	**80 874**			**80 874**	II.1.1. Generation of income account
K.1	Consumption of fixed capital										
B.1n/B.1*n	**Value added, net/Net domestic product**	**31 900**	**3 600**	**10 860**	**13 251**	**911**	**67 369**			**67 369**	
B.11	**External balance of goods and services**							**5 021**		**5 021**	
D.1	Compensation of employees				38 620		38 620	64		38 683	II.1.2. Allocation of primary income account
D.2-D.3	Net taxes on production and imports			9 937			9 937	165		10 102	
D.21-D.31	Net taxes on products			10 283			10 283	252		10 535	
D.29-D.39	Net taxes on production			1 220			- 346	- 87		- 433	
B.2g	**Gross operating surplus**	**17 319**	**2 028**	**1 452**		**78**	**17 189**			**17 189**	
B.3g	**Gross mixed income**				**14 973**		**14 973**			**14 973**	
B.2n	**Net operating surplus**	**10 115**	**1 295**	**- 74**		**- 201**	**7 446**			**7 446**	
B.3n	**Net mixed income**				**11 258**		**11 258**			**11 258**	
D.4	Property income	2 178	15 623	1 056	8 998	97	27 952	3 363		31 314	
P.119	Adjustment to the FISIM (Financial Intermediation Services Indirectly Measured)		- 3 688								
B.5g	**Gross national income/ Gross balance of primary incomes**	**11 561**	**1 787**	**7 379**	**59 614**	**137**	**80 479**			**80 479**	II.2. Secondary distribution income account
B.5n	**Net national income/ Net balance of primary incomes**	**4 357**	**1 054**	**5 853**	**55 899**	**- 142**	**67 022**			**67 022**	
D.5	Current taxes on income, wealth, etc			7 161			7 161			7 161	
D.61	Social contributions	1 339	1 473	8 851	42	13	11 718			11 718	
D.62	Social benefits other than social transfers in kind				11 629		11 629	30		11 659	
D.7	Other current transfers	444	1 063	7 690	4 376	1 272	14 845	892		15 737	
B.6g	**Gross disposable income**	**9 342**	**2 311**	**13 371**	**57 105**	**1 388**	**83 517**			**83 517**	II.3. Redistribution of income in kind account
B.6n	**Net disposable income**	**2 138**	**1 578**	**11 845**	**53 390**	**1 109**	**70 059**			**70 059**	
D.63	Social transfers in kind				10 177		10 177			10 177	
B.7g	**Gross adjusted disposable income**	**9 342**	**2 311**	**4 482**	**67 282**	**100**	**83 517**			**83 517**	II.4. Use of income account
B.7n	**Net adjusted disposable income**	**2 138**	**1 578**	**2 956**	**63 566**	**- 178**	**70 059**			**70 059**	
B.6g	**Gross disposable income**	**9 342**	**2 311**	**13 371**	**57 105**	**1 388**	**83 517**			**83 517**	
B.6n	**Net disposable income**	**2 138**	**1 578**	**11 845**	**53 390**	**1 109**	**70 059**			**70 059**	
P.4	Actual Final Consumption								66 225	66 225	
P.3	Final consumption expenditure								66 225	66 225	
D.8	Adjustment for the change in the net equity of households in pension funds reserves				752		752			752	
B.8g	**Gross saving**										
B.8n	**Net saving**										
B.12	**Current external balance**										
											Accumulation accounts Changes in liabilities and net worth
B.8g	**Gross saving**	**9 342**	**1 558**	**- 1 661**	**7 952**	**100**	**17 291**			**17 291**	III.1.1. Change in net worth due to saving and capital transfers account
B.8n	**Net saving**	**2 138**	**825**	**- 3 187**	**4 237**	**- 178**	**3 834**			**3 834**	
B.12	**Current external balance**							**2 331**		**2 331**	
D.9	Capital transfers, receivable	1 603	814	3 375	1 166	292	7 250	29		7 278	
D.9	Capital transfers, payable (-)	- 645	- 1 143	- 3 089	- 78	- 4	- 4 959	- 2 320		- 7 278	
B.10.1	**Changes in net worth due to saving and capital transfers**	**3 096**	**496**	**- 2 902**	**5 324**	**110**	**6 125**	**40**		**6 165**	III.1.2 Acquisitions of non-financial assets account
P.51	Gross fixed capital formation								18 457	18 457	
K.1	Consumption of fixed capital (-)										
P.52	Changes in inventories								1 026	1 026	
P.53	Acquisitions less disposals of valuables								140	140	
K.2	Acquisitions less disposals of non-produced non-financial assets								0	0	
B.9	**Net lending (+) /borrowing (-)**										
		S.11	**S.12**	**S.13**	**S.14 + S.15**		**S.1**	**S.2**			
	Net acquisition of financial assets\										III.2 Financial account
	Net incurrence of liabilities	5 844	18 044	5 704	5 438		35 030	9 217		44 247	
F.1	Monetary gold and SDRs										
F.2	Currency and deposits		12 961	1 317			14 278	3 010		17 287	
F.3	Securities other than shares	1 181	127	4 038			5 345	1 034		6 379	
F.4	Loans	2 145	134	545	4 626		7 450	1 295		8 745	
F.5	Shares and other equity	2 395	1 288				3 683	492		4 175	
F.6	Insurance technical reserves	150	3 213				3 362	37		3 400	
F.7	Other accounts receivable/payable	- 27	321	- 196	812		911	3 349		4 260	
B.9 F	**Net lending (+) /borrowing (-)**										
	Statistical discrepancy										

Table A.2.1a. Institutional Sector Accounts (in millions of euros) – (I) Production and (II.1.1.) Generation of Income Accounts – Uses

Total	Corresponding entries of the: Goods and services account (resources)	Corresponding entries of the: Rest of the world account	S.1 Total of the Economy	S.12 Financial Corporations	S.125 Insurance Corporations and Pension Funds	S.124 Financial Auxiliaries	S.123 Other Financial Intermediaries, except Insur. Corp. and Pens. F.	S.122 Other Monetary Financial Institutions	S.121 Central Bank	S.11 Non-Financial Corporations	S.13 General Government	S.1314 Social Security Funds	S.1313 Local Government	S.1311 Central Government	S.15 Non-Profit Institutions Serving Households (NPISHs)	S.14 Households	code	Transactions and other flows, stocks and balancing items
Uses																	**I: Production account**	
154 394	154 394																**P.1**	Output of goods and services
134 323	134 323																**P.11**	Market output
																	P.119	Adjustment to the FISIM (Financial Intermediation Services Indirectly Measured)
15 532	15 532																**P.13**	Other non-market output
4 539	4 539																**P.12**	Output produced for own final use
10 535	10 535																**D21-D31**	Net taxes on products
																	RI	*Total of resources*
84 102			84 102	1 631	431	132	165	873	29	64 959	3 003	74	627	2 302	1 527	9 294	**P.2**	Intermediate consumption
3 688			3 688														**P.119**	Adjustment to the FISIM (Financial Intermediation Services Indirectly Measured)
80 827	**80 827**		**80 827**	**4 333**	**673**	**117**	**363**	**3 173**	**7**	**39 105**	**12 386**	**247**	**1 964**	**10 175**	**1 190**	**16 966**	**B.1g**	**Gross added value/gross domestic product**
13 457			13 457	733	74	63	51	528	17	7 204	1 526	8	687	831	279	3 715	**K.1**	Consumption of fixed capital
67 369			**67 369**	**3 600**	**599**	**54**	**312**	**2 645**	**- 10**	**31 900**	**10 860**	**239**	**1 277**	**9 344**	**911**	**13 251**	**B.1n**	**Net value added /Net domestic product**
164 929			164 929	5 964	1 104	249	528	4 046	36	104 064	15 389	321	2 591	12 476	2 717	26 260	*EI*	*Total of uses*
Uses																	**II: Distribution and use of income account**	
																	II.1.1: Generation of income account	
																	B.1g	**Gross added value/gross domestic product**
																	B.1n	**Net value added /Net domestic product**
																	R2II	*Total of resources*
38 563			38 563	2 309	396	43	79	1 700	91	22 027	10 990	235	1 350	9 406	1 126	2 111	**D.1**	Compensation of employees
30 390			30 390	1 736	282	34	64	1 297	60	17 136	8 807	218	1 156	7 434	923	1 787	**D.11**	Wages and salaries
8 173			8 173	573	115	9	15	403	30	4 891	2 183	17	194	1 972	203	324	**D.12**	Employers' social contribution
11 802			11 802	12	2	2	1	6		201					1	223	**D.2**	Taxes on production and imports
11 364			11 364														**D.21**	Taxes on products
437			437	12	2	2	1	6		201					1	223	**D.29**	Other taxes on production
- 1 700			- 1 700	- 16	- 4		- 1	- 11		- 442	- 56		- 2	- 54	- 15	- 341	**D.3**	Subsidies, receivable
- 830			- 830														**D.31**	Subsidies on products
- 870			- 870	- 16	- 4		- 1	- 11		- 442	- 56		- 2	- 54	- 15	- 341	**D.39**	Other subsidies on production
17 189			**17 189**	**2 028**	**278**	**71**	**283**	**1 478**	**- 83**	**17 319**	**1 452**	**12**	**617**	**823**	**78**		**B.2g**	**Gross operating surplus**
14 973			**14 973**													**14 973**	**B.3g**	**Gross mixed income**
7 446			**7 446**	**1 295**	**204**	**9**	**232**	**951**	**- 101**	**10 115**	**- 74**	**4**	**- 70**	**- 8**	**- 201**		**B.2n**	**Net operating surplus**
11 258			**11 258**													**11 258**	**B.3n**	**Net mixed income**
67 369			67 369	3 600	599	54	312	2 645	- 10	31 900	10 860	239	1 277	9 344	911	13 251	*E2II*	*Total of uses*

Source: Instituto Nacional de Estatística

Table A.2.1b. Institutional Sector Accounts (in millions of euros) – (I) Production and (II.1.1.) Generation of Income Accounts – Resources

code	Transactions and other flows, stocks and balancing items	S.11	S.121	S.122	S.123	S.124	S.125	S.12	S.1311	S.1313	S.1314	S.13	S.14	S.15	S.1	Corresponding entries of the		Total
		Non-Financial Corporations	Central Bank	Other Monetary Financial Institutions	Other Financial Intermediaries, except Insur. Corp. and Pens. F.	Financial Auxiliaries	Insurance Corporations and Pension Funds	Financial Corporations	Central Government	Local Government	Social Security Funds	General Government	Households	Non-Profit Institutions Serving Households (NPISHs)	Total of the Economy	Rest of the world account	Goods and services account (uses)	
I: Production account																		**Resources**
P.1	Output of goods and services	104 064	36	4 046	528	249	1 104	5 964	12 476	2 591	321	15 389	26 260	2 717	154 394			154 394
P.11	Market output	103 638	36	4 046	528	249	1 104	5 964	713	420	11	1 145	22 148	1 430	134 323			134 323
P.119	Adjustment to the FISIM (Financial Intermediation Services Indirectly Measured)		33	3 367	287			3 688							3 688			3 688
P.13	Other non-market output								11 763	2 171	310	14 244		1 288	15 532			15 532
P.12	Output produced for own final use	426											4 113		4 539			4 539
D21-D31	Net taxes on products														10 535			10 535
RI	*Total of resources*	104 064	36	4 046	528	249	1 104	5 964	12 476	2 591	321	15 389	26 260	2 717	164 929			164 929
P.2	Intermediate consumption																84 102	84 102
P.119	Adjustment to the FISIM (Financial Intermediation Services Indirectly Measured)																	
B.1g	**Gross added value/gross domestic product**																	
K.1	Consumption of fixed capital																	
B.1n	**Net value added /Net domestic product**																	
EI	*Total of uses*																	
II: Distribution and use of income account																		**Resources**
II.1.1: Generation of income account																		
B.1g	**Gross added value/gross domestic product**	**39 105**	**7**	**3 173**	**363**	**117**	**673**	**4 333**	**10 175**	**1 964**	**247**	**12 386**	**16 966**	**1 190**	**80 827**			**80 827**
B.1n	**Net value added /Net domestic product**	**31 900**	**- 10**	**2 645**	**312**	**54**	**599**	**3 600**	**9 344**	**1 277**	**239**	**10 860**	**13 251**	**911**	**67 369**			**67 369**
R211	*Total of resources*	31 900	- 10	2 645	312	54	599	3 600	9 344	1 277	239	10 860	13 251	911	67 369			67 369
D.1	Compensation of employees																	
D.11	Wages and salaries																	
D.12	Employers' social contribution																	
D.2	Taxes on production and imports																	
D.21	Taxes on products																	
D.29	Other taxes on production																	
D.3	Subsidies, receivable																	
D.31	Subsidies on products																	
D.39	Other subsidies on production																	
B.2g	**Gross operating surplus**																	
B.3g	**Gross mixed income**																	
B.2n	**Net operating surplus**																	
B.3n	**Net mixed income**																	
E211	*Total of uses*																	

Source: Instituto Nacional de Estatística

Table A.2.2a. Institutional Sector Accounts (in millions of euros) – (II.1.2.) Allocation of Primary Income and (II.2.) Secondary Distribution of Income Accounts – Uses

Total	Corresponding entries of the: Goods and services account (resources)	Corresponding entries of the: Rest of the world account	S.1 Total of the Economy	S.12 Financial Corporations	S.125 Insurance Corporations and Pension Funds	S.124 Financial Auxiliaries	S.123 Other Financial Intermediaries, except Insur. Corp. and Pens. F.	S.122 Other Monetary Financial Institutions	S.121 Central Bank	S.11 Non-Financial Corporations	S.13 General Government	S.1314 Social Security Funds	S.1313 Local Government	S.1311 Central Government	S.15 Non-Profit Institutions Serving Households (NPISHs)	S.14 Households	code	Transactions and other flows, stocks and balancing items
Uses																	**II.1.2: Allocation of primary income account**	
																	B.2g	**Gross operating surplus**
																	B.3g	**Gross mixed income**
																	B.2n	**Net operating surplus**
																	B.3n	**Net mixed income**
120		120															**D.1**	Compensation of employees
120		120															**D.11**	Wages and salaries
																	D.12	Employers' social contribution
																	D.2	Taxes on production and imports
																	D.21	Taxes on products
																	D.29	Other taxes on production
																	D.3	Subsidies, payable
																	D.31	Subsidies on products
																	D.39	Other subsidies on production
31 314		3 123	28 191	12 175	1 101	19	1 282	9 034	740	7 936	5 066	11	178	4 878	38	2 976	**D.4**	Property income
26 944		2 683	24 260	10 565	12	3	1 164	8 646	740	5 669	5 065	11	177	4 877	38	2 923	**D.41**	Interest
																	P.119	Adjustment to the FISIM (Financial Intermediation Services Indirectly Measured)
2 575		373	2 202	523	12	16	119	377		1 673						5	**D.42**	Distributed income of corporations
419		67	352	12	2		- 1	12		340							**D.43**	Reinvested earnings on direct foreign investment
1 075			1 075	1 075	1 075												**D.44**	Property income attributed to insurance policy holders
302			302							253	1		1	1		48	**D.45**	Rent
80 479			**80 479**	**1 787**	**202**	**82**	**278**	**1 301**	**- 76**	**11 561**	**7 379**	**132**	**1 527**	**5 720**	**137**	**59 614**	**B.5g/B.5*g**	**Gross national income**
67 022			**67 022**	**1 054**	**128**	**19**	**227**	**773**	**- 93**	**4 357**	**5 853**	**124**	**840**	**4 889**	**- 142**	**55 899**	**B.5n/B.5*n**	**Net national income**
																	R212	*Total of resources*
95 213			95 213	13 230	1 229	38	1 509	9 807	647	12 293	10 919	135	1 017	9 767	- 104	58 875	*E212*	*Total of uses*
																	II.2: Secondary distribution income account	
																	B.5g/B.5*g	**Gross national income**
																	B.5n/B.5*n	**Net national income**
7 161			7 161	226	10	15	29	171		2 000					2	4 932	**D.5**	Current taxes on income, wealth, etc
6 864			6 864	222	8	14	29	170		1 795						4 848	**D.51**	Taxes on income
296			296	5	2	1		2		205					2	84	**D.59**	Other current taxes
11 718			11 718													11 718	**D.61**	Social contributions
11 659		29	11 630	720	653	1	1	51	14	1 339	9 515	8 757	66	693	13	42	**D.62**	Social benefits other than social transfers in kind
15 737		3 931	11 807	1 066	1 031		3	30	2	663	8 194	806	399	6 989	19	1 865	**D.7**	Other current transfers
1 158		33	1 126	21	9		1	11		435	4		2	2	14	652	**D.71**	Net non-life insurance premiums
1 047		25	1 022	1 022	1 022												**D.72**	Non-life insurance claims
6 866			6 866								6 866	493	262	6 111			**D.73**	Current transfers within general government
637		550	87								87			87			**D.74**	Current international cooperation
6 029		3 323	2 706	23	1		1	19	1	228	1 238	313	136	789	5	1 213	**D.75**	Miscellaneous current transfers
83 517			**83 517**	**2 311**	**963**	**67**	**249**	**1 110**	**- 78**	**9 342**	**13 371**	**- 102**	**2 509**	**10 965**	**1 388**	**57 105**	**B.6g**	**Gross disposable income**
70 059			**70 059**	**1 578**	**889**	**4**	**197**	**582**	**- 95**	**2 138**	**11 845**	**- 111**	**1 822**	**10 134**	**1 109**	**53 390**	**B.6n**	**Net disposable income**
																	R22	*Total of resources*
112 374			112 374	3 590	2 584	21	230	834	- 79	6 140	29 554	9 452	2 287	17 815	1 144	71 946	*E22*	*Total of uses*

Source: Instituto Nacional de Estatística

Table A.2.2b. Institutional Sector Accounts (in millions of euros) – (II.1.2.) Allocation of Primary Income and (II.2.) Secondary Distribution of Income Accounts – Resources

code	Transactions and other flows, stocks and balancing items	S.11	S.121	S.122	S.123	S.124	S.125	S.12	S.1311	S.1313	S.1314	S.13	S.14	S.15	S.1	Corresponding entries of the		Total
		Non-Financial Corporations	Central Bank	Other Monetary Financial Institutions	Other Financial Intermediaries, except Insur. Corp. and Pens. F.	Financial Auxiliaries	Insurance Corporations and Pension Funds	Financial Corporations	Central Government	Local Government	Social Security Funds	General Government	Households	Non-Profit Institutions Serving Households (NPISHs)	Total of the Economy	Rest of the world account	Goods and services account (uses)	
II.1.2: Allocation of primary income account																		Resources
B.2g	**Gross operating surplus**	**17 319**	**- 83**	**1 478**	**283**	**71**	**278**	**2 028**	**823**	**617**	**12**	**1 452**		**78**	**17 189**			**17 189**
B.3g	**Gross mixed income**												**14 973**		**14 973**			**14 973**
B.2n	**Net operating surplus**	**10 115**	**- 101**	**951**	**232**	**9**	**204**	**1 295**	**- 8**	**- 70**	**4**	**- 74**		**- 201**	**7 446**			**7 446**
B.3n	**Net mixed income**												**11 258**		**11 258**			**11 258**
D.1	Compensation of employees												38 620		38 620	64		38 683
D.11	Wages and salaries												30 447		30 447	64		30 510
D.12	Employers' social contribution												8 173		8 173			8 173
D.2	Taxes on production and imports								9 622	1 055	346	11 023			11 023	779		11 802
D.21	Taxes on products								9 517	723	346	10 586			10 586	779		11 364
D.29	Other taxes on production								105	332		437			437			437
D.3	Subsidies, payable								- 765	- 55	- 266	- 1 086			- 1 086	- 614		- 1 700
D.31	Subsidies on products								- 274	- 28		- 303			- 303	- 527		- 830
D.39	Other subsidies on production								- 491	- 27	- 266	- 783			- 783	- 87		- 870
D.4	Property income	2 178	781	12 224	1 564	30	1 025	15 623	917	88	51	1 056	8 998	97	27 952	3 363		31 314
D.41	Interest	1 364	773	12 013	1 452	29	660	14 928	598	21	51	670	7 233	18	24 213	2 731		26 944
P.119	Adjustment to the FISIM (Financial Intermediation Services Indirectly Measured)		- 33	- 3 367	- 287			- 3 688										
D.42	Distributed income of corporations	698	7	179	112		363	661	319	1		321	547	76	2 302	272		2 575
D.43	Reinvested earnings on direct foreign investment	37		30	1			30							67	352		419
D.44	Property income attributed to insurance policy holders	77		2			1	4					985	3	1 068	8		1 075
D.45	Rent	3							1	65		66	233		302			302
B.5g/B.5*g	**Gross national income**																	
B.5n/B.5*n	**Net national income**																	
R212	*Total of resources*	12 293	647	9 807	1 509	38	1 229	13 230	9 767	1 017	135	10 919	58 875	- 104	95 213			95 213
E212	*Total of uses*																	
II.2: Secondary distribution income account																		
B.5g/B.5*g	**Gross national income**	**11 561**	**- 76**	**1 301**	**278**	**82**	**202**	**1 787**	**5 720**	**1 527**	**132**	**7 379**	**59 614**	**137**	**80 479**			**80 479**
B.5n/B.5*n	**Net national income**	**4 357**	**- 93**	**773**	**227**	**19**	**128**	**1 054**	**4 889**	**840**	**124**	**5 853**	**55 899**	**- 142**	**67 022**			**67 022**
D.5	Current taxes on income, wealth, etc								6 808	353		7 161			7 161			7 161
D.51	Taxes on income								6 557	307		6 864			6 864			6 864
D.59	Other current taxes								250	46		296			296			296
D.61	Social contributions	1 339	14	51	1	1	1 406	1 473	703	68	8 080	8 851	42	13	11 718			11 718
D.62	Social benefits other than social transfers in kind												11 629		11 629	30		11 659
D.7	Other current transfers	444		10	2		1 050	1 063	5 415	1 026	1 248	7 690	4 376	1 272	14 845	892		15 737
D.71	Net non-life insurance premiums						1 042	1 042							1 042	116		1 158
D.72	Non-life insurance claims	386		9	1		8	18		1		1	578	12	995	52		1 047
D.73	Current transfers within general government								5 097	973	797	6 866			6 866			6 866
D.74	Current international cooperation								145		405	550			550	87		637
D.75	Miscellaneous current transfers	58		1	1			2	174	53	47	273	3 798	1 260	5 391	637		6 029
B.6g	**Gross disposable income**																	
B.6n	**Net disposable income**																	
R22	*Total of resources*	6 140	- 79	834	230	21	2 584	3 590	17 815	2 287	9 452	29 554	71 946	1 144	112 374			112 374
E22	*Total of uses*																	

Source: Instituto Nacional de Estatística

Table A.2.3a. Institutional Sector Accounts (in millions of euros) – (II.3.) Distribution of Income in Kind, (II.4.1.) Use of Disposable Income and (II.4.2.) Use of Adjusted Income Accounts – Uses

Total	Corresponding entries of the		S.1	S.12	S.125	S.124	S.123	S.122	S.121	S.11	S.13	S.1314	S.1313	S.1311	S.15	S.14	Transactions and other flows, stocks and balancing items	
	Goods and services account (resources)	Rest of the world account	Total of the Economy	Financial Corporations	Insurance Corporations and Pension Funds	Financial Auxiliaries	Other Financial Intermediaries, except Insur. Corp. and Pens. F.	Other Monetary Financial Institutions	Central Bank	Non-Financial Corporations	General Government	Social Security Funds	Local Government	Central Government	Non-Profit Institutions Serving Households (NPISHs)	Households	code	
Uses																	**II.3: Redistribution of income in kind account**	
																	B.6g	**Gross disposable income**
																	B.6n	**Net disposable income**
10 177			10 177								8 889	209	1 232	7 448	1 288		D.63	Social transfers in kind
1 157			1 157								1 157	62	30	1 065			D.631	Social benefits in kind
9 020			9 020								7 732	147	1 202	6 383	1 288		D.632	Transfers of individual non-market goods and services
83 517			**83 517**	**2 311**	**963**	**67**	**249**	**1 110**	**- 78**	**9 342**	**4 482**	**- 311**	**1 276**	**3 517**	**100**	**67 282**	**B.7g**	**Gross adjusted disposable income**
70 059			**70 059**	**1 578**	**889**	**4**	**197**	**582**	**- 95**	**2 138**	**2 956**	**- 319**	**589**	**2 686**	**- 178**	**63 566**	**B.7n**	**Net adjusted disposable income**
																	R23	*Total of resources*
80 236			80 236	1 578	889	4	197	582	- 95	2 138	11 845	- 111	1 822	10 134	1 109	63 566	*E23*	*Total of uses*
																	II.4.1: Use of disposable income	
																	B.6g	**Gross disposable income**
																	B.6n	**Net disposable income**
66 225			66 225								15 032	365	2 158	12 509	1 288	49 905	P.3	Final consumption
60 082			60 082								8 889	209	1 232	7 448	1 288	49 905	P.31	Individual consumption expenditure
6 143			6 143								6 143	157	926	5 061			P.32	Collective consumption expenditure
752			752	752	752												D.8	Adjustment for the change in the net equity of households in pension funds reserves
17 291			**17 291**	**1 558**	**211**	**67**	**249**	**1 110**	**- 78**	**9 342**	**- 1 661**	**- 468**	**350**	**- 1 544**	**100**	**7 952**	**B.8g**	**Gross saving**
3 834			**3 834**	**825**	**137**	**4**	**197**	**582**	**- 95**	**2 138**	**- 3 187**	**- 476**	**- 337**	**- 2 375**	**- 178**	**4 237**	**B.8n**	**Net saving**
2 331		**2 331**															**B.12**	**Current external balance**
																	R241	*Total of resources*
70 812			70 812	1 578	889	4	197	582	- 95	2 138	11 845	- 111	1 822	10 134	1 109	54 142	*E241*	*Total of uses*
																	II.4.2: Use of adjusted disposable income	
																	B.7g	**Gross adjusted disposable income**
																	B.7n	**Net adjusted disposable income**
66 225			66 225								6 143	157	926	5 061		60 082	P.4	Actual final consumption
60 082			60 082													60 082	P.41	Actual individual consumption
6 143			6 143								6 143	157	926	5 061			P.42	Actual collective consumption
752			752	752	752												D.8	Adjustment for the change in the net equity of households in pension funds reserves
17 291			**17 291**	**1 558**	**211**	**67**	**249**	**1 110**	**- 78**	**9 342**	**- 1 661**	**- 468**	**350**	**- 1 544**	**100**	**7 952**	**B.8g**	**Gross saving**
3 834			**3 834**	**825**	**137**	**4**	**197**	**582**	**- 95**	**2 138**	**- 3 187**	**- 476**	**- 337**	**- 2 375**	**- 178**	**4 237**	**B.8n**	**Net saving**
2 331		**2 331**															**B.12**	**Current external balance**
																	R242	*Total of resources*
70 812			70 812	1 578	889	4	197	582	- 95	2 138	2 956	- 319	589	2 686	- 178	64 319	*E242*	*Total of uses*

Source: Instituto Nacional de Estatística

Table A.2.3b. Institutional Sector Accounts (in millions of euros) – (II.3.) Distribution of Income in Kind, (II.4.1.) Use of Disposable Income and (II.4.2.) Use of Adjusted Income Accounts – Resources

code	Transactions and other flows, stocks and balancing items	S.11 Non-Financial Corporations	S.121 Central Bank	S.122 Other Monetary Financial Institutions	S.123 Other Financial Intermediaries, except Insur. Corp. and Pens. F.	S.124 Financial Auxiliaries	S.125 Insurance Corporations and Pension Funds	S.12 Financial Corporations	S.1311 Central Government	S.1313 Local Government	S.1314 Social Security Funds	S.13 General Government	S.14 Households	S.15 Non-Profit Institutions Serving Households (NPISHs)	S.1 Total of the Economy	Corresponding entries of the: Rest of the world account	Corresponding entries of the: Goods and services account (uses)	Total
II.3: Redistribution of income in kind account																		Resources
B.6g	**Gross disposable income**	9 342	- 78	1 110	249	67	963	2 311	10 965	2 509	- 102	13 371	57 105	1 388	83 517			83 517
B.6n	**Net disposable income**	2 138	- 95	582	197	4	889	1 578	10 134	1 822	- 111	11 845	53 390	1 109	70 059			70 059
D.63	Social transfers in kind												10 177		10 177			10 177
D.631	Social benefits in kind												1 157		1 157			1 157
D.632	Transfers of individual non-market goods and services												9 020		9 020			9 020
B.7g	**Gross adjusted disposable income**																	
B.7n	**Net adjusted disposable income**																	
R23	*Total of resources*	2 138	- 95	582	197	4	889	1 578	10 134	1 822	- 111	11 845	63 566	1 109	80 236			80 236
E23	*Total of uses*																	
II.4.1: Use of disposable income																		
B.6g	**Gross disposable income**	9 342	- 78	1 110	249	67	963	2 311	10 965	2 509	- 102	13 371	57 105	1 388	83 517			83 517
B.6n	**Net disposable income**	2 138	- 95	582	197	4	889	1 578	10 134	1 822	- 111	11 845	53 390	1 109	70 059			70 059
P.3	Final consumption																66 225	66 225
P.31	Individual consumption expenditure																60 082	60 082
P.32	Collective consumption expenditure																6 143	6 143
D.8	Adjustment for the change in the net equity of households in pension funds reserves												752		752			752
B.8g	**Gross saving**																	
B.8n	**Net saving**																	
B.12	**Current external balance**																	
R241	*Total of resources*	2 138	- 95	582	197	4	889	1 578	10 134	1 822	- 111	11 845	54 142	1 109	70 812			70 812
E241	*Total of uses*																	
II.4.2: Use of adjusted disposable income																		
B.7g	**Gross adjusted disposable income**	9 342	- 78	1 110	249	67	963	2 311	3 517	1 276	- 311	4 482	67 282	100	83 517			83 517
B.7n	**Net adjusted disposable income**	2 138	- 95	582	197	4	889	1 578	2 686	589	- 319	2 956	63 566	- 178	70 059			70 059
P.4	Actual final consumption																66 225	66 225
P.41	Actual individual consumption																60 082	60 082
P.42	Actual collective consumption																6 143	6 143
D.8	Adjustment for the change in the net equity of households in pension funds reserves												752		752			752
B.8g	**Gross saving**																	
B.8n	**Net saving**																	
B.12	**Current external balance**																	
R242	*Total of resources*	2 138	- 95	582	197	4	889	1 578	2 686	589	- 319	2 956	64 319	- 178	70 812			70 812
E242	*Total of uses*																	

Source: Instituto Nacional de Estatística

Table A.2.4a. Institutional Sector Accounts (in millions of euros) – (III) Accumulation Accounts – Changes in Assets

Total	Corresponding entries of the: Goods and services account (resources)	Corresponding entries of the: Rest of the world account	S.1 Total of the Economy	S.12 Financial Corporations	S.125 Insurance Corporations and Pension Funds	S.124 Financial Auxiliaries	S.123 Other Financial Intermediaries, except Insur. Corp. and Pens. F.	S.122 Other Monetary Financial Institutions	S.121 Central Bank	S.11 Non-Financial Corporations	S.13 General Government	S.1314 Social Security Funds	S.1313 Local Government	S.1311 Central Government	S.15 Non-Profit Institutions Serving Households (NPISHs)	S.14 Households	code	Transactions and other flows, stocks and balancing items
Changes in assets																		**III. Accumulation accounts**
																		III.1 Capital Account
																		III.1.1: Change in net worth due to saving and capital transfers account
																	B.8n	**Gross saving**
																	B.12	**Current external balance**
																	B.8n	**Net saving**
																	D.9	Capital transfers, receivable
																	D.91	Capital taxes
																	D.92	Investment grants
																	D.99	Other capital transfers
																	D.9	Capital transfers, payable
																	D.91	Capital taxes
																	D.92	Investment grants
																	D.99	Other capital transfers
6 165		**40**	**6 125**	**496**	**136**	**4**	**197**	**286**	**- 127**	**3 096**	**- 2 902**	**- 522**	**573**	**- 2 953**	**110**	**5 324**	B.10.1	**Changes in net worth due to saving and capital transfers**
																	R311	*Total of changes in liabilities and net worth*
6 165		40	6 125	496	136	4	197	286	- 127	3 096	- 2 902	- 522	573	- 2 953	110	5 324	*E311*	*Total of changes in assets*
																		III.1.2: Acquisitions of non-financial assets account
																	B.10.1	**Changes in net worth due to saving and capital transfers**
19 623			19 623	922	136	29	370	323	65	9 562	3 018	9	1 218	1 791	366	5 755	P.5	Gross capital formation
18 457			18 457	918	135	29	370	320	63	8 781	3 018	9	1 218	1 791	359	5 383	P.51	Gross fixed capital formation
- 13 457			- 13 457	- 733	- 74	- 63	- 51	- 528	- 17	- 7 204	- 1 526	- 8	- 687	- 831	- 279	- 3 715	K.1	Consumption of fixed capital
1 026			1 026							769					1	255	P.52	Changes in inventories
140			140	4				3	1	12					6	117	P.53	Acquisitions less disposals of valuables
				20	1		- 4	20	3	689	29		- 15	44		- 738	K.2	Acquisitions less disposals of non-produced non-financial assets
				18			- 5	19	3	695	25		- 15	40		- 738	K.21	Acquisitions less disposals of land and other tangible non-produced assets
				2	1			1		- 6	4			4			K.22	Acquisitions less disposals of intangible non-produced assets
		40	**- 40**	**287**	**73**	**38**	**- 117**	**472**	**- 178**	**49**	**- 4 423**	**- 523**	**58**	**- 3 957**	**23**	**4 023**	B.9	**Net lending (+)/ Net borrowing(-)**
																	R312	*Total of changes in liabilities and net worth*
6 125			6 125	496	136	4	197	286	- 127	3 096	- 2 902	- 522	573	- 2 953	110	5 324	*E313*	*Total of changes in assets*

Source: Instituto Nacional de Estatística

Table A.2.4b. Institutional Sector Accounts (in millions of euros) – (III) Accumulation Accounts – Changes in Liabilities and Net Worth

code	Transactions and other flows, stocks and balancing items	S.11 Non-Financial Corporations	S.121 Central Bank	S.122 Other Monetary Financial Institutions	S.123 Other Financial Intermediaries, except Insur. Corp. and Pens. F.	S.124 Financial Auxiliaries	S.125 Insurance Corporations and Pension Funds	S.12 Financial Corporations	S.1311 Central Government	S.1313 Local Government	S.1314 Social Security Funds	S.13 General Government	S.14 Households	S.15 Non-Profit Institutions Serving Households (NPISHs)	S.1 Total of the Economy	Corresponding entries of the: Rest of the world account	Corresponding entries of the: Goods and services account (uses)	Total
III. Accumulation accounts															Changes in liabilities and net worth			
III.1 Capital Account																		
III.1.1: Change in net worth due to saving and capital transfers account																		
B.8n	**Gross saving**	**9 342**	**- 78**	**1 110**	**249**	**67**	**211**	**1 558**	**- 1 544**	**350**	**- 468**	**- 1 661**	**7 952**	**100**	**17 291**			**17 291**
B.12	**Current external balance**															**2 331**		**2 331**
B.8n	**Net saving**	**2 138**	**- 95**	**582**	**197**	**4**	**137**	**825**	**- 2 375**	**- 337**	**- 476**	**- 3 187**	**4 237**	**- 178**	**3 834**			**3 834**
D.9	Capital transfers, receivable	1 603					814	814	2 239	1 113	22	3 375	1 166	292	7 250	29		7 278
D.91	Capital taxes								57			57			57			57
D.92	Investment grants	1 455					2	2	2 029	952	20	3 002	254	292	5 005	2		5 007
D.99	Other capital transfers	148					812	812	153	161	2	316	911		2 188	27		2 214
D.9	Capital transfers, payable	- 645	- 33	- 296			- 815	- 1 143	- 2 817	- 203	- 69	- 3 089	- 78	- 4	- 4 959	- 2 320		- 7 278
D.91	Capital taxes												- 57		- 57			- 57
D.92	Investment grants								- 2 541	- 197	- 69	- 2 806			- 2 806	- 2 201		- 5 007
D.99	Other capital transfers	- 645	- 33	- 296			- 815	- 1 143	- 276	- 7		- 283	- 21	- 4	- 2 096	- 118		- 2 214
B.10.1	**Changes in net worth due to saving and capital transfers**																	
R311	*Total of changes in liabilities and net worth*	3 096	- 127	286	197	4	136	496	- 2 953	573	- 522	- 2 902	5 324	110	6 125	40		6 165
E311	*Total of changes in assets*																	
III.1.2: Acquisitions of non-financial assets account																		
B.10.1	**Changes in net worth due to saving and capital transfers**	**3 096**	**- 127**	**286**	**197**	**4**	**136**	**496**	**- 2 953**	**573**	**- 522**	**- 2 902**	**5 324**	**110**	**6 125**	**40**		**6 165**
P.5	Gross capital formation																19 623	19 623
P.51	Gross fixed capital formation																18 457	18 457
K.1	Consumption of fixed capital																	
P.52	Changes in inventories																1 026	1 026
P.53	Acquisitions less disposals of valuables																140	140
K.2	Acquisitions less disposals of non-produced non-financial assets																	
K.21	Acquisitions less disposals of land and other tangible non-produced assets																	
K.22	Acquisitions less disposals of intangible non-produced assets																	
B.9	**Net lending (+)/ Net borrowing(-)**																	
R312	*Total of changes in liabilities and net worth*	3 096	- 127	286	197	4	136	496	- 2 953	573	- 522	- 2 902	5 324	110	6 125			6 125
E313	*Total of changes in assets*																	

Source: Instituto Nacional de Estatística

Table A.3a. Rest of the World Accounts (in millions of euros) – External Accounts (VI) of Goods and Services and (VII) of Primary Income and Current Transfers

Uses											Resources
S.2	S.22	S.21			Transactions and other flows, stocks and balancing items				S.21	S.22	S.2
			S.212	S.211			S.211	S.212			
Rest of the world	Non-member countries and international organisations	European Union	Institutions of the EU	member states of the EU	Code		Institutions of the EU	member states of the EU	European Union	Non-member countries and international organisations	Rest of the world
					V.I: External account of goods and services						
					P.7	Imports of goods and services	21 952		21 952	7 502	29 454
					P.71	Imports of goods	18 912		18 912	5 998	24 911
						goods	19 595		19 595	6 484	26 079
						c.i.f./f.o.b. margins	- 683		- 683	- 485	- 1 168
					P.72	Imports of services	3 040		3 040	1 504	4 543
						services	1 589		1 589	734	2 323
						c.i.f./f.o.b. margins	455		455	438	894
						Direct purchases abroad by residents	996		996	331	1 327
24 433	5 063	19 369		19 369	P.6	Exports of goods and services					
19 444	3 651	15 793		15 793	P.61	Exports of goods					
18 498	3 438	15 060		15 060		goods					
946	213	733		733		Direct purchases by non-residents in the domestic market					
4 989	1 413	3 576		3 576	P.62	Exports of services					
2 658	873	1 785		1 785		services					
- 275	- 47	- 228		- 228		c.i.f./f.o.b. margins					
2 605	586	2 019		2 019		Direct purchases by non-residents in the domestic market					
5 021	**2 438**	**2 583**		**2 583**	B.11	**External balance of goods and services**					
5 467	2 348	3 119		3 119		External balance of goods					
- 446	91	- 536		- 536		External balance of services					
					V.II: External account of primary income and current transfers						
					B.11	**External balance of goods and services**	**2 583**		**2 583**	**2 438**	**5 021**
120	56	64		64	D.1	Compensation of employees	37		37	26	64
120	56	64		64	D.11	Wages and salaries	37		37	26	64
					D.12	Employers' social contribution					
					D.2	Taxes on production and imports		779	779		779
					D21	Taxes on products		779	779		779
					D29	Other taxes on production					
					D.3	Subsidies		- 614	- 614		- 614
					D31	Subsidies on products		- 527	- 527		- 527
					D39	Other subsidies on production		- 87	- 87		- 87
3 123	1 342	1 781	47	1 734	D.4	Property income	1 945	347	2 292	1 070	3 363
2 683	1 153	1 530	47	1 483	D.41	Interest	1 491	347	1 837	893	2 731
373	103	270		270	D.42	Distributed income of corporations	188		188	84	272
67	86	- 19		- 19	D.43	Reinvested earnings on direct foreign investment				91	352
					D.44	Property income attributed to insurance policyholders				2	8
					D.45	Rents					
					D.5	Current taxes on income, wealth, etc.					
					D.51	Taxes on income					
					D.59	Other current taxes					
					D.61	Social contributions					
29	14	16		16	D.62	Social benefits other than social transfers in kind	18		18	12	30
3 931	1 532	2 398	544	1 855	D.7	Other current transfers	325	221	547	345	892
33	14	18		18	D.71	Net non-life insurance premiums				29	116
25	8	17		17	D.72	Non-life insurance claims				6	52
550	9	541	541		D.74	Current international cooperation				74	87
3 323	1 501	1 822	3	1 819	D.75	Miscellaneous current transfers				237	637
2 331	**948**	**1 383**	**142**	**1 241**	B.12	**Current External balance**					

Source: Instituto Nacional de Estatística

Table A.3b. Rest of the World Accounts (in millions of euros) – External Accumulation Accounts (VIII)

Uses											Resources
S.2	S.22	S.21	S.212	S.211	Transactions and other flows, stocks and balancing items		S.211	S.212	S.21	S.22	S.2
Rest of the world	Non-member countries and international organisations	European Union	Institutions of the EU	member states of the EU	Code		Institutions of the EU	member states of the EU	European Union	Non-member countries and international organisations	Rest of the world
					V.III. External accumulation accounts						
					V. III.1 Capital accounts						
					V. III.1.1: Change in net worth due to saving and capital transfers account						
					B.12	**Current External balance**	**1 241**	**142**	**1 383**	**948**	**2 331**
					D.9	Capital transfers, receivable	11		11	18	29
					D.91	Capital taxes					
					D.92	Investment grants				2	2
					D.99	Other capital transfers				16	27
					D.9	Capital transfers, payable	- 42	- 2 234	- 2 275	- 44	- 2 320
					D.91	Capital taxes					
					D.92	Investment grants	- 4	- 2 198	- 2 201		- 2 201
					D.99	Other capital transfers	- 38	- 36	- 74	- 44	- 118
40	**922**	**- 882**	**- 2 092**	**1 210**	**B.10.1**	**Changes in net worth due to saving and capital transfers**					
					V.III.1.2: Acquisition of non-financial assets account						
					B.10.1	**Changes in net worth due to saving and capital transfers**	**1 210**	**- 2 092**	**- 882**	**922**	**40**
					K.2	Acquisitions less disposals of non-financial non-produced assets					
					K21	Acquisitions less disposals of land and other tangible non-produced assets					
					K22	Acquisitions less disposals of intangible non-produced assets					
40	**922**	**- 882**	**- 2 092**	**1 210**	**B.9**	**Net lending (+) /borrowing (-)**					

Source: Instituto Nacional de Estatística

Table A.4a. Supply of products at basic prices (current prices in millions of euros) – Output of goods and services by activities 01-24

	Output of goods and services by activities (P.1)																	
Products	**01**	**02**	**05**	**10**	**11**	**12**	**13**	**14**	**15**	**16**	**17**	**18**	**19**	**20**	**21**	**22**	**23**	**24**
01	4 902	0	0	0	0	0	0	0	0	0	0	0	0	0	0	0	0	0
02	0	704	0	0	0	0	0	0	0	0	0	0	0	0	0	0	0	0
05	0	0	454	0	0	0	0	0	0	0	0	0	0	0	0	0	0	0
10	0	0	0	0	0	0	0	0	0	0	0	0	0	0	0	0	0	0
11	0	0	0	0	0	0	0	0	0	0	0	0	0	0	0	0	0	0
12	0	0	0	0	0	0	0	0	0	0	0	0	0	0	0	0	0	0
13	0	0	0	0	0	0	211	0	0	0	0	0	0	0	0	0	0	0
14	0	0	0	0	0	0	0	396	0	0	0	0	0	0	0	0	0	0
15	375	0	0	0	0	0	0	0	10 161	0	0	0	0	0	0	0	0	0
16	0	0	0	0	0	0	0	0	0	119	0	0	0	0	0	0	0	0
17	0	0	0	0	0	0	0	0	0	0	4 585	0	0	0	0	0	0	0
18	0	0	0	0	0	0	0	0	0	0	0	3 987	0	0	0	0	0	0
19	0	0	0	0	0	0	0	0	0	0	0	0	2 395	0	0	0	0	0
20	2	0	0	0	0	0	0	0	0	0	0	0	0	2 031	0	0	0	0
21	0	0	0	0	0	0	0	0	0	0	0	0	0	0	2 527	0	0	0
22	0	0	0	0	0	0	0	0	0	0	0	0	0	0	0	1 675	0	0
23	0	0	0	0	0	0	0	0	0	0	0	0	0	0	0	0	1 587	0
24	0	0	0	0	0	0	0	0	0	0	0	0	0	0	0	0	0	3 267
25	0	0	0	0	0	0	0	0	0	0	0	0	0	0	0	0	0	0
26	0	0	0	0	0	0	0	0	0	0	0	0	0	0	0	0	0	0
27	0	0	0	0	0	0	0	0	0	0	0	0	0	0	0	0	0	0
28	0	0	0	0	0	0	0	0	0	0	0	0	0	0	0	0	0	0
29	2	0	0	0	0	0	1	1	1	0	1	0	0	1	10	0	5	2
30	0	0	0	0	0	0	0	0	0	0	0	0	0	0	0	0	0	0
31	0	0	0	0	0	0	0	0	0	0	0	0	0	0	0	0	0	0
32	0	0	0	0	0	0	0	0	0	0	0	0	0	0	0	0	0	0
33	0	0	0	0	0	0	0	0	0	0	0	0	0	0	0	0	0	0
34	0	0	0	0	0	0	0	0	0	0	0	0	0	0	0	0	0	0
35	0	0	0	0	0	0	0	0	0	0	0	0	0	0	0	0	0	0
36	0	0	0	0	0	0	0	0	0	0	0	0	0	0	0	0	0	0
37	0	0	0	0	0	0	0	0	0	0	0	0	0	0	0	0	0	0
40	0	0	0	0	0	0	0	0	0	0	27	0	0	3	146	0	61	1
41	0	0	0	0	0	0	0	0	0	0	0	0	0	0	0	0	0	0
45	2	0	0	0	0	0	2	0	3	0	2	0	0	1	0	0	0	2
50	0	0	0	0	0	0	0	0	0	0	0	0	0	0	0	0	0	0
51	0	0	0	0	0	0	0	0	0	0	0	0	0	0	0	0	0	0
52	0	0	0	0	0	0	0	0	0	0	0	0	0	0	0	0	0	0
55	0	0	0	0	0	0	0	0	0	0	0	0	0	0	0	0	0	0
60	0	0	0	0	0	0	0	0	0	0	0	0	0	0	0	0	0	0
61	0	0	0	0	0	0	0	0	0	0	0	0	0	0	0	0	0	0
62	0	0	0	0	0	0	0	0	0	0	0	0	0	0	0	0	0	0
63	0	0	0	0	0	0	0	0	0	0	0	0	0	0	0	0	0	0
64	0	0	0	0	0	0	0	0	0	0	0	0	0	0	0	0	0	0
65	0	0	0	0	0	0	0	0	0	0	0	0	0	0	0	0	0	0
66	0	0	0	0	0	0	0	0	0	0	0	0	0	0	0	0	0	0
67	0	0	0	0	0	0	0	0	0	0	0	0	0	0	0	0	0	0
70	2	0	0	0	0	0	0	0	5	0	3	1	0	1	0	2	0	2
71	5	0	0	0	0	0	0	0	2	0	1	0	0	0	1	1	0	1
72	0	0	0	0	0	0	0	0	0	0	0	0	0	0	0	0	0	0
73	0	0	0	0	0	1	0	0	3	0	2	0	0	1	1	2	4	9
74	9	0	1	0	0	0	0	2	47	3	22	5	3	8	14	10	31	19
75	0	0	0	0	0	0	0	0	0	0	0	0	0	0	0	0	0	0
80	0	0	0	0	0	0	0	0	0	0	0	0	0	0	0	0	0	0
85	0	0	0	0	0	0	0	0	0	0	0	0	0	0	0	0	0	0
90	0	0	0	0	0	0	0	0	0	0	0	0	0	0	0	0	0	0
91	0	0	0	0	0	0	0	0	0	0	0	0	0	0	0	0	0	0
92	0	0	0	0	0	0	0	0	0	0	0	0	0	0	0	0	0	0
93	0	0	0	0	0	0	0	0	0	0	0	0	0	0	0	0	0	0
95	0	0	0	0	0	0	0	0	0	0	0	0	0	0	0	0	0	0
Adjustment items:																		
c.i.f./f.o.b. on imports	0	0	0	0	0	0	0	0	0	0	0	0	0	0	0	0	0	0
direct purchases abroad by residents	0	0	0	0	0	0	0	0	0	0	0	0	0	0	0	0	0	0
Total	**5 300**	**705**	**456**	**0**	**0**	**1**	**214**	**400**	**10 221**	**122**	**4 644**	**3 994**	**2 399**	**2 047**	**2 700**	**1 691**	**1 688**	**3 302**

Source: Instituto Nacional de Estatística

See Tables A.7 and A.8 for the description of codes and grouping of products and activities

Table A.4b. Supply of products at basic prices (current prices in millions of euros) – Output of goods and services by activities 25-51

	Output of goods and services by activities (P.1)																	
Products	25	26	27	28	29	30	31	32	33	34	35	36	37	40	41	45	50	51
01	0	0	0	0	0	0	0	0	0	0	0	0	0	0	0	0	0	0
02	0	0	0	0	0	0	0	0	0	0	0	0	0	0	0	0	0	0
05	0	0	0	0	0	0	0	0	0	0	0	0	0	0	0	0	0	0
10	0	0	0	0	0	0	0	0	0	0	0	0	0	0	0	0	0	0
11	0	0	0	0	0	0	0	0	0	0	0	0	0	0	0	0	0	0
12	0	0	0	0	0	0	0	0	0	0	0	0	0	0	0	0	0	0
13	0	0	0	0	0	0	0	0	0	0	0	0	0	0	0	0	0	0
14	0	0	0	0	0	0	0	0	0	0	0	0	0	0	0	0	0	0
15	0	0	0	0	0	0	0	0	0	0	0	0	0	0	0	0	0	0
16	0	0	0	0	0	0	0	0	0	0	0	0	0	0	0	0	0	0
17	0	0	0	0	0	0	0	0	0	0	0	0	0	0	0	0	0	0
18	0	0	0	0	0	0	0	0	0	0	0	0	0	0	0	0	0	0
19	0	0	0	0	0	0	0	0	0	0	0	0	0	0	0	0	0	0
20	0	0	0	0	0	0	0	0	0	0	0	0	0	0	0	0	0	0
21	0	0	0	0	0	0	0	0	0	0	0	0	0	0	0	0	0	0
22	0	0	0	0	0	0	0	0	0	0	0	0	0	0	0	0	0	0
23	0	0	7	0	0	0	0	0	0	0	0	0	0	0	0	0	0	0
24	0	0	0	0	0	0	0	0	0	0	0	0	0	0	0	0	0	0
25	1 333	0	0	0	0	0	0	0	0	0	0	0	0	0	0	0	0	0
26	0	2 921	0	0	0	0	0	0	0	0	0	0	0	0	0	0	0	0
27	0	0	1 212	0	0	0	0	0	0	0	0	0	0	0	0	0	0	0
28	0	0	1	1 556	0	0	0	0	0	0	0	0	0	0	0	1	0	0
29	1	3	1	1	1 746	0	2	2	0	1	1	0	0	0	0	9	0	2
30	0	0	0	0	0	209	0	0	0	0	0	0	0	0	0	0	0	0
31	0	0	0	0	0	0	1 634	0	0	0	0	0	0	0	0	0	0	0
32	0	0	0	0	0	0	0	1 238	0	0	0	0	0	0	0	0	0	0
33	0	0	0	0	0	0	0	0	327	0	0	0	0	0	0	0	0	0
34	0	0	0	0	0	0	0	0	0	2 466	0	0	0	0	0	2	0	0
35	0	0	0	0	0	0	0	0	0	0	667	0	0	0	0	0	0	0
36	0	0	0	0	0	0	0	0	0	0	0	1 699	0	0	0	0	0	0
37	0	0	0	0	0	0	0	0	0	0	0	0	88	0	0	0	0	0
40	0	2	0	0	0	0	0	0	0	0	0	0	0	4 609	0	0	0	0
41	0	0	0	0	0	0	0	0	0	0	0	0	0	0	391	0	0	0
45	0	2	0	1	1	0	1	0	0	1	4	1	0	28	17	14 191	2	1
50	0	0	0	0	0	0	0	0	0	0	0	0	0	0	0	0	4 243	0
51	0	0	0	0	0	0	0	0	0	0	0	0	0	0	0	0	0	9 306
52	0	0	0	0	0	0	0	0	0	0	0	0	0	0	0	0	0	0
55	0	0	0	0	0	0	0	0	0	0	0	0	0	0	0	0	0	0
60	0	0	0	0	0	0	0	0	0	0	0	0	0	0	2	0	0	0
61	0	0	0	0	0	0	0	0	0	0	0	0	0	0	0	0	0	0
62	0	0	0	0	0	0	0	0	0	0	0	0	0	0	0	0	0	0
63	0	0	0	0	0	0	0	0	0	0	0	0	0	0	0	0	0	0
64	0	0	0	0	0	0	0	0	0	0	0	0	0	0	0	0	0	0
65	0	0	0	0	0	0	0	0	0	0	0	0	0	0	0	0	0	0
66	0	0	0	0	0	0	0	0	0	0	0	0	0	0	0	0	0	0
67	0	0	0	0	0	0	0	0	0	0	0	0	0	0	0	0	0	0
70	0	1	0	1	1	0	1	0	0	0	0	1	0	0	0	0	13	0
71	0	3	0	0	0	0	0	0	0	1	2	0	0	0	0	0	3	10
72	0	0	0	0	0	0	0	0	0	0	0	0	0	0	0	0	0	0
73	1	1	0	2	5	1	8	14	1	1	5	0	0	6	0	0	0	1
74	5	32	1	5	5	0	14	14	2	19	3	3	0	45	1	0	21	130
75	0	0	0	0	0	0	0	0	0	0	0	0	0	0	0	0	0	0
80	0	0	0	0	0	0	0	0	0	0	0	0	0	0	0	0	0	0
85	0	0	0	0	0	0	0	0	0	0	0	0	0	0	0	0	0	0
90	0	0	0	0	0	0	0	0	0	0	0	0	0	0	48	0	0	0
91	0	0	0	0	0	0	0	0	0	0	0	0	0	0	0	0	0	0
92	0	0	0	0	0	0	0	0	0	0	0	0	0	0	0	0	0	0
93	0	0	0	0	0	0	0	0	0	0	0	0	0	0	0	0	0	0
95	0	0	0	0	0	0	0	0	0	0	0	0	0	0	0	0	0	0
Adjustment items:																		
c.i.f./f.o.b. on imports	0	0	0	0	0	0	0	0	0	0	0	0	0	0	0	0	0	0
direct purchases abroad by residents	0	0	0	0	0	0	0	0	0	0	0	0	0	0	0	0	0	0
Total	**1 341**	**2 964**	**1 223**	**1 566**	**1 758**	**210**	**1 660**	**1 268**	**331**	**2 489**	**682**	**1 705**	**88**	**4 688**	**459**	**14 204**	**4 283**	**9 451**

Table A.4c. Supply of products at basic prices (current prices in millions of euros) – Output of goods and services by activities 52-85

	Output of goods and services by activities (P.1)																	
Products	**52**	**55**	**60**	**61**	**62**	**63**	**64**	**65**	**66**	**67**	**70**	**71**	**72**	**73**	**74**	**75**	**80**	**85**
01	0	0	0	0	0	0	0	0	0	0	0	0	0	0	0	0	0	0
02	0	0	0	0	0	0	0	0	0	0	0	0	0	0	0	3	0	0
05	0	0	0	0	0	0	0	0	0	0	0	0	0	0	0	0	0	0
10	0	0	0	0	0	0	0	0	0	0	0	0	0	0	0	0	0	0
11	0	0	0	0	0	0	0	0	0	0	0	0	0	0	0	0	0	0
12	0	0	0	0	0	0	0	0	0	0	0	0	0	0	0	0	0	0
13	0	0	0	0	0	0	0	0	0	0	0	0	0	0	0	0	0	0
14	0	0	0	0	0	1	0	0	0	0	0	0	0	0	0	0	0	0
15	0	0	0	0	0	0	0	0	0	0	0	0	0	0	0	7	0	0
16	0	0	0	0	0	0	0	0	0	0	0	0	0	0	0	0	0	0
17	0	0	0	0	0	0	0	0	0	0	0	0	0	0	0	0	0	0
18	0	0	0	0	0	0	0	0	0	0	0	0	0	0	0	0	0	0
19	0	0	0	0	0	0	0	0	0	0	0	0	0	0	0	0	0	0
20	0	0	0	0	0	0	0	0	0	0	0	0	1	0	0	0	0	0
21	0	0	0	0	0	0	0	0	0	0	0	0	0	0	0	0	0	0
22	0	0	0	0	0	0	0	0	0	0	0	0	0	0	0	19	1	0
23	0	0	0	0	0	0	0	0	0	0	0	0	0	0	0	0	0	0
24	0	0	0	0	0	0	0	0	0	0	0	0	0	0	0	0	0	0
25	0	0	0	0	0	0	0	0	0	0	0	0	0	0	0	0	0	0
26	0	0	0	0	0	0	0	0	0	0	0	0	0	0	0	0	0	0
27	0	0	0	0	0	0	0	0	0	0	0	0	0	0	0	0	0	0
28	0	0	0	0	0	0	0	0	0	0	0	0	0	0	0	0	0	0
29	0	1	9	0	0	0	0	0	0	0	0	0	0	0	4	0	0	0
30	0	0	0	0	0	0	0	0	0	0	0	0	0	0	0	0	0	0
31	0	0	0	0	0	0	0	0	0	0	0	0	0	0	0	0	0	0
32	0	0	0	0	0	0	0	0	0	0	0	0	0	0	0	0	0	0
33	0	0	0	0	0	0	0	0	0	0	0	0	0	0	0	0	0	0
34	0	0	3	0	0	0	0	0	0	0	0	0	0	0	0	0	0	0
35	0	0	3	0	0	0	0	0	0	0	0	0	0	0	0	0	0	0
36	0	0	0	0	0	0	0	0	0	0	0	0	0	0	0	0	0	0
37	0	0	0	0	0	0	0	0	0	0	0	0	0	0	0	0	0	0
40	0	0	0	0	0	3	0	0	0	0	0	0	0	0	0	3	0	0
41	0	0	0	0	0	0	0	0	0	0	0	0	0	0	0	47	0	0
45	1	1	0	0	0	7	0	0	0	0	2	0	0	0	12	27	0	0
50	0	0	11	0	0	0	0	0	0	0	0	0	0	0	0	0	0	0
51	0	0	0	0	0	0	0	0	0	0	0	0	0	0	0	0	0	0
52	4 808	0	0	0	0	0	0	0	0	0	0	0	0	0	0	2	0	0
55	0	5 581	0	0	0	0	0	0	0	0	0	0	0	0	0	49	1	18
60	0	0	2 240	0	0	0	0	0	0	0	0	0	0	0	0	0	0	0
61	0	0	0	467	0	0	0	0	0	0	0	0	0	0	0	0	0	0
62	0	0	0	0	998	0	0	0	0	0	0	0	0	0	0	0	0	0
63	0	0	0	0	0	1 423	0	0	0	0	0	0	0	0	0	6	0	0
64	0	0	0	0	0	0	2 671	0	0	0	0	0	0	0	0	0	0	0
65	0	0	0	0	0	0	0	4 349	0	0	0	0	0	0	0	0	0	0
66	0	0	0	0	0	0	0	0	1 028	0	0	0	0	0	0	0	0	0
67	0	0	0	0	0	0	0	0	0	387	0	0	0	0	0	0	0	0
70	0	28	4	0	0	11	0	83	76	0	5 915	0	0	0	146	42	1	14
71	2	1	7	0	0	3	1	0	0	0	2	934	1	0	10	33	0	0
72	0	0	0	0	0	0	0	0	0	0	0	0	608	0	5	0	0	0
73	0	0	5	0	0	0	8	0	0	0	0	0	3	142	2	0	1	0
74	173	26	29	2	0	16	187	178	0	2	30	0	0	3	7 061	677	32	3
75	0	0	0	0	0	0	0	0	0	0	0	0	0	0	0	6 950	0	5
80	0	0	0	0	0	0	0	0	0	0	0	0	0	0	0	0	5 611	0
85	0	0	0	0	0	0	0	0	0	0	0	0	0	0	0	16	0	6 454
90	0	0	0	0	0	0	0	0	0	0	0	0	0	0	0	6	0	0
91	0	0	0	0	0	0	0	0	0	0	0	0	0	0	0	0	0	0
92	0	0	0	0	0	0	0	0	0	0	0	0	0	0	0	7	1	2
93	0	0	0	0	0	0	0	0	0	0	0	0	0	0	0	12	0	0
95	0	0	0	0	0	0	0	0	0	0	0	0	0	0	0	0	0	0
Adjustment items:																		
c.i.f./f.o.b. on imports	0	0	0	0	0	0	0	0	0	0	0	0	0	0	0	0	0	0
direct purchases abroad by residents	0	0	0	0	0	0	0	0	0	0	0	0	0	0	0	0	0	0
Total	**4 985**	**5 639**	**2 312**	**470**	**999**	**1 464**	**2 868**	**4 611**	**1 104**	**389**	**5 949**	**935**	**612**	**145**	**7 241**	**7 906**	**5 648**	**6 496**

Table A.4d. Supply of products at basic prices (current prices in millions of euros) – Output of goods and services by activities 90-95 and Total Output; Imports of goods and services; Total supply at basic prices; Trade and transport margins; Taxes and subsidies on products; Total supply at purchasers' prices

	Output of goods and services by activities (P.1)					Total of activities	Imports of goods and services (P.7)			Total of supply at basic prices	Trade and Transport Margins	Taxes on products (D.21)	Subsidies on products (D.31)	Total supply at purchasers' prices
Products	90	91	92	93	95		Imports of goods (P.71)	Imports of services (P.72)						
01	0	0	0	0	0	**4 903**	1 470	0	**1 470**	**6 373**	961	146	- 427	**7 052**
02	0	0	0	0	0	**707**	209	0	**209**	**916**	63	3	0	**982**
05	0	0	0	0	0	**454**	63	0	**63**	**517**	213	19	- 2	**746**
10	0	0	0	0	0	**0**	192	0	**192**	**193**	26	0	0	**219**
11	0	0	0	0	0	**0**	1 267	0	**1 267**	**1 267**	0	0	0	**1 267**
12	0	0	0	0	0	**0**	0	0	**0**	**0**	0	0	0	**0**
13	0	0	0	0	0	**211**	19	0	**19**	**230**	0	0	0	**230**
14	0	0	0	0	0	**397**	96	0	**96**	**493**	83	17	0	**592**
15	0	0	0	0	0	**10 543**	2 360	0	**2 360**	**12 904**	3 050	904	- 125	**16 733**
16	0	0	0	0	0	**119**	39	0	**39**	**157**	104	946	0	**1 207**
17	0	0	0	0	0	**4 585**	1 550	0	**1 550**	**6 135**	935	165	0	**7 235**
18	0	0	0	0	0	**3 987**	540	0	**540**	**4 527**	1 212	320	- 3	**6 056**
19	0	0	0	0	0	**2 395**	614	0	**614**	**3 009**	425	103	0	**3 537**
20	0	0	0	0	0	**2 034**	177	0	**177**	**2 211**	171	53	0	**2 435**
21	0	0	0	0	0	**2 527**	598	0	**598**	**3 125**	437	34	0	**3 597**
22	0	1	1	0	0	**1 698**	199	0	**199**	**1 896**	322	68	- 2	**2 284**
23	0	0	0	0	0	**1 594**	617	0	**617**	**2 211**	952	2 611	0	**5 773**
24	0	0	0	0	0	**3 267**	2 768	0	**2 768**	**6 035**	1 402	240	0	**7 677**
25	0	0	0	0	0	**1 333**	798	0	**798**	**2 131**	496	77	0	**2 703**
26	0	0	0	0	0	**2 921**	335	0	**335**	**3 256**	198	140	0	**3 594**
27	0	0	0	0	0	**1 212**	1 611	0	**1 611**	**2 823**	400	40	- 6	**3 258**
28	0	0	0	0	0	**1 560**	540	0	**540**	**2 100**	277	62	0	**2 440**
29	0	0	0	0	0	**1 809**	2 167	0	**2 167**	**3 976**	855	116	0	**4 947**
30	0	0	0	0	0	**209**	621	0	**621**	**830**	190	96	0	**1 117**
31	0	0	0	0	0	**1 634**	948	1	**949**	**2 583**	390	56	0	**3 030**
32	0	0	0	0	0	**1 238**	1 270	0	**1 270**	**2 508**	280	102	0	**2 889**
33	0	0	0	0	0	**327**	508	0	**508**	**835**	203	66	0	**1 105**
34	0	0	0	0	0	**2 472**	3 325	0	**3 325**	**5 796**	655	1 151	0	**7 602**
35	0	0	0	0	0	**670**	537	3	**540**	**1 210**	53	29	- 6	**1 286**
36	0	0	0	0	0	**1 699**	482	0	**482**	**2 181**	770	210	0	**3 161**
37	1	0	0	0	0	**89**	0	0	**0**	**89**	0	0	0	**89**
40	0	0	0	0	0	**4 854**	83	0	**83**	**4 937**	0	76	0	**5 013**
41	0	0	0	0	0	**438**	1	0	**1**	**439**	0	12	- 20	**431**
45	1	0	0	0	0	**14 317**	0	2	**2**	**14 319**	0	434	0	**14 754**
50	0	0	0	0	0	**4 254**	1	0	**2**	**4 256**	- 1 511	190	0	**2 934**
51	0	0	0	0	0	**9 306**	18	140	**159**	**9 465**	- 8 972	0	0	**492**
52	0	0	0	0	0	**4 811**	0	0	**0**	**4 811**	- 4 639	24	0	**196**
55	0	0	0	0	0	**5 649**	0	270	**270**	**5 920**	0	701	0	**6 620**
60	0	0	0	0	0	**2 243**	0	27	**27**	**2 270**	0	37	- 156	**2 150**
61	0	0	0	0	0	**467**	0	27	**27**	**494**	0	2	- 2	**494**
62	0	0	0	0	0	**998**	0	321	**321**	**1 319**	0	7	- 25	**1 300**
63	0	0	0	0	0	**1 430**	0	69	**69**	**1 499**	0	58	0	**1 557**
64	0	0	0	0	0	**2 671**	0	193	**193**	**2 865**	0	176	0	**3 041**
65	0	0	0	0	0	**4 349**	0	140	**140**	**4 489**	0	104	0	**4 593**
66	0	0	0	0	0	**1 028**	0	48	**48**	**1 076**	0	113	0	**1 189**
67	0	0	0	0	0	**387**	0	59	**59**	**446**	0	2	0	**448**
70	0	3	10	0	0	**6 367**	0	0	**1**	**6 368**	0	19	0	**6 387**
71	0	0	1	0	0	**1 026**	0	90	**90**	**1 115**	0	98	0	**1 213**
72	0	0	0	0	0	**613**	36	57	**93**	**706**	0	45	0	**751**
73	0	0	0	0	0	**233**	0	13	**13**	**246**	0	2	- 1	**247**
74	0	6	29	0	0	**8 930**	4	713	**717**	**9 647**	0	1 069	- 10	**10 705**
75	0	0	0	0	0	**6 955**	0	0	**0**	**6 955**	0	0	0	**6 955**
80	0	0	0	0	0	**5 611**	0	0	**0**	**5 611**	0	2	0	**5 613**
85	0	0	0	2	0	**6 472**	0	0	**0**	**6 472**	0	29	0	**6 501**
90	146	0	0	0	0	**199**	0	0	**0**	**199**	0	0	0	**199**
91	0	671	0	0	0	**671**	0	0	**0**	**671**	0	0	0	**671**
92	0	32	2 215	12	0	**2 269**	16	147	**163**	**2 432**	0	326	- 44	**2 714**
93	0	0	0	819	0	**831**	0	2	**2**	**833**	0	67	0	**901**
95	0	0	0	0	418	**418**	0	0	**0**	**418**	0	0	0	**418**
Adjustment items:														
c.i.f./f.o.b. on imports	0	0	0	0	0	**0**	- 1 168	894	**- 275**	**- 275**	0	0	0	**- 275**
direct purchases abroad by residents	0	0	0	0	0	**0**	0	1 327	**1 327**	**1 327**	0	0	0	**1 327**
Total	**147**	**713**	**2 257**	**834**	**418**	**154 394**	**24 911**	**4 543**	**29 454**	**183 848**	**0**	**11 364**	**- 830**	**194 383**

Source: Instituto Nacional de Estatística

See Tables A.7 and A.8 for the description of codes and grouping of products and activities

Table A.5a. Use of products at purchasers' prices (current prices in millions of euros) – Intermediate consumption by activities 01-26

	Intermediate consumption by activities (P.2)																			
Products	**01**	**02**	**05**	**10**	**11**	**12**	**13**	**14**	**15**	**16**	**17**	**18**	**19**	**20**	**21**	**22**	**23**	**24**	**25**	**26**
01	564	5	0	0	0	0	0	0	3 440	24	282	14	0	2	0	0	0	4	12	0
02	0	0	0	0	0	0	0	0	0	0	0	0	0	499	266	0	0	9	0	0
05	0	0	36	0	0	0	0	0	86	0	0	0	0	0	0	0	0	0	0	0
10	2	0	0	0	0	0	0	0	0	0	0	0	0	0	0	0	0	0	0	22
11	0	0	0	0	0	0	0	0	0	0	0	0	0	0	0	0	1 229	0	0	0
12	0	0	0	0	0	0	0	0	0	0	0	0	0	0	0	0	0	0	0	0
13	0	0	0	0	0	0	0	0	0	0	0	0	0	0	0	0	0	0	0	0
14	0	0	0	0	0	0	0	6	3	0	0	0	0	0	10	0	0	18	0	256
15	1 139	0	0	0	0	0	0	0	2 588	0	0	0	93	0	11	0	0	15	0	0
16	0	0	0	0	0	0	0	0	0	0	0	0	0	0	0	0	0	0	0	0
17	0	0	2	0	0	0	0	8	0	0	1 474	1 946	69	1	0	2	0	14	23	13
18	0	0	0	0	0	0	1	2	6	1	3	489	1	1	2	2	4	5	0	2
19	0	0	0	0	0	0	0	0	0	0	0	17	1 081	0	0	0	0	0	0	0
20	5	0	0	0	0	0	0	0	13	0	2	0	2	568	14	0	0	1	2	11
21	30	0	8	0	0	0	0	2	213	5	24	19	30	21	797	396	0	58	15	70
22	5	0	0	0	0	0	1	3	70	1	33	15	9	5	1	221	4	14	1	8
23	161	10	27	0	0	0	7	50	39	0	45	15	6	12	10	6	146	122	7	16
24	233	1	2	0	0	0	4	27	42	0	521	5	128	67	94	61	69	1 399	569	189
25	0	0	2	0	0	0	0	0	136	0	24	12	78	24	18	37	0	35	144	27
26	15	0	0	0	0	0	0	0	77	0	0	0	0	1	0	0	0	7	5	522
27	0	0	0	0	0	0	0	0	0	0	1	0	3	1	0	6	0	16	9	105
28	10	0	3	0	0	0	0	6	133	0	9	10	17	7	3	2	0	49	11	5
29	27	9	0	0	0	0	7	3	49	1	26	19	11	18	1	1	1	13	10	133
30	0	0	1	0	0	0	0	0	0	0	0	0	0	0	0	0	0	0	0	0
31	0	0	0	0	0	0	0	0	0	0	0	0	0	0	0	0	0	0	0	0
32	0	0	0	0	0	0	0	0	0	0	0	0	0	0	0	0	0	0	0	0
33	0	0	0	0	0	0	0	0	0	0	0	0	0	0	0	0	0	0	0	0
34	0	0	0	0	0	0	0	0	0	0	0	0	0	0	0	0	0	0	0	0
35	0	0	0	0	0	0	0	0	0	0	0	0	0	0	0	0	0	0	0	0
36	0	0	0	0	0	0	0	0	0	0	4	67	2	0	0	0	0	0	0	0
37	0	0	0	0	0	0	0	0	0	0	0	0	0	0	12	0	0	0	5	12
40	57	0	3	0	0	0	5	15	65	1	104	21	20	17	192	18	63	25	18	100
41	0	0	0	0	0	0	0	0	21	0	2	2	0	1	0	1	1	3	0	2
45	25	0	5	0	0	0	1	13	27	1	19	14	8	14	15	10	13	19	7	34
50	75	3	6	0	0	0	0	7	15	0	10	8	4	6	7	6	4	9	4	17
51	0	0	0	0	0	0	0	0	0	0	0	0	0	0	0	0	0	0	0	0
52	0	0	0	0	0	0	0	0	0	0	0	0	0	0	0	0	0	0	0	0
55	1	1	1	0	0	0	0	4	19	0	11	13	10	10	6	17	1	15	9	8
60	12	13	0	0	0	0	7	24	77	2	29	21	10	40	60	14	23	35	17	54
61	0	0	0	0	0	0	0	0	1	0	4	4	1	0	9	1	67	1	2	7
62	2	0	3	0	0	0	0	0	2	0	6	0	1	0	0	1	0	0	0	1
63	1	0	0	0	0	0	0	0	3	0	2	3	1	0	3	1	0	2	1	1
64	0	2	1	0	0	0	0	2	13	0	10	11	6	5	27	19	1	8	4	10
65	8	1	1	0	0	0	2	2	25	0	21	9	5	12	4	3	2	13	3	9
66	3	0	3	0	0	0	1	2	19	0	18	10	7	9	10	4	6	11	4	11
67	2	0	0	0	0	0	1	1	7	0	6	3	2	4	1	1	1	4	1	3
70	3	0	0	0	0	0	0	9	25	3	10	15	3	6	6	17	8	27	4	14
71	17	0	1	0	0	0	0	0	0	0	0	0	0	0	0	0	0	0	0	0
72	0	0	0	0	0	0	0	0	0	0	0	0	0	0	0	6	0	0	0	0
73	0	0	0	0	0	1	0	0	3	0	3	0	0	1	3	2	4	9	1	1
74	48	10	13	0	0	0	2	12	567	4	148	111	49	37	102	210	42	302	52	107
75	0	0	0	0	0	0	0	0	0	0	0	0	0	0	0	0	0	0	0	0
80	1	0	1	0	0	0	3	2	25	2	14	10	5	4	11	7	12	20	4	11
85	22	0	0	0	0	0	0	0	13	0	2	1	1	1	0	4	0	1	0	1
90	0	0	0	0	0	0	0	0	1	0	0	0	0	0	0	0	0	0	0	0
91	1	0	0	0	0	0	0	0	5	0	4	3	2	1	3	1	0	3	0	3
92	0	0	0	0	0	0	0	0	0	0	0	0	0	0	0	37	0	0	0	0
93	0	0	0	0	0	0	0	0	0	0	0	0	0	0	0	0	0	0	0	0
95	0	0	0	0	0	0	0	0	0	0	0	0	0	0	0	0	0	0	0	0
Adjustament items:																				
c.i.f./f.o.b. on exports	0	0	0	0	0	0	0	0	0	0	0	0	0	0	0	0	0	0	0	0
direct purchases abroad by residents	0	0	0	0	0	0	0	0	0	0	0	0	0	0	0	0	0	0	0	0
direct purchases by non-residents in the domestic market	0	0	0	0	0	0	0	0	0	0	0	0	0	0	0	0	0	0	0	0
Total	**2 472**	**58**	**121**	**0**	**0**	**2**	**44**	**201**	**7 826**	**47**	**2 871**	**2 885**	**1 665**	**1 395**	**1 700**	**1 114**	**1 702**	**2 287**	**947**	**1 785**
Gross added value (B1)	**2 828**	**647**	**334**	**0**	**0**	**0**	**169**	**198**	**2 395**	**75**	**1 773**	**1 109**	**733**	**652**	**1 000**	**576**	**- 14**	**1 015**	**394**	**1 179**
Compensation of employees[D.1(T.-S.2)]	490	29	134	0	0	1	27	118	1 261	23	1 009	815	484	368	295	371	50	557	237	629
Other net taxes on production (D.29-D.39)	- 163	0	- 7	- 2	0	0	0	- 1	- 18	0	5	2	- 9	- 7	- 1	- 8	2	4	- 3	- 4
Gross operating surplus/ Gross mixed income (B.2g/B.3g)	2 501	618	207	2	0	- 1	143	81	1 152	52	760	292	258	291	705	214	- 66	453	160	554
Consumption of fixed capital (K.1)	374	50	15	0	0	7	16	42	427	9	269	70	44	65	79	50	54	158	103	270
Net operating surplus/ Net mixed income (B.2n/B.3n)	2 127	568	193	2	0	- 9	127	39	725	43	490	221	215	226	626	164	- 119	295	57	285
Output of goods and serv. at basic prices (P.1)	**5 300**	**705**	**456**	**0**	**0**	**1**	**214**	**400**	**10 221**	**122**	**4 644**	**3 994**	**2 399**	**2 047**	**2 700**	**1 691**	**1 688**	**3 302**	**1 341**	**2 964**

Source: Instituto Nacional de Estatística

See Tables A.7 and A.8 for the description of codes and grouping of products and activities

Table A.5b. Use of products at purchasers' prices (current prices in millions of euros) – Intermediate consumption by activities 27-61

	Intermediate consumption by activities (P.2)																			
Products	27	28	29	30	31	32	33	34	35	36	37	40	41	45	50	51	52	55	60	61
01	0	0	0	0	0	0	0	1	0	0	0	0	0	0	0	0	0	290	0	0
02	0	0	0	0	0	0	0	0	0	2	0	0	0	0	0	0	0	0	0	0
05	0	0	0	0	0	0	0	0	0	0	0	0	0	0	0	0	0	79	0	0
10	24	0	0	0	0	0	0	0	0	0	0	158	0	0	0	0	0	0	0	0
11	0	0	0	0	0	0	0	0	0	0	0	0	0	0	0	0	0	0	0	0
12	0	0	0	0	0	0	0	0	0	0	0	0	0	0	0	0	0	0	0	0
13	17	2	0	0	0	0	0	0	0	0	0	0	0	0	0	0	0	0	0	0
14	2	1	0	0	0	0	0	0	0	0	0	0	0	210	0	0	0	5	0	0
15	0	0	0	0	0	0	0	0	0	0	0	0	0	0	0	0	0	1 930	0	0
16	0	0	0	0	0	0	0	0	0	0	0	0	0	0	0	0	0	0	0	0
17	0	0	0	0	0	0	0	29	0	105	0	0	0	84	50	64	24	76	1	0
18	2	2	2	0	4	3	0	8	1	7	0	12	0	6	2	15	4	18	1	1
19	0	0	0	0	0	0	0	1	0	13	0	0	0	0	0	8	2	0	0	0
20	1	31	2	0	1	1	0	3	1	205	0	23	0	467	0	53	30	2	0	0
21	1	11	15	0	5	6	2	5	4	27	9	0	1	3	69	86	34	14	0	0
22	11	20	2	0	1	2	2	1	0	10	0	1	2	46	62	97	114	1	11	6
23	8	19	9	0	3	1	1	4	2	28	1	198	10	420	93	49	46	212	395	22
24	4	37	26	0	43	5	4	41	13	51	2	1	17	195	39	60	46	38	2	0
25	0	35	64	0	163	84	36	97	5	79	0	0	1	139	78	140	54	2	16	0
26	0	11	24	0	13	0	10	91	1	12	0	1	0	1 734	9	33	15	30	0	0
27	414	769	292	0	220	5	3	177	148	213	25	4	3	428	0	0	0	0	0	0
28	6	82	107	17	6	5	2	129	5	32	0	6	1	560	46	179	55	29	0	0
29	4	40	511	3	16	7	1	34	27	9	1	0	9	242	26	22	7	20	0	0
30	0	0	0	106	0	4	0	0	0	0	0	0	0	0	0	10	2	3	5	0
31	0	0	114	2	386	134	8	127	2	0	0	29	0	387	103	69	22	110	0	0
32	0	0	31	10	69	631	30	20	0	0	0	0	0	22	40	0	0	0	0	0
33	0	0	24	0	7	14	45	31	0	5	0	31	0	0	0	39	12	4	0	0
34	0	0	3	0	0	0	0	1 152	3	0	0	0	0	0	317	8	3	0	29	0
35	0	0	0	0	0	0	0	0	72	1	0	0	0	0	5	3	1	3	2	1
36	0	1	2	0	0	0	0	38	9	159	0	1	0	100	23	126	55	58	0	0
37	59	0	0	0	0	0	0	0	0	0	0	0	0	0	0	0	0	0	0	0
40	50	29	17	0	10	5	2	13	10	15	1	1 830	17	45	38	178	70	148	27	0
41	0	1	1	0	1	0	0	1	1	0	0	0	48	9	3	19	9	32	2	0
45	6	11	7	0	4	3	1	7	2	6	1	5	3	3 394	11	73	25	35	57	8
50	4	6	4	0	2	2	0	4	1	3	0	0	5	48	93	242	101	61	57	4
51	0	0	0	0	0	0	0	0	0	0	0	0	0	0	0	347	0	0	0	0
52	0	0	0	0	0	0	0	0	0	8	0	0	0	0	0	0	0	16	0	0
55	3	20	17	1	7	6	2	5	3	13	0	3	2	96	36	286	83	31	11	1
60	17	13	18	0	16	6	2	8	2	15	1	0	1	48	58	212	99	1	70	2
61	0	5	0	0	0	0	0	3	8	0	0	0	0	2	2	30	10	0	0	129
62	0	0	0	0	1	1	0	2	1	1	0	0	0	0	17	135	48	0	0	0
63	0	1	1	0	1	1	0	1	0	1	0	1	18	4	46	307	169	38	3	50
64	1	9	7	0	4	3	1	4	1	6	0	12	5	48	24	182	110	20	15	1
65	1	3	20	0	3	3	2	3	2	7	0	16	0	30	20	29	25	11	5	0
66	2	6	5	0	3	2	1	5	4	5	0	12	0	45	14	42	9	7	28	3
67	0	1	6	0	1	1	1	1	1	2	0	4	0	16	6	14	13	3	1	0
70	6	7	8	0	7	10	1	6	11	4	0	5	1	99	72	141	150	59	25	24
71	0	0	0	0	0	0	0	0	0	0	0	0	0	0	0	195	99	36	0	0
72	0	0	4	0	1	1	0	0	0	0	0	28	1	0	0	18	12	2	55	5
73	0	2	6	1	10	21	2	1	7	0	0	6	0	0	0	2	0	0	6	0
74	28	60	57	4	38	48	15	53	15	86	1	124	22	372	318	563	268	199	84	16
75	0	0	0	0	0	0	0	0	0	0	0	0	0	0	0	0	0	0	0	0
80	6	8	9	0	12	12	1	15	9	4	0	1	2	24	11	34	9	15	13	1
85	0	1	1	0	0	0	0	1	0	1	0	0	0	6	3	11	6	6	1	0
90	0	0	0	0	0	0	0	0	0	0	0	0	0	0	0	1	0	1	0	0
91	1	1	1	0	1	0	0	1	1	1	0	5	0	8	4	13	20	4	3	1
92	0	0	0	0	0	0	0	0	0	0	0	0	0	0	0	9	5	12	0	0
93	0	0	0	0	0	0	0	0	0	0	0	0	0	0	0	2	1	41	0	0
95	0	0	0	0	0	0	0	0	0	0	0	0	0	0	0	0	0	0	0	0
Adjustament items:																				
c.i.f./f.o.b. on exports	0	0	0	0	0	0	0	0	0	0	0	0	0	0	0	0	0	0	0	0
direct purchases abroad by residents	0	0	0	0	0	0	0	0	0	0	0	0	0	0	0	0	0	0	0	0
direct purchases by non-residents in the domestic market	0	0	0	0	0	0	0	0	0	0	0	0	0	0	0	0	0	0	0	0
Total	**680**	**1 246**	**1 419**	**145**	**1 061**	**1 023**	**176**	**2 116**	**373**	**1 135**	**46**	**2 516**	**171**	**9 337**	**1 737**	**4 145**	**1 865**	**3 704**	**925**	**273**
Gross added value (B1)	**543**	**320**	**339**	**66**	**599**	**245**	**154**	**372**	**309**	**570**	**43**	**2 172**	**288**	**4 867**	**2 545**	**5 306**	**3 119**	**1 935**	**1 387**	**197**
Compensation of employees[D.1(T.-S.2)]	245	285	245	29	431	172	67	346	223	385	16	430	139	2 589	862	2 259	1 673	1 106	923	45
Other net taxes on production (D.29-D.39)	1	- 5	2	0	- 4	- 1	- 1	0	- 2	1	0	8	- 1	- 25	- 2	- 12	- 14	- 10	- 55	- 4
Gross operating surplus/ Gross mixed income (B.2g/B.3g)	296	40	92	36	172	74	88	26	88	183	27	1 733	150	2 303	1 685	3 058	1 461	839	519	156
Consumption of fixed capital (K.1)	41	97	131	2	125	105	20	203	45	41	3	355	87	569	312	294	359	307	529	103
Net operating surplus/ Net mixed income (B.2n/B.3n)	255	- 57	- 39	34	47	- 31	68	- 177	43	143	24	1 378	64	1 734	1 373	2 764	1 102	533	- 10	53
Output of goods and serv. at basic prices (P.1)	**1 223**	**1 566**	**1 758**	**210**	**1 660**	**1 268**	**331**	**2 489**	**682**	**1 705**	**88**	**4 688**	**459**	**14 204**	**4 283**	**9 451**	**4 985**	**5 639**	**2 312**	**470**

Table A.5c. Use of products at purchasers' prices (current prices in millions of euros) – Intermediate consumption by activities 62-100

	Intermediate consumption by activities (P.2)																			
Products	**62**	**63**	**64**	**65**	**66**	**67**	**70**	**71**	**72**	**73**	**74**	**75**	**80**	**85**	**90**	**91**	**92**	**93**	**95**	**100**
01	0	0	0	0	0	0	0	0	0	0	0	0	1	73	0	0	0	0	0	0
02	0	0	0	0	0	0	0	0	0	0	0	1	1	0	0	0	0	0	0	0
05	0	0	0	0	0	0	0	0	0	0	0	3	0	0	0	0	0	0	0	0
10	0	0	0	0	0	0	0	0	0	0	0	0	0	0	0	0	0	0	0	0
11	0	0	0	0	0	0	0	0	0	0	0	0	0	0	0	0	0	0	0	0
12	0	0	0	0	0	0	0	0	0	0	0	0	0	0	0	0	0	0	0	0
13	0	0	0	0	0	0	0	0	0	0	0	0	0	0	0	0	0	0	0	0
14	0	0	0	0	0	0	0	0	0	0	0	1	1	0	0	0	0	0	0	0
15	0	0	0	0	0	0	0	0	0	0	0	51	30	304	0	0	0	0	0	0
16	0	0	0	0	0	0	0	0	0	0	0	0	0	0	0	0	0	0	0	0
17	0	0	0	0	0	0	0	0	0	0	2	4	1	151	0	0	0	9	0	0
18	9	2	17	0	0	0	1	0	0	0	12	1	2	36	0	0	38	0	0	0
19	1	0	0	0	0	0	0	0	0	0	0	0	0	0	0	0	0	0	0	0
20	0	0	0	0	0	0	0	0	0	0	10	1	0	0	0	0	17	46	0	0
21	0	6	0	4	1	0	9	1	8	2	177	33	22	10	0	9	11	3	0	0
22	43	62	14	83	10	5	113	20	18	1	298	28	32	68	0	24	19	10	0	0
23	52	52	10	1	4	0	23	13	3	2	52	257	39	310	9	19	13	10	0	0
24	0	1	0	2	0	0	5	0	1	6	31	14	12	552	0	12	29	102	0	0
25	0	0	0	0	0	0	0	0	3	0	119	3	2	0	0	0	13	0	0	0
26	0	1	0	0	0	0	0	0	0	1	19	28	5	1	0	0	0	0	0	0
27	0	0	0	0	0	0	0	0	0	0	0	0	0	0	0	0	0	0	0	0
28	1	0	1	9	0	2	0	0	0	0	90	20	6	19	0	0	15	0	0	0
29	0	0	0	0	0	0	0	16	0	0	0	75	2	8	0	0	0	0	0	0
30	2	1	1	46	0	8	0	0	0	0	0	17	7	0	0	0	2	0	0	0
31	0	2	54	7	24	1	0	0	0	0	0	28	7	9	1	2	0	0	0	0
32	0	0	77	0	0	0	0	0	0	0	0	5	2	0	0	0	24	0	0	0
33	0	0	0	0	0	0	0	0	0	2	5	4	3	62	0	0	74	0	0	0
34	0	0	0	0	0	0	0	0	0	0	1	11	1	3	1	1	0	0	0	0
35	31	0	0	0	0	0	0	0	0	0	0	22	0	0	0	0	0	0	0	0
36	0	0	0	0	0	0	3	0	0	0	2	21	22	13	0	8	26	4	0	0
37	0	0	0	0	0	0	0	0	0	0	0	0	0	0	0	0	0	0	0	0
40	2	26	19	49	6	1	51	1	1	3	153	132	66	48	2	43	22	21	0	0
41	0	4	1	3	1	0	4	0	0	1	5	29	18	18	1	13	4	8	0	0
45	15	40	17	34	0	6	423	9	4	1	49	38	14	33	0	14	14	14	0	0
50	5	17	6	6	0	1	15	14	2	0	27	37	8	36	1	2	6	5	0	0
51	0	0	0	0	0	0	0	0	0	0	0	0	0	0	0	0	0	0	0	0
52	0	0	0	0	0	0	0	6	0	0	0	0	0	0	0	0	0	0	0	0
55	1	68	2	63	18	4	23	3	10	2	178	143	52	47	0	10	14	5	0	0
60	1	82	7	5	0	0	17	1	2	1	60	25	18	7	5	21	4	2	0	0
61	0	0	2	0	0	0	2	0	0	1	20	0	3	1	0	0	0	0	0	0
62	139	13	6	0	0	0	21	1	3	0	54	20	15	9	0	21	8	2	0	0
63	115	16	0	0	0	0	6	1	2	0	19	7	1	44	2	0	3	1	0	0
64	7	82	477	164	36	6	32	5	4	1	63	85	49	41	0	105	22	7	0	0
65	2	2	9	27	0	6	5	6	2	0	51	33	3	6	0	0	17	1	0	3 688
66	4	3	5	7	5	0	2	14	1	0	12	3	2	2	0	1	2	0	0	0
67	1	1	3	65	183	0	1	2	1	0	15	0	1	1	0	0	5	0	0	0
70	8	30	23	107	32	20	143	11	16	0	97	42	25	27	0	9	26	7	0	0
71	0	1	0	34	5	1	0	0	2	2	84	45	107	73	1	28	8	0	0	0
72	11	14	36	80	0	3	33	11	4	0	70	40	16	45	0	3	15	9	0	0
73	0	0	8	0	0	0	0	0	3	7	2	11	4	0	0	0	0	0	0	0
74	33	132	184	241	106	68	501	50	96	32	1 563	281	268	501	22	151	440	86	0	0
75	0	0	0	0	0	0	0	0	0	0	0	0	0	0	0	0	0	0	0	0
80	28	10	74	23	0	0	2	1	2	0	23	22	4	1	0	0	10	0	0	0
85	0	2	0	0	0	0	5	2	2	0	26	1	8	167	0	0	6	1	0	0
90	0	0	0	0	0	0	0	0	0	0	0	9	1	3	0	1	0	0	0	0
91	1	2	5	0	0	0	1	2	1	0	7	1	1	2	0	0	1	0	0	0
92	0	0	0	11	0	1	2	0	3	0	599	17	0	1	0	93	97	0	0	0
93	0	0	0	0	0	0	1	0	0	0	0	5	40	27	0	8	87	10	0	0
95	0	0	0	0	0	0	0	0	0	0	0	0	0	0	0	0	0	0	0	0
Adjustament items:																				
c.i.f./f.o.b. on exports	0	0	0	0	0	0	0	0	0	0	0	0	0	0	0	0	0	0	0	0
direct purchases abroad by residents	0	0	0	0	0	0	0	0	0	0	0	0	0	0	0	0	0	0	0	0
direct purchases by non-residents in the domestic market	0	0	0	0	0	0	0	0	0	0	0	0	0	0	0	0	0	0	0	0
Total	**512**	**670**	**1 057**	**1 067**	**431**	**132**	**1 442**	**190**	**193**	**67**	**3 998**	**1 652**	**923**	**2 761**	**48**	**599**	**1 091**	**363**	**0**	**3 688**
Gross added value (B1)	**487**	**794**	**1 810**	**3 543**	**673**	**257**	**4 507**	**745**	**420**	**79**	**3 243**	**6 254**	**4 725**	**3 736**	**99**	**114**	**1 166**	**471**	**418**	**- 3 688**
Compensation of employees[D.1(T.-S.2)]	156	447	750	1 870	396	43	215	92	252	82	1 262	5 116	4 188	2 709	59	128	919	92	418	0
Other net taxes on production (D.29-D.39)	0	- 21	- 1	- 4	- 1	2	- 25	6	1	- 1	6	- 2	- 53	- 2	0	- 6	0	0	0	0
Gross operating surplus/ Gross mixed income (B.2g/B.3g)	331	368	1 061	1 678	278	211	4 317	647	167	- 2	1 975	1 141	590	1 029	39	- 8	247	379	0	- 3 688
Consumption of fixed capital (K.1)	243	76	236	597	74	63	3 590	186	34	20	166	1 188	271	284	39	20	527	13	0	0
Net operating surplus/ Net mixed income (B.2n/B.3n)	88	292	825	1 082	204	149	727	461	133	- 22	1 809	- 48	318	745	1	- 28	- 280	366	0	- 3 688
Output of goods and serv. at basic prices (P.1)	**999**	**1 464**	**2 868**	**4 611**	**1 104**	**389**	**5 949**	**935**	**612**	**145**	**7 241**	**7 906**	**5 648**	**6 496**	**147**	**713**	**2 257**	**834**	**418**	**0**

Table A.5d. Use of products at purchasers' prices (current prices in millions of euros) – Total intermediate consumption by activities; Final consumption; Gross capital formation; Exports of goods and services; Total uses at purchasers' prices

Products	(P.2) Total of activities	Final consumption (P.3)				Gross capital formation (P.5)				Exports of goods and serv. (P.6)			Total uses at purchasers' prices
		General Government (S.13)	Households (S.14)	NPISHs (S.15)		Gross fixed capital formation(P.51)	Changes in inventories (P.52)	Acquisitions less disposals of valuables(P.53)		Exports of goods (P.61)	Exports of services (P.62)		
01	4 712	18	1 977	0	1 995	195	38	0	233	112	0	112	7 052
02	777	0	67	0	67	32	55	0	87	51	0	51	982
05	205	0	502	0	502	0	- 2	0	- 2	42	0	42	746
10	206	0	0	0	0	0	12	0	12	0	0	0	219
11	1 229	0	0	0	0	0	38	0	38	0	0	0	1 267
12	0	0	0	0	0	0	0	0	0	1	0	1	0
13	19	0	0	0	0	0	0	0	0	211	0	211	230
14	512	0	7	0	7	0	23	0	23	50	0	50	592
15	6 161	0	9 362	0	9 362	0	8	0	8	1 202	0	1 202	16 733
16	0	0	1 198	0	1 198	0	4	0	4	5	0	5	1 207
17	4 152	0	1 137	0	1 137	9	76	0	85	1 862	0	1 862	7 235
18	725	0	2 801	0	2 801	0	20	0	20	2 510	0	2 510	6 056
19	1 122	0	905	0	905	0	24	0	24	1 487	0	1 487	3 537
20	1 513	0	84	0	84	3	18	0	21	816	0	816	2 435
21	2 277	0	138	0	138	0	90	0	90	1 093	0	1 093	3 597
22	1 629	0	603	0	603	0	6	0	6	46	0	46	2 284
23	3 067	0	2 130	0	2 130	0	- 13	0	- 13	590	0	590	5 773
24	4 802	623	1 354	0	1 977	0	20	0	20	878	0	878	7 677
25	1 670	0	594	0	594	62	51	0	112	327	0	327	2 703
26	2 666	0	128	0	128	0	17	0	17	783	0	783	3 594
27	2 842	0	1	0	1	0	143	65	208	208	0	208	3 258
28	1 697	0	70	0	70	168	22	0	189	484	0	484	2 440
29	1 408	0	448	0	448	2 327	16	0	2 342	748	0	748	4 947
30	217	0	59	0	59	804	0	0	804	36	0	36	1 117
31	1 630	0	84	0	84	192	5	0	197	1 119	0	1 119	3 030
32	961	0	460	0	460	439	67	0	506	962	0	962	2 889
33	361	0	179	0	179	344	8	1	353	212	0	212	1 105
34	1 534	0	3 196	0	3 196	1 000	43	0	1 043	1 829	0	1 829	7 602
35	141	0	157	0	157	552	41	0	593	392	3	395	1 286
36	747	0	1 637	0	1 637	319	17	56	392	384	0	384	3 161
37	89	0	- 2	0	- 2	0	2	0	2	0	0	0	89
40	3 876	0	1 085	0	1 085	0	0	0	0	53	0	53	5 013
41	272	5	153	0	159	0	0	0	0	0	0	0	431
45	4 606	0	74	0	74	9 921	152	0	10 072	0	1	1	14 754
50	1 009	0	1 638	0	1 638	287	0	0	287	0	1	1	2 934
51	347	0	0	0	0	0	18	0	18	2	125	127	492
52	31	0	165	0	165	0	0	0	0	0	0	0	196
55	1 395	1	5 143	0	5 144	0	0	0	0	0	81	81	6 620
60	1 284	36	493	0	529	0	0	0	0	0	338	338	2 150
61	318	0	18	0	18	0	0	0	0	0	158	158	494
62	534	0	90	0	90	0	0	0	0	0	676	676	1 300
63	877	0	443	0	443	0	0	0	0	0	237	237	1 557
64	1 757	0	1 029	0	1 029	0	0	0	0	0	255	255	3 041
65	4 160	0	267	0	267	0	0	0	0	0	166	166	4 593
66	373	0	776	0	776	0	0	0	0	0	39	39	1 189
67	384	0	32	0	32	0	0	0	0	0	32	32	448
70	1 412	2	4 185	8	4 196	779	0	0	779	0	0	0	6 387
71	741	0	456	0	456	0	0	0	0	0	16	16	1 213
72	522	0	22	0	22	172	3	0	176	1	31	32	751
73	129	71	0	35	105	0	0	0	0	0	12	12	247
74	8 945	4	650	0	654	712	5	0	716	0	390	391	10 705
75	0	6 791	88	75	6 955	0	0	0	0	0	0	0	6 955
80	517	4 127	906	64	5 096	0	0	0	0	0	0	0	5 613
85	303	3 249	2 693	256	6 198	0	0	0	0	0	0	0	6 501
90	18	51	130	0	181	0	0	0	0	0	0	0	199
91	116	0	245	310	555	0	0	0	0	0	0	0	671
92	886	53	978	541	1 571	139	3	18	160	2	94	96	2 714
93	222	1	677	0	678	0	0	0	0	0	1	1	901
95	0	0	418	0	418	0	0	0	0	0	0	0	418
Adjustament items:													
c.i.f./f.o.b. on exports	0	0	0	0	0	0	0	0	0	0	- 275	- 275	- 275
direct purchases abroad by residents	0	0	1 327	0	1 327	0	0	0	0	0	0	0	1 327
direct purchases by non-residents in the domestic market	0	0	- 3 552	0	- 3 552	0	0	0	0	946	2 605	3 552	0
Total	84 102	15 032	49 905	1 288	66 225	18 457	1 026	140	19 623	19 444	4 989	24 433	194 383
Gross added value (B1)	70 292												
Compensation of employees[D.1(T.-S.2)]	38 563												
Other net taxes on production (D.29-D.39)	- 433												
Gross operating surplus/ Gross mixed income (B.2g/B.3g)	32 161												
Consumption of fixed capital (K.1)	13 457												
Net operating surplus/ Net mixed income (B.2n/B.3n)	18 704												
Output of goods and serv. at basic prices (P.1)	154 394												

Source: Instituto Nacional de Estatística

See Tables A.7 and A.8 for the description of codes and grouping of products and activities

Table A.6. "From whom to whom" matrices (in millions of euros)

D71 - net non-life insurance premiums

	S.14	S.11	S.12	S.13	S.15	S1	S.2	Total
S.14						0		0
S.11						0		0
S.12	652	327	13	4	14	1 010	33	1 042
S.13						0		0
S.15						0		0
S.1	652	327	13	4	14	1 010	33	1 042
S.2		108	8			116		
Total	652	435	21	4	14	1 126		

D72 - non-life insurance claims

	S.14	S.11	S.12	S.13	S.15	S1	S.2	Total
S.14			578			578		578
S.11			362			362	23	386
S.12			16			16	2	18
S.13			1			1		1
S.15			12			12		12
S.1	0	0	970	0	0	970	25	995
S.2			52			52		
Total	0	0	1 022	0	0	1 022		

D75 - miscellaneous current transfers

	S.14	S.11	S.12	S.13	S.15	S1	S.2	Total
S.14	386	10		138		535	3 264	3 798
S.11		58	0			58		58
S.12		2				2		2
S.13	100	108	2		4	214	59	273
S.15	310	50	21	878	0	1 260		1 260
S.1	797	228	23	1 016	5	2 069	3 323	5 391
S.2	416			222		637		
Total	1 213	228	23	1 238	5	2 706		

D92 - investment grants

	S.14	S.11	S.12	S.13	S.15	S1	S.2	Total
S.14				204		204	50	254
S.11				579		579	877	1 455
S.12				2		2		2
S.13				1 729		1 729	1 273	3 002
S.15				291		291	1	292
S.1	0	0	0	2 804	0	2 804	2 201	5 005
S.2				2		2		2
Total	0	0	0	2 806	0	2 806		

D99 - other capital transfers

	S.14	S.11	S.12	S.13	S.15	S1	S.2	Total
S.14			812	2		814	97	911
S.11				128		128	20	148
S.12		484	328			812		812
S.13	6	161	3	141	4	314	2	316
S.15						0		0
S.1	6	645	1 143	271	4	2 069	118	2 188
S.2	15			12		27		27
Total	21	645	1 143	283	4	2 096		

Source: Instituto Nacional de Estatística

Table A.7a. Description of codes and grouping of Products – Codes

Code[16]	Description
01	Products of agriculture, hunting and related services
02	Products of forestry, logging and related services
05	Fish and other fishing products, services incidental to fishing
10	Coal and lignite; peat
11	Crude petroleum and natural gas; services incidental to oil and gas extraction excluding surveying
12	Uranium and thorium ores
13	Metal ores
14	Other mining and quarrying products
15	Food products and beverages
16	Tobacco products
17	Textiles
18	Wearing apparel; furs
19	Leather and leather products
20	Wood and products of wood and cork (except furniture), articles of straw and plaiting materials
21	Pulp, paper and paper products
22	Printed matter and recorded media
23	Coke, refined petroleum products and nuclear fuel
24	Chemicals, chemical products and man-made fibres
25	Rubber and plastic products
26	Other non-metallic mineral products
27	Basic metals
28	Fabricated metal products, except machinery and equipment
29	Machinery and equipment n.e.c.
30	Office machinery and computers
31	Electrical machinery and apparatus n.e.c
32	Radio, television and communication equipment and apparatus
33	Medical, precision and optical instruments, watches and clocks
34	Motor vehicles, trailers and semi-trailers
35	Other transport equipment
36	Furniture; other manufactured goods n.e.c.
37	Recovered secondary raw materials
40	Electrical energy, gas, steam and hot water
41	Collected and purified water, distribution services of water
45	Construction work
50	Trade, maintenance and repair services of motor vehicles and motorcycles; retail trade services of automotive fuel
51	Wholesale trade and commission trade, except of motor vehicles and motorcycles
52	Retail trade, except of motor vehicles and motorcycles; repair of personal and household goods

[16] CPA codes, the Classification of Products by Activity that shows the principal products of activities according to NACE Rev.1 (General Industrial Classification of Economic Activities within the European Union).

Code	Description
55	Hotels and restaurants
60	Land transport; transport via pipelines
61	Water transport
62	Air transport
63	Supporting and auxiliary transport activities; activities of travel agencies
64	Post and telecommunications
65	Financial intermediation, except insurance and pension funding
66	Insurance and pension funding, except compulsory social security
67	Activities auxiliary to financial intermediation
70	Real estate activities
71	Renting of machinery and equipment without operator and of personal and household goods
72	Computer and related activities
73	Research and development
74	Other business activities
75	Public administration and defence; compulsory social security
80	Education
85	Health and social work
90	Sewage and refuse disposal, sanitation and similar activities
91	Activities of membership organisations n.e.c.
92	Recreation, cultural and sporting activities
93	Other service activities
95	Private households with employed persons

Table A.7b. Description of codes and grouping of Products – Groups

Group	Code	Description
1	01-05	Products of agriculture, hunting, forestry, fisheries and aquaculture
2	10-41	Products from mining and quarrying, manufactured products and energy products
3	45	Construction work
4	50-64	Wholesale and retail trade services; repair services, hotel and restaurant services, transport and communication services
5	65-74	Financial intermediation services, real estate, renting and business services
6	75-95	Other services

Table A.8a. Description of codes and grouping of Activities – Codes

Code[17]	Description
01	Agriculture, hunting and related activities
02	Forestry, logging and related service activities
05	Fishing, operation of fish hatcheries and fish farms; service activities incidental to fishing
10	Mining of coal and lignite; extraction of peat
11	Extraction of crude petroleum and natural gas; service activities incidental to oil and gas extraction excluding surveying
12	Mining of uranium and thorium ores
13	Mining of metal ores
14	Other mining and quarrying
15	Manufacture of food products and beverages
16	Manufacture of tobacco products
17	Manufacture of textiles
18	Manufacture of wearing apparel; dressing and dyeing of fur
19	Tanning and dressing of leather; manufacture of luggage, handbags, saddlery, harness and footwear
20	Manufacture of wood and of products of wood and cork, except furniture; manufacture of articles of straw and plaiting materials
21	Manufacture of pulp, paper and paper products
22	Publishing, printing and reproduction of recorded media
23	Manufacture of coke, refined petroleum products and nuclear fuel
24	Manufacture of chemicals and chemical products
25	Manufacture of rubber and plastic products
26	Manufacture of other non-metallic mineral products
27	Manufacture of basic metals
28	Manufacture of fabricated metal products, except machinery and equipment
29	Manufacture of machinery and equipment n.e.c.
30	Manufacture of office machinery and computers
31	Manufacture of electrical machinery and apparatus n.e.c.
32	Manufacture of radio, television and communication equipment and apparatus
33	Manufacture of medical, precision and optical instruments, watches and clocks
34	Manufacture of motor vehicles, trailers and semi-trailers
35	Manufacture of other transport equipment
36	Manufacture of furniture; manufacturing n.e.c.
37	Recycling
40	Electricity, gas, steam and hot water supply
41	Collection, purification and distribution of water
45	Construction
50	Sale, maintenance and repair of motor vehicles and motorcycles; retail sale of automotive fuel
51	Wholesale trade and commission trade, except of motor vehicles and motorcycles

[17] NACE Rev.1 code, the classification of economic activities within the European Union.

Code	Description
52	Retail trade services, except of motor vehicles and motorcycles; repair services of personal and household goods
55	Hotel and restaurant services
60	Land transport; transport via pipeline services
61	Water transport services
62	Air transport services
63	Supporting and auxiliary transport services; travel agency services
64	Post and telecommunication services
65	Financial intermediation services, except insurance and pension funding services
66	Insurance and pension funding services, except compulsory social security services
67	Services auxiliary to financial intermediation
70	Real estate services
71	Renting of machinery and equipment without operator and of personal and household goods
72	Computer and related services
73	Research and development services
74	Other business services
75	Public administration and defence services; compulsory social security services
80	Education services
85	Health and social work services
90	Sewage and refuse disposal services, sanitation and similar services
91	Membership organisation services n.e.c.
92	Recreational, cultural and sporting services
93	Other services
95	Private households with employed persons

Table A.8b. Description of codes and grouping of Activities – Groups

Group	Code	Description
1	01-05	Agriculture, hunting and forestry; fishing and operation of fish hatcheries and fish farms
2	10-41	Industry, including energy
3	45	Construction
4	50-64	Wholesale and retail trade, repair of motor vehicles and household goods, hotels and restaurants; transport and communications
5	65-74	Financial, real-estate, renting and business activities
6	75-95	Other service activities

Note: In the Use of Products at purchasers' prices – Tables A.5 – there is also an activity 100 considered as a fictitious activity for the uses of the Financial Intermediation Services Indirectly Measured (FISIM), the intermediate consumption of which was added to the intermediate consumption by the group 5 activities of the group 5 products of the SAM.

Appendix B

Identifying the items and balances of the various internal accounts of the SNA in the aggregate SAM

As mentioned in Chapter 2, (Section 2.2), the SNA is the basic source of information for the construction of the SAM used in this work; therefore, almost all the flows that are part of the former are integrated into the latter.

Next, the items and balances of the several (T) accounts of the Portuguese SNA for 1995 (Appendix A), represented in the matrix format by the NAM (National Accounting Matrix – Table B.1) will be identified in the SAM (Tables 1, 2 or 15), each of them referring to an aspect of the economic circuit (see Outline 1). The cells of the basic SAM (Table 1) and the basic NAM (Table 2) will be referred to when the SAM and the NAM accounts, respectively, are to be analysed. As uses (outlays, expenditures or changes in assets) and resources (incomes, receipts or changes in liabilities and net worth), which are always recorded in millions of euros, we will use the designations that we used for the various accounts of the SAM. We will add a " ´ " to the SAM balances.

The author will deal with gross balances and will not therefore take into account the consumption of fixed capital.

Besides the external transactions of the rest of the world account, the author will also work upon the goods and services account, at current prices, the current accounts and the accumulation accounts (with the exception of SNA account III.3 – other changes in assets account), which are the accounts made available by the Portuguese National Accounts.

Goods and Services Account (SNA account 0) – balanced by definition:

Resources

Trade and transport margins (total) (1,1)		0
Output of goods and services (2,1)		154 394
Imports of goods and services (8,1)		29 454
Net taxes on products (2,1)		10 535
– paid to Portuguese institutions	10 283	
– paid to European Union institutions	252	
Total		194 383

Uses

Trade and transport margins (total) (1,1)	0
Intermediate consumption (1,2)	84 102
Final consumption expenditure (1,5)	66 225
Gross capital formation (1,6)	19 623
Exports of goods and services (1,8)	24 433
Total	194 383

This account can be associated with the SAM's "products" account, belonging to the group of "production" accounts.

Thus:

Resources

Intermediate consumption (3,2)	84 102
Trade and transport margins (total) (3,3)	0
Final consumption expenditure of the national institutions in the economy (3,4)	64 898
Gross capital formation (3,5)	19 623
Exports of goods and services (3,7)	24 433
Aggregate demand	193 056

Uses

Output of goods and services (2,3)		154 394
Trade and transport margins (total) (3,3)		0
Net taxes on products paid to Portuguese institutions (4,3)		10 283
Imports of goods and services plus net taxes on products paid to European Union institutions (7,3)		28 379
– imports of goods and services	28 127	
– net taxes on products paid to European Union institutions	252	
Aggregate supply		193 056

The difference between these two accounts is in the "direct purchases abroad by residents" (1327), considered in the SAM as a "current transfer to the rest of the world", since it does not represent an expenditure in the economy and should not therefore be considered in the final consumption sub-matrix (see Outline 1).

Production Account (SNA account I) – which describes the transactions that constitute the appropriately named production process:

Resources
Output of goods and services (2,1) 154 394
Net taxes on products (2,1) 10 535
– paid to Portuguese institutions 10 283
– paid to European Union institutions 252
Total 164 929

Uses
Intermediate Consumption (1,2) 84 102
(B1g) Gross added value/gross domestic product (3,2) ... 80 827
Total 164 929

We associated this account with the SAM's "activities" account:

Resources
Production (output of goods and services) (2,3) 154 394

Uses
Intermediate consumption (3,2) 84 102
Net taxes on production .... – 433
– paid to Portuguese institutions (4,2) .... – 346
– paid to European Union institutions (7,2) .... – 87
(B1g´) Gross added value/gross domestic product, at factor cost (1,2) 70 725
Total costs 154 394

We therefore have:

Gross added value/gross domestic product, at factor cost (B1g´) = Gross domestic product (at market prices, B1g) – net indirect taxes or net taxes on products and imports (70 725 = 80 827 – (10 535-433)).

In the SAM, the GDP (gross domestic product) at market prices can be calculated by adding to the GDP at factor cost the net indirect taxes paid to the Portuguese government and to the European Union institutions: 70 725 + (-346-87) + (10283+252) = 80 827.

Primary Distribution of Income Accounts (SNA account II.1) – which show how primary incomes, i.e. incomes that accrue as a result of involvement in processes of production or the ownership of assets that may be needed for production purposes, are distributed among institutions and activities:

– Generation of income account (SNA account II.1.1)

Resources

(B1g) Gross added value/gross domestic product		80 827

Uses

Compensation of employees paid by Portuguese institutions		38 563
– to Portuguese institutions	38 500	
– to the rest of the world	64	
Net taxes on production and imports paid by Portuguese institutions		10 102
– to Portuguese institutions	9 937	
– to the rest of the world	165	
(B2g + B3g) Gross operating surplus + Gross mixed income		32 161
Total		80 827

– Allocation of primary income account (SNA account II.1.2)

Resources

(B2g + B3g) Gross operating surplus + Gross mixed income		32 161
Compensation of employees received by Portuguese institutions		38 620
– from Portuguese institutions	38 500	
– from the rest of the world	120	
Net taxes on production and imports received/paid by Portuguese institutions		9 937
Property income received by Portuguese institutions		27 952

– from Portuguese institutions 24 829
– from the rest of the world 3 363
Total 108 670

Uses
Property income paid by Portuguese institutions 28 191
– to Portuguese institutions 24 829
– to the rest of the world 3 363
(B5g) Gross national income 80 479
Total 108 670

– (Summary) Primary distribution of income account (generation and allocation – SNA account II.1)

Resources
(B1g) Gross added value/gross domestic product (3,1) ... 80 827
Property income received by Portuguese institutions from Portuguese institutions (3,3) 24 828
Primary income from the rest of the world (3,8) 3 243
– compensation of employees 120
– property income 3 123
Total 108 898

Uses
Property income paid by Portuguese institutions to Portuguese institutions (3,3) 24 828
Primary income to the rest of the world (8,3) 3 591
– compensation of employees 64
– property income 3 363
– net taxes on production and imports 165
(B5g) Gross national income (4,3) 80 479
Total 108 898

We can associate these accounts with the SAM's "factors of production" account, which has the following composition:

Resources
(B1g´) Gross added value /gross domestic product, at factor cost (1,2) 70 725
– Labour (compensation of employees paid by Portuguese institutions) 38 563

– Others ((B2g´ + B3g´) Gross operating surplus + Gross mixed income)	32 161	
Compensation of factors from the rest of the world (1,7)		3 243
– Labour (compensation of employees)		120
– Others (property income)	3 123	
Aggregate Income of Factors		73 968

Uses

(B5g´) Gross national income, at factor cost (4,1)		70 542
– Labour (compensation of employees received by Portuguese institutions)	38 620	
– Other compensation of factors	31 922	
Compensation of factors to the rest of the world (7,1)		3 426
– Labour (wages and salaries)	64	
– Other (property income)	3 363	
Aggregate Income of Factors		73 968

In establishing the connection between those accounts, we have:

Gross national income, at factor cost (B5g´) = Gross national income (at market prices, B5g) – net indirect taxes or net taxes on production and imports received/paid by Portuguese institutions (70 542 = 80 479 – 9 937).

Secondary Distribution of Income, Redistribution of Income in Kind and Use of Income Accounts. The first two accounts show how the balance of primary incomes (national income) is transformed into disposable income through the receipt and payment of current transfers; the third account shows how gross disposable income is distributed between final consumption and saving.

– Secondary distribution of income and redistribution of income in kind accounts (SNA accounts II.2 and 3)

Resources

(B5g) Gross national income (4,3)	80 479
Current transfers within Portuguese institutions[18] (4,4)	51 569

[18] Total Current transfers (resources) = 51 569 + 3960 = 55 529:

Current taxes on income, wealth, etc. received by Portuguese institutions	7 161

Current transfers from the rest of the world[18] (4,8)	3 960
Total	136 008

Uses

Current transfers within Portuguese institutions[19] (4,4) ...	51 569
Current transfers to the rest of the world[19] (8,4)	922
(B6/7g) Gross disposable income (5,4)	83 517
Total	136 008

– Use of income account (SNA account II.4)

Resources

(B6/7g) Gross disposable income (5,4)	83 517
Adjustment for the change in the net equity of households in pension fund reserves (5,5)	752
Total	84 269

Uses

Final consumption (1,5)	66 225
Adjustment for the change in the net equity of households in pension fund reserves (5,5)	752
(B8g) Gross saving (6,5)	17 291
Total	84 269

Here is the SAM's "current" account of the Institutions:

Resources

(B5g´) Gross national income, at factor cost (4,1)		70 542
– Compensation of employees	38 620	
– other compensations of factors	31 922	

Social contributions and benefits received by Portuguese institutions	33 523
Other current transfers received by Portuguese institutions	14 845

[19] Total current transfers (uses) = 51 569 + 922 = 52 491:

Current taxes on income, wealth, etc. paid by Portuguese institutions	7 161
Social contributions and benefits paid by Portuguese institutions.	33 524
Other current transfers paid by Portuguese institutions	11 807

Other net taxes on production paid to Portuguese institutions (4,2)	– 346
Net taxes on products paid to Portuguese institutions (4,3)	10 283
Current transfers within Portuguese institutions[20] (4,4) ...	42 145
Current transfers from the rest of the world (4,7)	3 960
Aggregate income	126 583

Uses

Final consumption in the economy (3,4)		64 898
Current transfers within Portuguese institutions[20] (4,4) ...		42 145
Current transfers to the rest of the world (7,4)		2 249
– current transfers to the rest of the world	922	
– direct purchases abroad by residents	1 327	
(B8g´) Gross saving (5,4)		17 291
Aggregate income		126 583

We thus have the total of the SAM's current account, which we have called aggregate income, corresponding to the sum of the items:

Gross national income (B5g) + current transfers within Portuguese institutions + current transfers from the rest of the world (126 583 = 80 479 + 42 145 + 3 960)

or

Gross disposable income (B6/7g) + current transfers within Portuguese institutions + current transfers to the rest of the world (126 583 = 83 517 + 42 145 + 922).

Capital Account (SNA account III.1) – which records non-financial investment transactions and capital transfers, considered as the partition of property transactions:

Changes in liabilities and net worth (resources)

(B8g) Gross saving (6,5)	17 291
Capital transfers within Portuguese institutions (6,6)	4 930
Capital transfers from the rest of the world (6,8)	2 320
Total	24 541

[20] Includes "Adjustment for the change in the net equity of households in pension fund reserves".

Changes in assets (uses)	
Gross capital formation (1,6)	19 623
Capital transfers within Portuguese institutions (6,6)	4 930
Capital transfers to the rest of the world (8,6)	29
– Acquisitions less disposals of non-produced non-financial assets ... 0	
(B9) Net borrowing/lending (7,6)	– 40
Total	24 541

We have the following SAM's "capital" account:

Changes in liabilities and net worth (resources)	
(B8g') Gross saving (5,4)	17 291
Capital transfers within Portuguese institutions (5,5)	4 930
Capital transfers from the rest of the world (5,7)	2 320
(B9') – Net borrowing/lending (5,6)	40
Investment Funds	24 582

Changes in assets (uses)	
Gross Capital Formation (3,5)	19 623
Capital transfers within Portuguese institutions (5,5)	4 930
Capital transfers to the rest of the world (7,5)	29
– Acquisitions less disposals of non-produced non-financial assets ... 0	
Aggregate Investment	24 582

The only difference between these two accounts is in the way in which net borrowing/lending is considered. In the SAM's capital account, it is considered as a component of investment funds, required/not required to cover the aggregate investment, in other words, it is the financing requirement/capacity of the economy that will be covered/absorbed by financial transactions (from/to the rest of the world, since the national funds are not enough/in excess).

Financial Account (SNA account III.2) – records the transactions in financial assets and liabilities between institutional units, and between these and the rest of the world:

Changes in liabilities and net worth (resources)	
Financial transactions within Portuguese institutions (7,7)	35 030

Financial transactions from the rest of the world (7,8)	9 257
(B9F) Net borrowing/lending (7,6)	– 40
Total	44 247

Changes in assets (uses)

Financial transactions within Portuguese institutions (7,7)	35 030
Financial transactions to the rest of the world (8,7)	9 217
Total	44 247

We have the following SAM's "financial" account:

Changes in liabilities and net worth (resources)

Financial transactions within Portuguese institutions (6,6)	35 030
Financial transactions from the rest of the world (6,7)	9 257
Total	44 287

Changes in assets (uses)

Financial transactions within Portuguese institutions (6,6)	35 030
Financial transactions to the rest of the world (7,6)	9 217
(B9´F) – Net borrowing/lending (5,6)	40
Total	44 287

The explanation for the difference between these accounts is, once again, in the way in which net borrowing/lending is considered. In the SAM's financial account, it is considered as a use because it is used to cover/absorb the financing requirement/capacity of the economy, with financial transactions from/to the rest of the world (an amount that represents a liability with the rest of the world, in the case of the financing requirement).

Rest of the World Account (SNA account V) – records transactions between resident and non-resident units.

Resources / changes in liabilities and net worth

Imports of goods and services (8,1)		29 454
– goods and services	28 127	
– direct purchases abroad by residents	1 327	
Primary income to the rest of the world (8,3)		3 591
– compensation of employees	64	
– property income	3 363	
– net taxes on production and imports	165	

Current transfers to the rest of the world (8,4)		922
– social benefits other than social transfers in kind	30	
– others	892	
Capital transfers to the rest of the world (8,6)		29
– Acquisitions less disposals of non-produced nonfinancial assets	0	
Financial transactions to the rest of the world (8,7)		9 217
Total		43 213

Uses / changes in assets

Exports of goods and services (1,8)		24 433
Primary income from the rest of the world (3,8)		3 243
– compensation of employees	120	
– property income	3 123	
Current transfers from the rest of the world (4,8)		3 960
– social benefits other than social transfers in kind	29	
– others	3 931	
Capital transfers from the rest of the world (6,8)		2 320
Financial transactions from the rest of the world (7,8)		9 257
– Net lending	– 40	
Total		43 213

In the SAM's "rest of the world" account:

Resources / changes in liabilities and net worth

Compensation of factors to the rest of the world (7,1)		3 426
– Labour (wages and salaries)	64	
– Others (property income)	3 363	
Net taxes on production paid to European Union institutions (7,2)		– 87
Imports of goods and services plus net taxes on products paid to European Union institutions (7,3)		28 379
– imports of goods and services	28 127	
– net taxes on products paid to European Union institutions	252	
Current transfers to the rest of the world (7,4)		2 249
– current transfers to the rest of the world	922	
– direct purchases abroad by residents	1 327	
Capital transfers to the rest of the world (7,5)		29
– Acquisitions less disposals of non-produced non-financial assets	0	

Financial transactions to the rest of the world (7,6)		9 217
Total		43 213

Uses / changes in assets

Compensation of factors from the rest of the world (1,7)		3 243
– Labour (wages and salaries)	120	
– Others (property income)	3 123	
Exports of goods and services (3,7)		24 433
Current transfers from the rest of the world (4,7)		3 960
Capital transfers from the rest of the world (5,7)		2 320
Financial transactions from the rest of the world (6,7)		9 257
– Net lending	40	
Total		43 213

There is a close relationship between both accounts.

Therefore, generally speaking, if it were not for indirect taxation, the association of SAM accounts with national (T) accounts would be perfect – with the aggregate SAM being calculated from these accounts. The latter could also be calculated from the former, which may not be true if some disaggregation is undertaken. "SAMs are an extension of the core national accounts as presented in the European System of Accounts (ESA95) and the System of National Accounts (SNA 93)" (LEG, 2003).

The author also systematises, in a more detailed fashion, the differences between the matrix format of the National Accounts and the SAM in her works "Better policy analysis with better data. Constructing a Social Accounting Matrix from the European System of National Accounts" (Santos, 2006a) and "Macro-SAMs for Modelling Purposes. An Application to Portugal in 2003" (Santos, 2007a).

Thus, one of the many advantages of the SAM approach could be referred to here, using the words of Pyatt (1991):

> "by sticking to essentials, the relationship between economic concepts and principles, on the one hand, and on the other, the accounting structure they give rise to, can be kept clearly in the open".

Table B.1 summarises what was seen for the Portuguese national accounts in 1995.

Table B.1. Portuguese Basic NAM (National Accounting Matrix) for 1995 (in millions of euros)

SNA Account		(1)	(2)	(3)	(4)	(5)	(6)	(7)	(8)
0. Goods and services	(1)	Trade and transport margins (0)	Intermediate consumption (84 102)			Final consumption (66 225)	Gross capital formation (19 623)		Exports of goods and services (24 433)
I. Production	(2)	Output of goods and services + Net taxes on products (154 394 + 10 535)							
II.1. Primary distribution of income	(3)		Gross added value (80 827)	Property income (24 828)					Primary income from the RW (3 243)
II.2, II.3. Secondary distribution of income and redistribution of income in kind	(4)			Gross national income (89 479)	Current Transfers (51 569)				Current transfers from the RW (3 960)
II.4. Use of income	(5)				Gross disposable income (83 517)	Adjustment for the change in the net equity of households in the pension fund reserve (752)			
III.1. Capital	(6)					Gross saving (17 291)	Capital transfers (4 930)		Capital transfers from the RW (2 320)
III.2. Financial	(7)						Net borrowing (- 40)	Financial transactions (35 030)	Financial transactions from the RW (9 257)
V. Rest of the world	(8)	Imports of goods and services (29 454)		Primary income to the RW (3 591)	Current transfers to the RW (922)		Capital transfers to the RW (29)	Financial transactions to the RW (9 217)	
Total		194 383	164 929	108 898	136 008	84 269	24 541	44 247	43 213

Source: Round (2003); Keuning (1996); ESA 95; Portuguese National Accounts (Appendix A).
Row totals match column totals.

Appendix C

Portuguese Pilot-National Accounting Matrix (NAM) for 1995

Table C.1. Aggregate Pilot-NAM (in millions of euros)

Account		Goods and services	Production	Generation of income	Allocation of primary income	Secondary distribution of income	Use of income	Capital	Gross fixed capital formation	Financial	RW (current)	RW (capital)	Total
	codes	1	2	3	4	5	6	7	8	9	10	11	12
Goods and services	1	TRADE AND TRANSPORT MARGINS 0	INTERMEDIATE CONSUMPTION 85 979				FINAL CONSUMPTION 67 703	CHANGES IN INVENTORIES (1) 1 191	GROSS FIXED CAPITAL FORMATION 18 869		EXPORTS OF GOODS AND SERVICES (2) 25 259		199 001
Production	2	OUTPUT 157 526											157 526
Generation of income	3	TAXES LESS SUBSIDIES ON PRODUCTS 11 084	NET VALUE ADDED 57 789								COMPENSATION OF EMPLOYEES FROM THE R.O.V. 123		68 996
Allocation of primary income	4			NET GENERATED INCOME 68 762	PROPERTY INCOME 25 383						PROPERTY INCOME (3) FROM THE R.O.V. 3 193		97 338
Secondary distribution of income	5				NET NATIONAL INCOME 68 518	CURRENT TRANSFERS 42 825					CURRENT TRANSFERS FROM THE R.O.V. 4 048		115 391
Use of income	6					NET DISPOSABLE INCOME 71 623	ADJUSTMENT FOR CHANGE IN NET EQUITY ON PENSION 769				ADJUSTMENT FOR CHANGE IN NET EQUITY ON PENSION FUNDS FROM THE 0		72 392
Capital	7						NET SAVING 3 920	CAPITAL TRANSFERS (4) 4 945		NET INCURRENCE OF LIABILITIES 37 278		CAPITAL TRANSFERS FROM THE R.O.V. 2 371	48 514
Gross fixed capital formation	8		CONSUMPTION OF FIXED CAPITAL 13 758					NET FIXED CAPITAL FORMATION 5 112					18 870
Financial	9							NET ACQUISITIONS OF FINANCIAL ASSESTS 37 137				NET LENDING OF THE R.O.V. 141	37 278
RW (current)	10	IMPORTS OF GOODS AND SERVICES (5) 30 392		COMPENSATION OF EMPLOYEES TO THE R.O.V. 233	PROPERTY INCOME (3) TO THE R.O.V. 3 438	CURRENT TRANSFERS TO THE R.O.V. 943	ADJUSTMENT FOR CHANGE IN NET EQUITY ON PENSION 0						35 006
RW (capital)	11							CAPITAL TRANSFERS TO THE R.O.V. 29			CURRENT EXTERNAL BALANCE 2 383		2 412
Statistical discrepancy	SD							Statistical Discrepancy 100				- 100	- 100
Total	12	199 002	157 526	68 995	97 338	115 391	72 392	48 414	18 869	37 278	35 006	2 412	852 624

Source : Instituto Nacional de Estatística

(1) Including acquisition less disposable of valuables
(2) Including purchases in domestic market by non-residents
(3) Including taxes less subsidies on production from the Rest of the World
(4) Including acquisitions less disposals of non-produced non-financial assets
(5) Including purchases abroad by residents

Table C.2[21].1. Disaggregated Pilot-NAM cells (in millions of euros) – Cell (1,6) Final Consumption

Goods and services (CPA groups)		Use of income (Institutional sectors)								Total
		Non-financial corporations	Financial corporations	General government	Households (by main source of income)				Non-profit institutions serving households	
					Wages and salaries	Mixed income (including property income)	Income in connection with old age (retirement)	Other transfers income (including other households)		
	code	6a	6b	6c	6d-1	6d-2	6d-3	6d-4	6e	6f
Products of agriculture, hunting, forestry, fisheries and aquaculture (CPA A/B)	1a			18	1 465	491	533	73	0	2 581
Products from mining and quarrying, manufactured products and energy products (CPA C/D/E)	1b			642	17 395	5 564	4 117	918	0	28 637
Construction work (CPA F)	1c			0	41	10	22	3	0	75
Wholesale and retail trade services; repair services, hotel and restaurant services, transport and communication services (CPA G/H/I)	1d			38	5 264	1 559	891	250	0	8 002
Financial intermediation services, real estate, renting and business services (CPA J/K)	1e			79	3 711	1 574	861	183	44	6 451
Other services (CPA L to P)	1f			14 590	3 986	1 080	874	154	1 273	21 957
Total	1g			15 368	31 861	10 278	7 298	1 581	1 316	67 703

Source : Instituto Nacional de Estatística

[21] a) See the methodological details on the cell's calculation in LEG (2003), pp. 159-163.

b) Due to the unavailability of certain data in this version, some values of cells from former versions were also used, although they are not presented here.

Table C.2.2. Disaggregated Pilot-NAM cells (in millions of euros) – Cell (4,3) Generated Income

Allocation of primary income (Institutional sectors)			Generation of income (value added categories)																Total
			Compensation of employees						Net mixed income						Net operating surplus	Other taxes less subsidies on production	FISIM	
			Male			Female			Male			Female						
			Primary/lower secondary (ISCED 1-2)	Upper or post secondary (ISCED 3-4)	Tertiary (ISCED 5-6)	Primary/lower secondary (ISCED 1-2)	Upper or post secondary (ISCED 3-4)	Tertiary (ISCED 5-6)	Primary/lower secondary (ISCED 1-2)	Upper or post secondary (ISCED 3-4)	Tertiary (ISCED 5-6)	Primary/lower secondary (ISCED 1-2)	Upper or post secondary (ISCED 3-4)	Tertiary (ISCED 5-6)				
		codes	3a-1	3a-2	3a-3	3a-4	3a-5	3a-6	3b-1	3b-2	3b-3	3b-4	3b-5	3b-6	3c	3d	3e	3f
Non-financial corporations		4a													10 097			10 097
Financial corporations		4b													1 324		- 3 770	- 2 447
General government		4c													- 76	10 473		10 398
Households classified by main source of income	*Wages and salaries*	4d-1	13 463	4 100	6 003	7 599	3 253	2 848	1 031	297	271	926	220	155	260			40 426
	Mixed income (including property income)	4d-2	235	127	38	515	274	97	4 649	560	268	1 676	298	35	117			8 888
	Income in connection with old age (retirement)	4d-3	121	79	17	166	80	66	84	66	13	196	39	4	58			987
	Other transfers income (including other households)	4d-4	96	48	45	159	45	13	71	33	8	73	12	0	15			618
Non-profit institutions serving households		4e													- 205			- 205
Total		4f	13 916	4 354	6 103	8 438	3 652	3 025	5 835	955	559	2 871	569	194	11 589	10 473	- 3 770	68 762

Source: Instituto Nacional de Estatística

Table C.2.3. Disaggregated Pilot-NAM cells (in millions of euros) – Cell (4,4) Property Income; Cell (5,4) Net National Income

CELL (4,4)

Allocation of primary income (Institutional sectors)			Allocation of primary income (Institutional sectors)								Total
			Non-financial corporations	Financial corporations	General government	Households: *Wages and salaries*	Households: *Mixed income (including property income)*	Households: *Income in connection with old age (retirement)*	Households: *Other transfers income (including other households)*	Non-profit institutions serving households	
		codes	4a	4b	4c	4d-1	4d-2	4d-3	4d-4	4e	4f
Non-financial corporations		4a	901	878	3	16	4	0	1	0	1 803
Financial corporations		4b	5 111	2 240	3 062	2 237	527	51	148	34	13 410
General government		4c	321	629	9	4	1	0	0	5	969
Households classified by main source of income	*Wages and salaries*	4d-1	142	2 233	469	14	5	1	2	0	2 865
	Mixed income (including property income)	4d-2	298	3 558	906	16	5	1	3	0	4 787
	Income in connection with old age (retirement)	4d-3	15	695	180	1	0	0	0	0	891
	Other transfers income (including other households)	4d-4	4	553	17	0	0	0	0	0	575
Non-profit institutions serving households		4e	54	29	0	0	0	0	0	0	83
Total		4f	6 846	10 815	4 646	2 288	542	53	154	39	25 383

CELL (5,4)

Secondary distribution of income (Institutional sectors)			Allocation of primary income (Institutional sectors)								Total
			Non-financial corporations	Financial corporations	General government	Households: *Wages and salaries*	Households: *Mixed income (including property income)*	Households: *Income in connection with old age (retirement)*	Households: *Other transfers income (including other households)*	Non-profit institutions serving households	
		codes	4a	4b	4c	4d-1	4d-2	4d-3	4d-4	4e	4f
Non-financial corporations		5a	4 211								4 211
Financial corporations		5b		1 078							1 078
General government		5c			6 298						6 298
Households classified by main source of income	*Wages and salaries*	5d-1				41 037					41 037
	Mixed income (including property income)	5d-2					13 194				13 194
	Income in connection with old age (retirement)	5d-3						1 809			1 809
	Other transfers income (including other households)	5d-4							1 036		1 036
Non-profit institutions serving households		5e								- 145	- 145
Total		5f	4 211	1 078	6 298	41 037	13 194	1 809	1 036	- 145	68 518

Source : Instituto Nacional de Estatística

Table C.2.4. Disaggregated Pilot-NAM cells (in millions of euros) – Cell (5,5) Current Transfers among Residents; Cell (6,5) Net Disposable Income

CELL (5,5)

Secondary distribution of income (Institutional sectors)			Secondary distribution of income (Institutional sectors)								Total
			Non-financial corporations	Financial corporations	General government	Households				Non-profit institutions serving households	
						Wages and salaries	*Mixed income (including property income)*	*Income in connection with old age (retirement)*	*Other transfers income (including other households)*		
		codes	5a	5b	5c	5d-1	5d-2	5d-3	5d-5	5e	5f
Non-financial corporations		5a	59	384	0	313	125	900	31	0	1 812
Financial corporations		5b	401	37	4	1 698	221	143	42	13	2 558
General government		5c	2 496	276	7 019	12 197	1 094	854	174	7	24 117
Households classified by main source of income	*Wages and salaries*	5d-1	319	427	2 288	127	50	18	16	3	3 247
	Mixed income (including property income)	5d-2	126	93	905	53	21	7	7	1	1 214
	Income in connection with old age (retirement)	5d-3	900	498	6 385	39	15	5	5	9	7 855
	Other transfers income (including other households)	5d-4	34	295	260	72	28	10	9	0	707
Non-profit institutions serving households		5e	51	34	897	220	66	17	28	1	1 314
Total		5f	4 386	2 044	17 758	14 719	1 620	1 954	310	34	42 825

CELL (6,5)

Use of income (Institutional sectors)			Allocation of primary income (Institutional sectors)								Total
			Non-financial corporations	Financial corporations	General government	Households				Non-profit institutions serving households	
						Wages and salaries	*Mixed income (including property income)*	*Income in connection with old age (retirement)*	*Other transfers income (including other households)*		
		codes	5a	5b	5c	5d-1	5d-2	5d-3	5d-5	5e	5f
Non-financial corporations		6a	1 601								1 601
Financial corporations		6b		1 571							1 571
General government		6c			12 933						12 933
Households classified by main source of income	*Wages and salaries*	6d-1				31 629					31 629
	Mixed income (including property income)	6d-2					13 448				13 448
	Income in connection with old age (retirement)	6d-3						7 816			7 816
	Other transfers income (including other households)	6d-4							1 491		1 491
Non-profit institutions serving households		6e								1 134	1 134
Total		6f	1 601	1 571	12 933	31 629	13 448	7 816	1 491	1 134	71 623

Source : Instituto Nacional de Estatística

Table C.2.5. Disaggregated Pilot-NAM cells (in millions of euros) – Cell (7,6) Net Saving

CELL (7,6) A DETAILED NET SAVING MATRIX

Capital (Institutional sectors)			Use of income (Institutional sectors)								Total
			Non-financial corporations	Financial corporations	General government	Households				Non-profit institutions serving households	
						Wages and salaries	*Mixed income (including property income)*	*Income in connection with old age (retirement)*	*Other transfers income (including other households)*		
		codes	6a	6b	6c	6d-1	6d-2	6d-3	6d-6	6e	6f
Non-financial corporations		7a	1 601								1 601
Financial corporations		7b		802							802
General government		7c			- 2 435						- 2 435
Households	Wages and salaries	7d-1				320					320
	Mixed income (including property income)	7d-2					3 319				3 319
	Income in connection with old age (retirement)	7d-3						556			556
	Other transfers income (including other households)	7d-4							- 62		- 62
Non-profit institutions serving households		7e								- 182	- 182
Total		7f	1 601	802	- 2 435	320	3 319	556	- 62	- 182	3 920

Source : Instituto Nacional de Estatística

Table C.3. Description of the grouping of labour – male and female

Group	ISCED[22] level	Description
Lower	1&2	Primary and lower secondary school
Medium	3	Upper and post-secondary school
Higher	4&5	Tertiary education

Table C.4. Description of codes and grouping of households

Group	Code[23]	Description (in accordance with the main source of income)
Employees	S143	Wages and salaries
Employers (including own account workers)	S141+S142 S1441	Mixed income including property income – employers (including own account workers) – recipients of property income
Recipients of pensions	S1442	Income in connection with old age (retirement)
Others	S1443 S145	Other transfer incomes (including other households) – recipients of other transfers incomes – other household[s24]

[22] International Standard Classification of Education (LEG, 2003).

[23] ESA 95 (Eurostat, 1996) Household Classification (LEG, 2003).

[24] Consists of persons permanently living in institutions. Such persons "are classified separately because the criterion of largest source of income does not allow a meaningful classification of these persons" (ESA 95, paragraph 2.84; LEG, 2003).

Appendix D

Additional data[25]

[25] This Appendix has all the additional data that were collected to estimate the parameters of the model and that are not contained in the tables of Appendix A or C.

Table D.1. Employment and compensation of employees in Portugal, by activities in 1995 (in millions of euros)

	Employees	Own-account workers	**Employment**	Wages and salaries D.11	Employers' social contribution D.12	**Compensation of employees D.1**
Activities	thousands of persons			millions of euros		
01	79	435	**514**	398	92	**490**
02	4	7	**11**	22	7	**29**
05	17	6	**23**	101	33	**134**
10	0	0	**0**	0	0	**0**
11	0	0	**0**	0	0	**0**
12	0	0	**0**	1	0	**1**
13	1	0	**1**	21	6	**27**
14	13	1	**13**	94	25	**118**
15	132	18	**151**	964	297	**1 261**
16	1	0	**1**	13	10	**23**
17	135	12	**147**	783	226	**1 009**
18	130	10	**140**	644	172	**815**
19	68	4	**72**	373	110	**484**
20	50	7	**56**	289	79	**368**
21	16	0	**16**	222	73	**295**
22	28	1	**29**	289	82	**371**
23	1	0	**1**	33	17	**50**
24	28	0	**28**	426	132	**557**
25	24	0	**24**	191	45	**237**
26	58	2	**59**	481	148	**629**
27	21	0	**21**	183	62	**245**
28	38	4	**42**	222	63	**285**
29	22	1	**23**	189	55	**245**
30	3	0	**4**	23	6	**29**
31	36	1	**37**	340	91	**431**
32	12	0	**12**	135	37	**172**
33	6	0	**6**	51	16	**67**
34	20	0	**20**	270	76	**346**
35	16	0	**16**	173	50	**223**
36	49	7	**56**	300	86	**385**
37	2	0	**2**	12	4	**16**
40	19	0	**19**	313	118	**430**
41	13	0	**13**	115	24	**139**
45	276	113	**390**	2 144	445	**2 589**
50	85	24	**109**	671	191	**862**
51	182	41	**223**	1 757	503	**2 259**
52	207	132	**339**	1 327	346	**1 673**
55	147	48	**195**	878	228	**1 106**
60	73	7	**79**	702	221	**923**
61	3	0	**3**	35	10	**45**
62	6	0	**6**	120	36	**156**
63	25	1	**26**	346	102	**447**
64	35	0	**36**	575	174	**750**
65	70	0	**70**	1 420	449	**1 870**
66	14	0	**14**	282	115	**396**
67	2	32	**33**	34	9	**43**
70	19	5	**23**	169	46	**215**
71	8	1	**9**	70	21	**92**
72	13	14	**27**	193	59	**252**
73	6	1	**7**	69	12	**82**
74	117	79	**197**	967	295	**1 262**
75	365	0	**365**	3 833	1 283	**5 116**
80	239	29	**268**	3 549	639	**4 188**
85	196	29	**225**	2 221	488	**2 709**
90	7	0	**7**	53	7	**59**
91	17	0	**17**	104	24	**128**
92	56	6	**62**	732	187	**919**
93	14	61	**75**	75	17	**92**
95	124	0	**124**	394	24	**418**
	3 345	**1 138**	**4 484**	**30 390**	**8 173**	**38 563**

Source: Instituto Nacional de Estatística (National Accounts – Supplementary Tables)
See Table A.8 for the description of codes of activities.

Table D.2. Portuguese persons by types of labour and households in 1995

Type of Households (by main source of income)		Type of labour												Total
		Employees						Self employed						
		Male			Female			Male			Female			
		Primary/lower secondary (ISCED 1-2)	Upper or post secondary (ISCED 3-4)	Tertiary (ISCED 5-6)	Primary/lower secondary (ISCED 1-2)	Upper or post secondary (ISCED 3-4)	Tertiary (ISCED 5-6)	Primary/lower secondary (ISCED 1-2)	Upper or post secondary (ISCED 3-4)	Tertiary (ISCED 5-6)	Primary/lower secondary (ISCED 1-2)	Upper or post secondary (ISCED 3-4)	Tertiary (ISCED 5-6)	
	codes	3a-1-ps	3a-2-ps	3a-3-ps	3a-4-ps	3a-5-ps	3a-6-ps	3b-1-ps	3b-2-ps	3b-3-ps	3b-4-ps	3b-5-ps	3b-6-ps	3c-ps
Wages and salaries	4d-1-ps	1353381	219835	147202	903764	254838	146112	162850	20103	18875	159017	15689	12840	3.414.506
Mixed income (including property income)	4d-2-ps	47586	12930	1946	75557	28695	10085	388470	25628	12451	190168	12359	4504	810.379
Income in connection with old age (retirement)	4d-3-ps	22853	7400	489	34577	10262	6405	30764	4052	739	43594	2847	738	164.719
Other transfers income (including other households)	4d-4-ps	16346	4765	1925	28582	5761	1128	12805	3067	1006	14776	1035	85	91.280
Total	4e-ps	1.440.166	244.929	151.561	1.042.480	299.555	163.730	594.889	52.850	33.071	407.555	31.929	18.167	4.480.884

Source: Instituto Nacional de Estatística (Pilot-NAM – Supplementary Tables)

Table D.3. Portuguese population in 1995

	Population
Active	*4 734 164*
– Employed	4 483 700
• employees	3 345 300
• employers, own-account workers and other occupational status	1 138 400
– Unemployed	*250 464*
Inactive	*5 186 596*
Total 9 920 760	

Source: Instituto Nacional de Estatística (National Accounts – Supplementary Tables, Projections of Resident Population, Employment Survey)

Notes: – The figures in italics were estimated from the Employment Survey.
– In accordance with labour market statistics, the occupational status of the employed population, besides the employees (fle – see conventions), the employers and the own-account workers, includes the "members of producers' cooperatives" and "another situation", which are considered jointly here with employers and own-account workers (foal – see conventions).

Table D.4. Gross fixed capital formation in Portugal by products and institutional sector in 1995 (in millions of euros)

	Products	**S.11** Non-Financial Corporations	**S.12** Financial Corpora-tions	**S.13** General Gover-nment	**S.14** Households	**S.15** Non-Profit Institutions Serving Households (NPISHs)	**S.1** **Total of the Economy**
1	Products of agriculture, forestry, fisheries and aquaculture	62	0	3	162	0	**228**
	Equipment:	**4 648**	**339**	**447**	**473**	**239**	**6 145**
2	Metal products and machinery	3 420	308	375	324	167	**4 594**
3	Transport equipment	1 228	31	72	149	72	**1 552**
4+5	Construction	**2 703**	**437**	**2 552**	**4 110**	**119**	**9 921**
6	Other products	1 368	142	16	637	0	**2 164**
	Total	**8 781**	**918**	**3 018**	**5 383**	**359**	**18 457**

Source: Instituto Nacional de Estatística (National Accounts – Supplementary Tables)

Appendix E

Sources and methodology by (macro) SAM's blocks of sub-matrices

E.1. Compensation of factors of production

Sources

- SAM: generation of income and allocation of primary income accounts of the institutions (II.1.1 and II.1.2, in integrated economic accounts or in institutional sector accounts – Tables A.1., A.2.1.and A.2.2.); external account of primary income and current transfers (V.II, in rest of the world accounts – Table A.3.); use of products at purchasers' prices (current prices) (Table A.5.).
- Parameters and exogenous variables (besides the SAM): employment and compensation of employees by activities (Table D.1); Portuguese persons by types of labour and households in 1995 (Table D.2); Portuguese population in 1995 (Table D.3).

Methodology

The other compensation of factors, in the gross national income sub-matrix, is the sum of the gross operating surplus and the balance of the income from property. The gross operating surplus is the gross added value (production minus intermediate consumption) minus the taxes paid on production plus the subsidies received on production minus the paid compensation of employees.

The values of the Portuguese persons (Table D.2.) by types of labour (used in Chapters 3, 5 and 6) and households (used in Chapters 5 and 6) were adjusted to the values of the Portuguese population (Table D.3.), using the RAS method.

E.2. Production

Sources

Production account of institutions (I, in integrated economic accounts or in institutional sector accounts – Tables A.1., A.2.1.); supply of products at basic prices (current prices) (Table A.4.); goods and services account (see related columns of integrated economic accounts – Table A.1.).

E.3. External Trade

Sources

Supply of products at basic prices (current prices) (Table A.4.), for imports; use of products at purchasers' prices (current prices) (Table A.5.), for exports; external account of goods and services (V.I, in the rest of the world accounts – Table A.3a.); goods and services account (see related columns of the integrated economic accounts – Table A.1.).

E.4. Net Indirect Taxes or Net Taxes on Production and Imports

E.4.1. *Net Taxes on Production*

Sources

Primary distribution of income accounts of the institutions (II.1., in integrated economic accounts or in institutional sector accounts – Tables A.1., A.2.1. and A.2.2.); external account of primary income and current transfers account (V.II, in rest of the world accounts – Table A.3.); use of products at purchasers' prices (current prices) (Table A.3.).

Methodology

The totals by activity/ies are calculated from the use of the products table.

The totals for the government and for the rest of the world are calculated from the table showing the allocation of the primary income account of the institutions (the totals for the rest of the world may also be calculated from the external account of the primary income and current transfers account, and this must be the case if some disaggregation is needed).

The values by activity/ies for the rest of the world are calculated by applying the share of the activity/ies in the total to the total value of the rest of the world. The values (by activity/ies) for the government are calculated by the difference between the total value (by activity/ies) and the rest of the world's value.

E.4.2. *Net Taxes on Products*

Sources

Production account and primary distribution of income accounts of institutions (I and II.1, in integrated economic accounts or in institutional sector accounts – Tables A.1., A.2.1. and A.2.2.); external account of the primary income and current transfers account (V.II, in the rest of the world accounts – Table A.3.); supply of products at basic prices (current prices) (Table A.4.); goods and services account (see related columns of integrated economic accounts – Table A.1.).

Methodology

The totals by product(s) are calculated from the supply of products table.

The totals for the government and for the rest of the world are calculated from the table showing the allocation of the primary income account of the institutions (the totals for the rest of the world may also be calculated from the external account of the primary income and current transfers account, and this must always be the case if some disaggregation is needed).

The values by product(s) for the rest of the world, which will be added to imports (the external trade block), are calculated by applying the share of the product(s) in the total to the total value of the rest of the world. The values (by product(s)) for the government are calculated by the difference between the total value (by product(s)) and the rest of the world's value.

E.5. Trade and Transport Margins

Sources

Supply of products at basic prices (current prices) (Table A.4.).

E.6. Domestic Trade

E.6.1. *Intermediate Consumption*

Sources

Production account of institutions (I, in integrated economic accounts or in institutional sector accounts – Tables A.1. and A.2.1.); use of products at purchasers' prices (current prices) (Table A.5.); goods and services account (see related columns of integrated economic accounts – Table A.1.).

E.6.2. *Final Consumption*

Sources

Use of products at purchasers' prices (current prices) (Table A.5.); use of disposable income (II.4, in integrated economic accounts or in institutional sector accounts – Tables A.1. and A.2.3.).

E.6.3. *Gross Capital Formation*

Sources

Capital account of the institutions (III.1, in integrated economic accounts or in institutional sector accounts – Tables A.1 and A.2.4.); use of products at purchasers' prices (current prices) (Table A.5.); goods and services account (see related columns of integrated economic accounts – Table A.1.); gross fixed capital formation by products and institutional sector (Table D.4).

Methodology

The total gross capital formation by product(s) was calculated from the use of products table.

The total gross capital formation by institution(s) was calculated from the capital account of the institutions table.

The gross fixed capital formation by product(s) and institution(s) was calculated from the table with the same name.

The changes in inventories and the acquisitions less disposals of valuables by product(s) and institution(s) were calculated by applying the share of the product(s) in the total to the total value of the institution(s).

E.7. Current Transfers

Sources

Secondary distribution of income and use of disposable income accounts of the institutions (II.2 and II.4, in integrated economic accounts or in institutional sector accounts – Tables A.1., A.2.2. and A.2.3.); external account of primary income and current transfers account (V.II, in rest of the world accounts – Table A.3); "from whom to whom" matrices, made available particularly by the Portuguese Statistical Institute, for the inter-institutional flows (Table A.6.).

E.8. Capital Transfers

Sources

Capital accounts of the institutions (III.1, in integrated economic accounts or in institutional sector accounts – Tables A.1. and A.2.4.); capital accounts, in the external accumulation accounts (V.III.1, in the rest of the world accounts – Table A.3.); "from whom to whom" matrices, made available particularly by the Portuguese Statistical Institute, for the interinstitutional flows (Table A.6.).

E.9. Gross Saving

Sources

Use of disposable income account of the institutions (II.4, in integrated economic accounts or in institutional sector accounts – Tables A.1. and A.2.3.).

E.10. Financial Transactions

Sources

Financial account of the institutions (III.2, in integrated economic accounts – Table A.1.).

E.11. Net borrowing/lending

Sources

Capital account of the institutions (III.1, in integrated economic accounts or in institutional sector accounts – Tables A.1. and A.2.4.); external accumulation accounts (V.III, in the rest of the world accounts – Table A.3.).

Methodology

These values can be taken directly from the sources or calculated as the balance between the totals of the components of investment funds and aggregate investment or as the difference between the financial transactions from and to the rest of the world.

Appendix F

Conventions and declarations

Sets (set indices: lower-case subscripts)

f ε Factors of production

- Labour – employees (**fle**) [with low education level (**flel**), with medium education level (**flem**), with high education level (**fleh**)]
- Own assets (**foa**)
  - Labour – employers and/or own-account workers (**foal**) [with low education level (**foall**), with medium education level (**foalm**), with high education level (**foalh**)]
  - Capital – interests, profits, rents (**foak**)

a **ε Activities** [agriculture, hunting and forestry; fishing and operation of fish hatcheries and fish farms (group1, ***a*1**); industry, including energy (group 2, ***a*2**); construction (group 3, ***a*3**); wholesale and retail trade, repair of motor vehicles and household goods, hotels and restaurants; transport and communications (group 4, ***a*4**); financial, real-estate, renting and business activities (group 5, ***a*5**); other service activities (group 6, ***a*6**)]

p ε Products [products of agriculture, hunting, forestry, fisheries and aquaculture (group1, **p1**); products from mining and quarrying, manufactured products and energy products (group 2, **p2**); construction work (group 3, **p3**); wholesale and retail trade services, repair services, hotel and restaurant services, transport and communication services (group 4, **p4**); financial intermediation services, real estate, renting and business services (group 5, **p5**); other services (group 6, **p6**)]

di ε **Domestic Institutions**

- **dic** (current account of di) [households (**dich**): employees (group 1, **dich1**), employers and own account works (group 2, **dich2**), recipients of pensions (group 3, **dich3**), others (group 4; **dich4**); non-financial corporations (**dicnfc**); financial corporations (**dicfc**); general government (**dicg**); non-profit institutions serving households (**dicnp**-NPISHs)]
- **dik** (capital account of di) [households (**dikh**), non-financial corporations (**diknfc**), financial corporations (**dikfc**), general government (**dikg**), and non-profit institutions serving households (**diknp**-NPISHs)]
- **dif** (financial account of di)

rw ε rest of the world

In variables and parameters with **two indices**, the **first** represent the **row** and the **second** the **column accounts** (both indices may be equal).

Parameters (lower-case, italics)

α .. share of the production of each group of activities in the value of production of each group of products

β .. proportion of gross added value in the value of production of each group of activities

γ .. proportion of intermediate consumption in the value of production of each group of activities

adv.. share of the value of acquisitions less disposals of valuables of each group of products by each group of domestic institutions in the total value of acquisitions less disposals of valuables by these institutions

advc .. coefficient of acquisitions less disposals of valuables: amount expended by each group of domestic institutions on acquisitions less disposals of valuables per unit of gross saving

apc .. average propensity to consume of each group of domestic institutions: amount of final consumption per unit of (gross) disposable income

b2gp.. proportion of capital compensation (gross operating surplus) in labour compensation

b3gc.. gross mixed income coefficient: amount of gross mixed income per employer and/or own-account worker

b3s.. share of compensation of employers and/or own-account workers (gross mixed income) in the gross added value
ce .. coefficient of main source of income of domestic institutions (households) recipients of compensation of employees
cgfcf .. rate of coverage of gross fixed capital formation of each group of domestic institutions by investment grants received by these institutions
chinv .. share of the value of changes in inventories of each group of products by each group of domestic institutions in the total value of changes in inventories of that group of products
chinvc .. coefficient of changes in inventories: amount of change in inventories of each group of products per unit of supply
clr .. share of compensation of employees paid by activities and sent to the rest of the world
coa .. coefficient of main source of income of domestic institutions (households) recipients of compensation of employers and/or own-account workers
d1s .. share of compensation of employees in the gross added value
d5s .. share of current tax on income, wealth, etc. paid by each group of domestic institutions to each group of domestic institutions (Portuguese general government), in the total of current tax on income, wealth, etc. paid by the former
d61s .. share of social contributions paid by each group of domestic institutions to each group of domestic institutions in the total of social contributions paid by the former
d62s .. share of social benefits other than social transfers in kind paid by each group of domestic institutions to each group of domestic institutions in the total of social benefits other than social transfers in kind paid by the former
d62rws.. share of social benefits other than social transfers in kind paid by each group of domestic institutions to the rest of the world in the total of social benefits other than social transfers in kind paid by the former
d7 .. share of other current transfers paid by each group of domestic institutions to each group of domestic institutions in the total of other current transfers paid by the former
d7rws .. share of other current transfers paid by each group of domestic institutions to the rest of the world in the total of social benefits other than social transfers in kind paid by the former
d91 .. share of capital taxes paid by each group of domestic institutions (households) to each group of domestic institutions

(Portuguese general government) in the total of capital taxes paid by the former

d92.. share of investment grants paid by each group of domestic institutions (Portuguese general government) to each group of domestic institutions in the total of investment grants received by the latter

d92rw.. share of investment grants paid by the rest of the world to each group of domestic institutions in the total of investment grants received by the latter

d99.. share of other capital transfers paid by each group of domestic institutions to each group of domestic institutions in the total of other capital transfers received by the latter

d99rw.. share of other capital transfers paid by the rest of the world to each group of domestic institutions in the total of other capital transfers received by the latter

esc .. employers' social contributions (actual and imputed social contributions) coefficient: amount of social contributions (transaction D12 of the National Accounts) paid by the employers of each group of activities to the government per employee

fcs .. proportion of expenditure on final consumption in each group of products in the total value of the final consumption of each group of domestic institutions

fcsrw .. proportion of expenditure on final consumption in the rest of the world in the total value of the final consumption of each group of domestic institutions

gfcf .. share of the value of gross fixed capital formation in each group of products by each group of domestic institutions in the total value of gross fixed capital formation by these institutions

icp .. coefficient of the intermediate consumption of products: proportion of intermediate consumption of each group of products per unit of intermediate consumption of each group of activities

ntag .. share of net taxes on production paid by each group of activities and received by domestic institutions (Portuguese general government)

ntarw .. share of net taxes on production paid by each group of activities and received by the rest of the world (European Union institutions)

ntpg .. share of net taxes on each group of products received by domestic institutions (Portuguese general government) *ntprw* .. share of net taxes on each group of products received by the rest of the world (European Union institutions)

sc .. social contribution rate: social contributions paid by domestic institutions, per unit of received gross national income

si .. saving identity special

sk.. share of compensation of capital received by domestic institutions

ti .. direct tax rate: current taxes on income, wealth, etc. paid by domestic institutions, per unit of received aggregate income

tk .. rate of capital tax levied on other capital transfers received by domestic institutions

tm .. rate of trade and transport margins on each group of domestically transacted products: amount of trade and transport margins per unit of value of domestically transacted products

tmc .. trade and transport margins coefficient of correction

tp .. (net) tax rate on each group of products: amount of (net) taxes on products per unit of the value of domestically transacted products

w .. wages and salary (in cash or in kind) coefficient: amount of wages/salary (transaction D11 of the National Accounts) paid by each group of activities to each employee

Exogenous variables (upper-case, italics)

AP .. active population

CFR.. compensation of the factors of production received from the rest of the world

CFS.. compensation of the factors of production sent to the rest of the world

D1RW.. compensation of employees (transaction D1 of the National Accounts) received from the rest of the world

D4PRW .. property income (transaction D4 of the National Accounts) sent to the rest of the world

D4RW .. property income (transaction D4 of the National Accounts) received from the rest of the world

D62P .. social benefits other than social transfers in kind (transaction D62 of the National Accounts) paid by domestic institutions

D62RW .. social benefits other than social transfers in kind (transaction D62 of the National Accounts) received by domestic institutions from the rest of the world

D7P .. other current transfers (transaction D7 of the National Accounts) paid by domestic institutions

D7RW .. other current transfers (transaction D7 of the National Accounts) received by domestic institutions from the rest of the world

D8 .. adjustment made for the change in the net equity of households in pension fund reserves (transaction D8 of the National Accounts)

D92P .. investment grants (transaction D92 of the National Accounts) paid by domestic institutions (Portuguese general government) to the rest of the world

D99P .. other capital transfers (transaction D99 of the National Accounts) paid by domestic institutions to the rest of the world

D99R .. other capital transfers (transaction D99 of the National Accounts) received by domestic institutions

EX .. value of exports (transaction P6 of the National Accounts, at f.o.b. prices)

FT .. financial transactions (transactions F1 to F7 of the National Accounts), except those received from the rest of the world

IM .. value of imports (transaction P7 of the National Accounts, at c.i.f. prices)

K2 .. acquisitions less disposals of non-financial non-produced assets (transaction K2 of the National Accounts)

NTAA .. net taxes on production paid by each group of activities

P.. total population

P51 .. value of gross fixed capital formation (transaction P51 of the National Accounts)

Endogenous variables (upper-case, at least the first letter, normal)

AD .. value of aggregate demand (at market prices)

AFIP .. aggregate factors income (paid)

AFIR .. aggregate factors income (received)

AI .. aggregate income (received)

AINV .. aggregate investment

AIP .. aggregate income (paid)

AS .. aggregate supply (value at market prices)

B2g .. gross operating surplus (balance B2g of the National Accounts)

B3g ..	gross mixed income (balance B3g of the National Accounts)
CB ..	current balance (balance of payments – current account – total)
Cfctm ..	trade and transport margins component of the final consumption value
Cfcntp..	net taxes on products component of the final consumption value
Cfcbcif ..	basic-c.i.f. component of the final consumption value
Cfe..	factor cost component – labour (employees): amount relating to the compensation of employees in the value of production of each group of products
Cfoa..	factor cost component – labour (employers and/or own-account workers): amount relating to the compensation of employers and/or own-account workers in the value of production of each group of products
Cfk..	factor cost component – capital: amount relating to the compensation of capital in the value of production of each group of products
CFS..	compensation of the factors of production sent to the rest of the world (except, property income sent to the rest of the world)
Cgcftm ..	trade and transport margins component of the value of gross capital formation
Cgcfntp..	net taxes on products component of the value of gross capital formation
Cgcfbcif..	basic-c.i.f. component of the value of gross capital formation
Cic ..	intermediate consumption component: amount relating to intermediate consumption in the value of production of each group of products
Cnta ..	net taxes on production component: amount relating to net taxes on production in the value of production of each group of products
CT ..	current transfers
CTB ..	current transfers balance (balance of payments – current account – current transfers)
CTP ..	(total) current transfers paid by each group of domestic institutions to (all) domestic institutions
CTR ..	(total) current transfers received by each group of domestic institutions from (all) domestic institutions

Cvictm.. trade and transport margins component of the value of intermediate consumption
Cvicntp.. net taxes on products component of the value of intermediate consumption
Cvicbcif.. basic-c.i.f. component of the value of intermediate consumption
DI .. (gross) disposable income
Didi .. percentage of gross disposable income received by domestic institutions
Digav .. percentage of income generated by the factors production
Digavfle .. percentage of income generated by employees, by level of education
Digavfoal .. percentage of income generated by employers and/or own-account workers, by level of education
Digni.. percentage of generated income (gross national income) received by domestic institutions
DT.. value of domestically transacted products, at basic-c.i.f. prices
DTmp .. value of domestically transacted products, at market prices
D1 .. compensation of employees (transaction D1 of the National Accounts)
D5 .. current taxes on income, wealth, etc. (transaction D5 of the National Accounts)
D61 .. social contributions (transaction D61 of the National Accounts)
D91P .. capital taxes (transaction D91 of the National Accounts) paid by domestic institutions
D92R .. investment grants (transaction D92 of the National Accounts) received by domestic institutions
E .. employed population
FB .. financial balance (balance of payments – financial account + errors and omissions)
FC .. value of final consumption (transaction P3 of the National Accounts), at market prices
FTRW .. financial transactions (transactions F1 to F7 of the National Accounts) received by domestic institutions from the rest of the world
GAV .. gross added value, at factor cost
GCF .. value of gross capital formation (transaction P5 of the National Accounts), at market prices
GDP.. gross domestic product, at market prices

GNI ..	gross national income, at factor cost
GNIMP..	gross national income, at market prices
GSB ..	goods and services balance (balance of payments – current account – goods and services)
IB ..	income balance (balance of payments – current account – income)
INVF ..	investment funds
KT ..	capital transfers
KB ..	capital balance (balance of payments – capital account)
KTP ..	(total) capital transfers paid by each group of domestic institutions to (all) domestic institutions
KTR ..	(total) capital transfers received by each group of domestic institutions from (all) domestic institutions
LE	labour – employees
LOA	labour – employers and/or own-account workers
NLB ..	net lending / borrowing
NTA ..	net taxes on production (transaction D29-D39 of the National Accounts)
NTP ..	net taxes on products (transaction D21-D31 of the National Accounts)
PcDI ..	gross disposable income *per capita* (in euros)
PcFC ..	final consumption *per capita* (in euros)
PcS ..	saving *per capita* (in euros)
Ptm..	proportion of trade and transport margins in the value of domestically transacted products (at market prices)
Pntp..	proportion of net taxes on products in the value of domestically transacted products (at market prices)
Pbcif..	proportion of basic-c.i.f. component in the value of domestically transacted products (at market prices)
P52 ..	value of changes in inventories (transaction P52 of the National Accounts)
P53 ..	value of acquisitions less disposals of valuables (transaction P53 of the National Accounts)
S ..	gross saving
TFTP ..	total financial transactions (paid)
TFTR ..	total financial transactions (received)
TM ..	trade and transport margins (without correction)
TMc ..	trade and transport margins – correction
TMT ..	trade and transport margins with correction
TVRWP ..	value of transactions to the rest of the world
TVRWR ..	transactions value from the rest of the world

Ur..	unemployment rate
UdiFC ..	percentage of gross disposable income used in final consumption by domestic institutions
UdiS ..	percentage of gross disposable income used in (gross) saving by domestic institutions
VCT ..	value of total costs (at basic prices)
VIC ..	value of intermediate consumption (transaction P2 of the National Accounts) at market prices
VP ..	value of production (transaction P1 of the National Accounts), at basic prices
VPT..	total production value (at basic prices)
Wgav ..	amount of income generated by worker, by level of education
Wgavfle ..	amount of income generated by employee
Wgavfoal..	amount of income generated by employer and/or own-account worker